CHARTING T

for

COLLABORATIVE
Teams

Lessons From **Priority Schools** in a PLC at Work®

Joe **CUDDEMI** · Diane **KERR** · Tammy **MILLER**
Gerry **PETERSEN-INCORVAIA** · Dana **RENNER** · Michael **ROBERTS**
Tamie **SANDERS** · Sarah **SCHUHL**

SHARON V. KRAMER | EDITOR

Solution Tree | Press
a division of
Solution Tree

555 North Morton Street
Bloomington, IN 47404
800.733.6786 (toll free) / 812.336.7700
FAX: 812.336.7790

email: info@SolutionTree.com
SolutionTree.com

Visit **go.SolutionTree.com/PLCbooks** to download the free reproducibles in this book.

Printed in the United States of America

Library of Congress Cataloging-in-Publication Data

Names: Kramer, Sharon V., editor.
Title: Charting the course for collaborative teams : lessons from priority
   schools in a PLC at work / Sharon V. Kramer, Joe Cuddemi, Diane Kerr,
   Tammy Miller, Gerry Petersen-Incorvaia, Dana Renner, Michael Roberts,
   Tamie Sanders, Sarah Schuhl.
Description: Bloomington, IN : Solution Tree Press, [2021] | Includes
   bibliographical references and index.
Identifiers: LCCN 2021006444 (print) | LCCN 2021006445 (ebook) | ISBN
   9781951075576 (paperback) | ISBN 9781951075583 (ebook)
Subjects: LCSH: Professional learning communities. | School improvement
   programs. | Educational equalization. | School management teams.
Classification: LCC LB1731 .C437 2021 (print) | LCC LB1731 (ebook) | DDC
   370.71/1--dc23
LC record available at https://lccn.loc.gov/2021006444
LC ebook record available at https://lccn.loc.gov/2021006445

Solution Tree
Jeffrey C. Jones, CEO
Edmund M. Ackerman, President

Solution Tree Press
President and Publisher: Douglas M. Rife
Associate Publisher: Sarah Payne-Mills
Art Director: Rian Anderson
Managing Production Editor: Kendra Slayton
Copy Chief: Jessi Finn
Senior Production Editor: Todd Brakke
Content Development Specialist: Amy Rubenstein
Proofreader: Kate St. Ives
Text and Cover Designer: Laura Cox
Editorial Assistants: Sarah Ludwig and Elijah Oates

Acknowledgments

A simple thank you cannot describe my gratitude and appreciation for the individuals who made this book a reality. Writing a book or chapter is one of the most difficult tasks that anyone can embark upon, and it would be an impossible task without the support and hard work of the Solution Tree Press. The constant encouragement of Douglas Rife, president and publisher, is a gift that keeps on giving. He and the entire press team are so appreciated for their intellect, enthusiasm, integrity, and energy that propelled this project to fruition. I began this book with a simple idea, and content development specialist Amy Rubinstein helped to shape my thinking and focus my efforts as a first-time anthology editor. Our work was then furthered by senior production editor Todd Brakke as he transformed our drafts into finished chapters. The entire project was coordinated under the very capable direction of associate publisher Sarah Payne-Mills. And finally, I am grateful to art director Rian Anderson and cover designer Laura Cox for the thoughtful and most fitting artwork that adorns the cover of this book.

Jeff Jones, the CEO of Solution Tree, is a dream maker in the true sense of the word. His ability to grow options and opportunities to directly impact districts, schools, teachers, and, most importantly, student learning worldwide is like none other. His vision, commitment, and integrity is evident as he approaches every task. He is a transformational influence on education.

The authors who contributed to this anthology are exceptionally busy and are sought after by schools and districts for their expertise and support. Each of them could have thought of a million reasons or excuses not to participate in this process. I extend my deepest appreciation to Joe Cuddemi, Diane Kerr, Tammy Miller, Gerry Peterson-Incorvaia, Dana Renner, Michael Roberts, Tamie Sanders, and Sarah Schuhl. This is a truly amazing team of educators, consultants, authors, and PLC experts.

I am also grateful for all educators working every day in support of the students that need us the most. These educators create breakthrough moments and opportunities that have lasting, lifelong impacts on their students. They are saving lives on a daily basis.

Finally, I want to acknowledge the support and unending love of my family. My work and writing is a direct result of the inspiration my husband, children, and grandchildren give me. This is the true measure of a life well lived.

Solution Tree Press would like to thank the following reviewers:

Jordan Edgerly
Math Teacher
Waukee High School
Waukee, Iowa

Lorraine Perez
Science Teacher
Russellville High School
Russellville, Alabama

Eric Lindblad
English Teacher
Andover High School
Andover, Minnesota

Ringnolda Jofee' Tremain
PreK–8 Principal
Trinity Basin Preparatory
Fort Worth, Texas

Visit **go.SolutionTree.com/PLCbooks** to download the free reproducibles in this book.

Table of Contents

Reproducibles are in italics.

6 Working Together to Ensure All Students Learn Mathematics 131
Sarah Schuhl

7 Understanding the Story Data Tell 149
Dana Renner

8 Moving From a Flooded to a Balanced Intervention Pyramid. 171
Gerry Petersen-Incorvaia

About the Editor

 **Sharon V. Kramer, PhD,** knows firsthand the demands and rewards of working in a professional learning community (PLC). As a leader in the field, she has done priority schools work with districts across the United States, emphasizing the importance of creating and using quality assessments and utilizing the PLC continuous-improvement process to raise student achievement. Sharon served as assistant superintendent for curriculum and instruction of Kildeer Countryside Community Consolidated School District 96 in Illinois. In this position, she ensured all students were prepared to enter Adlai E. Stevenson High School, a model PLC started and formerly led by PLC architect Richard DuFour.

A seasoned educator, Sharon has taught in elementary and middle school classrooms, and she has served as principal, director of elementary education, and university professor. In addition to her PLC experience, Sharon has completed assessment training by Rick Stiggins, Steve Chappuis, Larry Ainsworth, and the Center for Performance Assessment (now the Leadership and Learning Center). She has presented a variety of assessment workshops at institutes and summits and for state departments of education. Sharon has also worked with school districts across the United States to determine their power standards and develop assessments.

She has been a Comprehensive School Reform consultant to schools that have received grant funding to implement the PLC process as their whole-school reform model, and her customized PLC coaching academies have empowered school and district leadership teams across the United States. Sharon has presented at state and national conferences sponsored by Learning Forward, the National Association for Gifted Children, the American Federation of Teachers, and California State University. She has been instrumental in facilitating professional development initiatives focused on standards-based learning and teaching, improved understanding and utilization of assessment data, interventions and differentiation that meet the needs of all learners, and strengthened efforts to ensure K–12 literacy.

Sharon is the author of *How to Leverage PLCs for School Improvement* and coauthor of *School Improvement for All: A How-To Guide for Doing the Right Work*; *Best Practices at Tier 2: Supplemental Interventions for Additional Student Support, Elementary*; and *Best Practices at Tier 2: Supplemental Interventions for Additional Student Support, Secondary*. She also contributed to the books *It's About Time: Planning Interventions and Extensions in Elementary School, The Teacher as Assessment Leader*, and *The Collaborative Teacher: Working Together as a Professional Learning Community.*

Sharon earned a doctorate in educational leadership and policy studies from Loyola University Chicago.

To learn more about Sharon's work, follow @DrKramer1 on Twitter.

To book Sharon V. Kramer for professional development, contact pd@SolutionTree.com.

Introduction

Sharon V. Kramer

> The greatest challenge to school improvement is the overwhelming perception that no matter what the teachers and administrators do, there seems to be no way out of failing results.
>
> —*Sharon V. Kramer*

Educators are the hardest-working individuals on this earth! They work tirelessly on behalf of their students and families, always searching for ways to meet all students' needs. Many spend weekends and evenings planning and preparing lessons, activities, and assessments and providing feedback to students. Additionally, educators attend after-school activities and meetings in support of students and their families. There is a reason educators have summer vacation; it's because they work a full twelve months in about nine months. Plus, many educators take on additional responsibilities for summer learning or spend time preparing for the upcoming school year during the school break. Educators know they will be working hard and that the school year is rapidly paced with too much to teach in too little time. They do not shy away from hard work, long hours, or the draconian accountability measures they often face. But the truth is, even with their best effort and time-consuming planning, students do not always make the progress educators hope for. Educators are frustrated and, given the amount of effort they put forth daily, understandably so. This is especially true of educators who work in schools where students chronically underperform.

As an educator, you know this. Chances are, you've either heard your colleagues voice the following frustrations or said or thought them yourself.

- "I have tried everything, but the students still don't get it."
- "My students are so far below grade level they can't even read the text."
- "These students had three different teachers last year, so I am starting all over."
- "Teacher and administrator turnover is a real factor here."
- "You know, we *are* a Title I school."

Yes, these frustrations are real. Educators often feel judged and fear they may be doing something wrong. This work of improving learning is not about right or wrong or good or bad. School improvement as part of a professional learning community (PLC) is about asking the question, "How can we do this work even better?"

I believe all educators, including you and your collaborative team members, want to use the knowledge they have to be the best educators they can be for the students they serve. As Maya Angelou (2018) said, "Do the best you can until you know better. Then when you know better, do better." Feelings and statements like those listed in this introduction constitute an outcry for help and support, not an excuse or a desire to do less work. As part of a PLC, you and your colleagues employ best practices and do everything you can to help all students learn at high levels. You care deeply for your students and understand the importance of preparing them for life beyond classroom walls.

This begs the overwhelmingly compelling question, Is it really possible to get *all* students to learn at grade level and beyond? And if the answer is a resounding *yes*, then how? This inevitably leads to even more questions: What strategies, practices, policies, and procedures need to be in place to ensure high levels of learning for *all*? Where do educators begin? What is proven to work with the students who are often missing essential prerequisite skills and knowledge to even begin to learn grade- or course-level content? How can teachers accelerate learning instead of using remediation to address students' needs? What strategies are effective in supporting special education students and students who are learning English?

In *How to Leverage PLCs for School Improvement* (Kramer, 2015), I outline the five greatest challenges facing underperforming schools and districts.

1. Create a culture of success.
2. Engage in the right work.
3. Shift from all to each.
4. Develop leadership for learning.
5. Engage students in owning their learning.

Through this list, I acknowledge the barriers to reaching the goal of high levels of learning for all. It also emphasizes strategies for turning these specific challenges into opportunities for improvement. Most of all, this list reflects a journey through the challenges of the lowest-performing high school in the state of Oklahoma as it became a model for the work of a PLC. This journey is important to you because it illustrates how teachers can accomplish this work anywhere. The practices, procedures, and strategies are replicable across all schools and districts.

To show the value of this work, several colleagues and I formed a priority schools team focused on continuous-improvement efforts in Oklahoma. As we facilitated success, our team expanded its work to support and coach schools and districts in need of improvement throughout North America and abroad. It quickly became clear to us that our work is most effective at getting real results when it's clearly articulated and widely available to all educators asking to do better and be better for the students they serve. To further this aim, educational consultant, PLC expert, and author Sarah Schuhl and I wrote *School Improvement for All* (Kramer & Schuhl, 2017) to complement and greatly expand on *How to Leverage PLCs for School Improvement* (Kramer, 2015). It is the result of and foundation for our school improvement efforts and contains many of the resources necessary to do the work of a PLC in a struggling school.

This anthology further expands on those two previous books' content and details specific strategies its contributors have used to address barriers and challenges educators and collaborative teams encounter as they engage in the work of continuous improvement. This collection of chapters, each from an expert in supporting and coaching schools in need of improvement (which we refer to as *priority schools*), represents lessons learned as all of us who contributed to it continue to move the right work forward. Each chapter describes a problem of practice that many schools and districts face and provides tried, true, and research-affirmed strategies schools in need of improvement have successfully employed. The following sections provide core information about the work of a PLC in priority schools and about the specific contents of this book.

The Work of a PLC in Priority Schools

To be clear, all the books and work I've referenced up to this point hinge on understanding the PLC process and culture, which is best detailed in *Learning by Doing* (DuFour, DuFour, Eaker, Many, & Mattos, 2016). If schools and districts are not operating as PLCs, no amount of effort or work to improve will have success. PLCs are not about buying a new program or offering more and more staff training; they are about engaging a school organization's people in doing the right work. To get the most out of this book, it is vital that you and your collaborative team members understand and adhere to the following core concepts of PLCs (DuFour et al., 2016).

- **The three big ideas of a PLC:** (1) A focus on learning, (2) a collaborative culture and collective responsibility, and (3) a results orientation

- **The four pillars of a PLC:** (1) Mission (why we exist), (2) vision (what we must become), (3) values and commitments (how we must behave), and (4) goals (how we will mark our progress)

- **The four critical questions of a PLC:** (1) What do we want students to learn? (2) How will we know if they've learned it? (3) How will we respond when some students do not learn? and (4) How will we extend learning for students who are already proficient?

By embedding these ideas, pillars, and critical questions deeply into the work of continuous improvement, teams impact results and ensure higher achievement levels for all students. *School Improvement for All* (Kramer & Schuhl, 2017) specifically expands on and customizes these PLC concepts and processes to meet the unique needs of underperforming or priority schools. School improvement is not something different from the work of a PLC; it is doing PLCs right, not lite. This anthology both supports educators in implementing the PLC process deeply enough to get real results in student achievement and tailors recommendations for common challenges, barriers, and pitfalls associated with priority schools.

For this book's purposes, we define *priority schools* as schools that a district, state, or province identifies as in need of improvement or schools whose data are flat, showing little or no progress over time. Individual states and provinces use a variety of labels to describe priority schools, with each designation deriving from a specific ranking and rating system. Common labels refer to schools and districts on a five-star scale, use designations like *improvement required* (IR) or *schools in need of assistance* (SINA), or rank schools on an A–F scale. When low achievement persists at such schools, state and provincial entities commonly take over and manage them.

It's an unfortunate reality that labels associated with priority schools frame and define students and staff as deficient without highlighting the hard work, dedication, and love the educators devote to their students, families, and school community. As such, it is important to view these schools and districts through a strengths-based lens. Even in the absence of these designations, this book is useful for educators seeking improvement. The practices, strategies, and protocols you will find in each chapter are essential for some and good for all. Priority schools represent an enormous opportunity for growth that is indescribably rewarding for all educators that have the good fortune of supporting them. As student achievement increases, the entire school and broader community regain hope and a healthy, positive culture.

About This Book

This anthology adds to the body of knowledge about engaging in the right work and provides specific how-to suggestions, strategies, and templates to support a collaborative team's continuous improvement. As you will see in each chapter, this anthology features research-supported practices, which is important, but always keep in mind the best, most actionable books provide both the knowledge and the means to easily apply their contents to real-world situations. Although my coauthors and I intend for you to read the book in its entirety, it can also serve to address specific issues or problems present in a school or collaborative team, as each chapter offers specific and targeted support. Each individual chapter is comprehensive and provides learning experiences you can share within your collaborative team, with your leadership team, or with an entire staff. You will also find individual resources to expand your team's and individual teachers' impact. My coauthors reference and provide high-quality resources throughout every chapter so that readers can explore the specific topics in depth.

Before I address chapter specifics, it's important that you understand something. Consider that as educators do the work of improving schools and districts, and as educators continue to grow and learn along with the teams and administrators they work with, they commonly face several barriers to growth, especially poverty. Luis Cruz (2020), author and educational consultant, often characterizes educators as an elite team with the arduous task of breaking students free from the cycle of poverty. I would add that educators are an elite team with the arduous task of breaking students free from poverty *and*, in doing so, equipping them with the skills and knowledge necessary to be successful in life.

In this book, each chapter's author is an educator who represents an ongoing commitment to the students, teachers, schools, and districts he or she supports. I carefully selected these educators to share their knowledge and expertise because they have successfully implemented and used the strategies they write about to turn around their own underperforming schools and districts. All the authors have been in the trenches and understand the work from the inside out. They have also been successful in replicating and implementing the same strategies as coaches at other schools, helping those schools obtain the results they hope for and are working hard to achieve. The schools and districts they describe in this collection are diverse in their sizes, demographics, grade spans, geographical locations, and resources available to them. These authors are an elite team dedicated to achieving high levels of learning for all students, even in the face of backbreaking student poverty and other challenges. Their practical insights and lived examples conveyed in each chapter are invaluable in making progress toward educators' collective purpose and vision of all students' learning at grade level and beyond. The topics covered may not be new, but the value of each chapter lies in the practical applications and examples each presents to address the ongoing issues that plague schools and get in the way of real improvement.

The following list introduces each chapter and explains the problem of practice it addresses.

- **Chapter 1, "Teaching the Behaviors You Expect," by Joe Cuddemi:** This chapter describes a process to identify, teach, and monitor essential academic and social behaviors. Without a definitive system of support, the typical outcry in priority schools centers on student behaviors that get in the way of learning. Often, teachers do not recognize social learning as important to academic outcomes or even as a component of their work. This process establishes collective responsibility for academic and social behaviors while keeping the focus on learning.

- **Chapter 2, "Rethinking SMART Goals to Accelerate Learning," by Gerry Petersen-Incorvaia:** SMART goals are goals that are strategic and specific, measurable, attainable, results oriented, and time bound (Conzemius & O'Neill, 2014). Collaborative teams usually create SMART goals by determining merely what is safe and absolutely attainable for improving the results of a small number of students. This chapter focuses on the *A* in the SMART goal acronym and describes how a little rethinking can lead to teams' making SMART goals not only attainable but also audacious. Gerry presents a process of looking at the zone of opportunity in student data, through which collaborative teams can reliably increase achievement and ensure students on the cusp of proficiency factor into SMART goal creation.

- **Chapter 3, "Adopting the Ten-Day Collaborative Cycle," by Tamie Sanders and Dana Renner:** The real work of collaborative teams is to deeply answer the four critical questions of a PLC in recurring cycles of instruction, unit by unit. This chapter describes the most effective and succinct ways to answer these questions with a laser-sharp focus on learning. Tamie and Dana provide examples from successful teams to demonstrate how to engage in a ten-day collaborative cycle.

- **Chapter 4, "Answering the First Critical Question From an English Learner's Point of View," by Diane Kerr:** This chapter provides teams with a process for examining the academic language of their essential standards during the unwrapping (unpacking) process and creating language objectives in the domains of reading, writing, speaking, and listening as appropriate to the standards' purpose. This leads teams to develop a plan for explicitly teaching vocabulary and incorporating language-engagement strategies.

- **Chapter 5, "Getting Students to Grade-Level Reading Fast," by Tammy Miller:** This chapter focuses on a viable solution to the reading crisis in priority schools. Students require literacy, and early literacy learning is key to success in school and life. By following Tammy's continuum of skills based on a system of acceleration, collaborative teams can create an effective pathway for classroom reading instruction and intervention and monitor for mastery.

- **Chapter 6, "Working Together to Ensure All Students Learn Mathematics," by Sarah Schuhl:** This chapter describes the actions necessary to accelerate mathematics learning in a priority school. Often, students miss key concepts in their learning journey, which gets in the way of understandings in subsequent grade levels or courses. So, how do teams fill those gaps while also keeping students in the current grade level or course? Sarah describes specific steps and actions based on high-level understanding of the most important concepts that will accelerate student learning.

- **Chapter 7, "Understanding the Story Data Tell," by Dana Renner:** This chapter looks at data through a nine-step process aimed at understanding the story behind the numbers. The protocols and discussion questions in this chapter are the key to giving data a social context, making them into actionable information. This deep and targeted analysis is the pathway to real improvement.

- **Chapter 8, "Moving From a Flooded to a Balanced Intervention Pyramid," by Gerry Petersen-Incorvaia:** Often, between 40 and 80 percent or more of priority schools' students are in need of intensive remediation. Schools usually do not have the necessary resources, such as enough time, money, and teachers, to support the sheer number of students in need. Ideally, schools have between 5 and 8 percent of students in need of this support. This chapter focuses on teams' using strategies and repurposing resources to accelerate the learning and create a three-tier intervention system that is balanced, not flooded.

- **Chapter 9, "Making Proficient Students a Priority," by Michael Roberts:** This chapter focuses on the fourth critical question of a PLC (DuFour et al., 2016): How will we respond when students have learned? In every priority school, some students demonstrate proficiency and spend an inordinate amount of time waiting to learn something new while watching others learn. Michael offers teacher and team strategies and supports for students who demonstrate proficiency or learn quickly so that all learners engage in continuous learning.

Since 2006, it has been my privilege and honor to work side by side with all the authors whose work appears in this collection. Their respective schools have each earned model PLC status, and one of their schools received the first DuFour Award (recognition as the top-performing PLC in the world) for its staff's work to improve student achievement. These authors have their specific areas of expertise, present their ideas in their unique ways, and offer effective strategies for bringing about significant school improvement. But the common thread throughout this book is the deeply held belief that even at priority schools, *all* students can learn at high levels, and it is every team's responsibility to get them there. You will witness this dedication in each chapter, as these practitioners offer a results-driven look at their work.

This book is a clear call to action for teachers and collaborative teams. I hope that educators will use their own collective wisdom and knowledge, purposeful actions, and shared commitments to make a difference in the lives of the students they serve. Real school improvement cannot come from the outside in. Instead, it must come from the inside out. It is the responsibility and commitment of the educators within a school that can and does make this happen. When teachers understand that this is the right work and make it their job to do it, achievement soars. In the end, any school or district must harness the power within to achieve its goal of *learning for all when all really means* all.

References and Resources

Angelou, M. [@DrMayaAngelou]. (2018, August 12). "Do the best you can until you know better. Then when you know better, do better." — #MayaAngelou [Tweet]. *Twitter*. Accessed at https://twitter.com/drmayaangelou/status/1028663286512930817?lang=en on September 30, 2020.

Conzemius, A. E., & O'Neill, J. (2014). *The handbook for SMART school teams: Revitalizing best practices for collaboration* (2nd ed.). Bloomington, IN: Solution Tree Press.

Cruz, L. (2020, August 26). *Welcome back and are we ready to show the world what we are capable of accomplishing?* Presentation to White River School District, Buckley, WA.

DuFour, R., DuFour, R., Eaker, R., Many, T. W., & Mattos, M. (2016). *Learning by doing: A handbook for Professional Learning Communities at Work* (3rd ed.). Bloomington, IN: Solution Tree Press.

Kramer, S. V. (2015). *How to leverage PLCs for school improvement.* Bloomington, IN: Solution Tree Press.

Kramer, S. V., & Schuhl, S. (2017). *School improvement for all: A how-to guide for doing the right work.* Bloomington, IN: Solution Tree Press.

Joe Cuddemi has over thirty-five years of experience in education, serving as a teacher, counselor, and principal in a wide variety of educational settings and as an adjunct professor at Colorado State University. Since 2015, Joe has been an educational consultant, serving hundreds of districts and schools across the United States. Joe delivers keynotes, facilitates workshops, and coaches educators in the Professional Learning Community (PLC) at Work® process, school culture transformation, Response to Intervention (RTI) at Work™, priority schools, and social-emotional learning.

Joe has taught at schools in Jamaica, in Colorado, and on the Fort Belknap Reservation in Montana. As counselor, Joe created an award-winning experiential educational program that included horsemanship for students facing high levels of adversity. As principal, Joe opened Kinard Middle School in Fort Collins, Colorado in 2003. During his principalship, Kinard received several national recognitions, including the 2015 Blue Ribbon Award, which recognizes outstanding schools with high-performing student achievement, the 2013 Green Ribbon Award, which recognizes schools that improve the health, performance, and equity for all students, and the schoolwide model PLC designation in 2012.

Joe earned a bachelor's degree in biology from Boston College, a master's degree in the art of teaching mathematics from Northern Arizona University, and a principal licensure from Colorado State University.

To book Joe Cuddemi for professional development, contact pd@SolutionTree.com.

Teaching the Behaviors
You Expect

Joe Cuddemi

Educators need to prepare their students
for the future, not the past.
—Sharon V. Kramer and Sarah Schuhl

In 1989, I was a mathematics teacher at Conrad Ball Middle School in Loveland, Colorado. After having taught for nine years, I contemplated leaving the teaching profession. My inability to reach and teach students who lacked the motivation and appropriate behaviors to succeed in school left me increasingly frustrated; the school system seemed like it was designed to push out our students most at risk by punishing them with increasingly stiff consequences, resulting in their removal from school.

As I continued to reflect, I fondly remembered my first two years of teaching on the Fort Belknap Reservation in Hays, Montana, from 1980–1982. Among the many powerful learning experiences I experienced there, I learned about riding and training horses. Rejuvenated at the memory, I spent the remainder of the summer of 1989 writing and raising funds for what I called the *Horsemanship Program*: *Meeting the Social and Emotional Needs of Students at Risk*. The program's purpose was to support students who were unsuccessful in school and struggling to manage their behaviors. It provided these students with an experiential learning opportunity, outside the school building, to learn necessary skills for respecting others and being responsible for their choices.

As part of this program, we established a partnership with Sylvan Dale Ranch, a working ranch in Loveland, Colorado, owned and operated by Morris Jessup, a former educator and an advocate for students at risk. In our first year, we identified the ten students we determined to be most at risk, the students who had the lowest attendance rates, most disciplinary referrals, and the lowest grade point averages. The number of students who participated in the program grew very rapidly, and by the third year of implementation, we were supporting up to one hundred students a year at Sylvan Dale Ranch. It was amazing to see students who had no hope for their future, and who had lost trust in people, instantly bond and connect with their horses. Through their relationships with the horses, and in this school without walls, students learned skills such as responsible decision making, self-management, self-awareness, and relationship skills, all core competencies identified in the Collaborative for Academic, Social, and Emotional Learning (n.d.) framework for social-emotional learning.

As a result of this program, I became the school's at-risk coordinator. From 1990–1999, I committed myself to doing whatever it took to keep students in school. In time, I realized that this program was neither sustainable nor replicable. The following factors all played a role in this conclusion.

- Not every school has access to horses.

- Interventions can't cure a toxic school culture.

- No one person could be the school's interventionist and still reach every student in need.

- Many teachers believed that we were rewarding students for bad behavior.

- Some of the students I pulled out of class fell further behind academically.

- Students started asking me how many office referrals and Fs they needed to get into the Horsemanship Program. (This was when I knew things were really taking a wrong turn!)

These were all legitimate concerns, but the results of this experience reinforced my belief that *all* students, regardless of background, are *capable* of learning how to behave in order to learn in the classroom if they receive additional support. As we tracked the progress of the students who participated in the program, we noticed a significant overall increase in their attendance rates, grades, and a reduction in their disciplinary referrals. In the final analysis, I needed an equally effective strategy that any teacher or teacher team could use in any school, district, or region. I ultimately concluded any approach to supporting students at risk required a focus on providing behavioral supports.

If priority schools and districts are to improve their results, they must clarify the learning outcomes they desire for the students they serve. In my work as a consultant with priority schools, we focus on not only clarifying the essential academic content standards that all students must learn but also the essential *behavioral* skills that students need to learn in order to be successful academically and in life. One of the first questions that I ask educators in priority schools is, "What do you want school to provide *your* child?" The responses that I typically receive include the following descriptors.

- A safe and orderly learning environment

- Positive and respectful relationships

- Teachers who both support and challenge students to learn the skills they'll need to be successful in school and in life

I then ask educators, "Would you agree that if a school isn't good enough for your own child, then it isn't good enough for anyone's child?" They all agree, at least philosophically, that they want the very best for every student that they serve. Educators want *all* their students to be successful in school, to be successful in the world of work, and to also enjoy the many benefits derived from having healthy and nurturing relationships.

A plethora of research and evidence supports the idea that student learning occurs at higher levels when the school provides a safe and positive learning environment (Buffum, Mattos, & Malone, 2018; Jensen, 2019; Lezotte & Snyder, 2011). In this chapter, I use the research-based PLC process, with its emphasis on the four critical questions of a PLC (DuFour, DuFour, Eaker, Many, & Mattos, 2016; see page 3), to guide collaborative teacher teams to coordinate schoolwide and teach the essential behavioral skills that students must learn to be successful in school and life. The process is simple but not easy. The factors that contribute to the complexity of this work include the following.

- The health of the school's culture, which includes the health of the relationships (Buffum et al., 2018)

- The clarity, skills, and effectiveness of the educators who model and teach the behavioral expectations and skills (Weber, 2018)

- The presence of a multitiered system of support (MTSS) or response to intervention (RTI) framework for students whose needs exceed what any one individual classroom teacher can do to support them (Buffum et al., 2018)

- The necessary resources to support students coming from home environments that are counterproductive to learning and have high levels of adverse circumstances, such as poverty, abuse, and neglect that contribute to students lacking the skills necessary to manage their dysregulation and behavior (Harris, 2018)

The following sections explore an easy-to-learn process for teacher teams to teach essential behavioral skills and address behavioral concerns. While this process is easy to learn, it requires recurring cycles of teaching and learning in order to meet every student's learning needs. To maximize the benefits of this process, teacher teams must continuously clarify why there is a need for the school's culture to be healthy, why they require a collective understanding of terms and concepts (clarity precedes competence), and how teams can use the four critical questions of a PLC as the foundation for students learning the essential behavioral skills. Throughout this process, individual teachers will learn and benefit from the support that occurs through collaborative teaming.

The Need for a Healthy Schoolwide Culture

You can't create a sustainable process to teach and monitor student behavior without a healthy school culture. In this context, I adhere to Kent D. Peterson's (2002) approach, in which he defines *school culture* as "the set of norms, values, and beliefs, rituals, ceremonies, symbols, and stories that make up the 'persona' of the school" (p. 10). My big assumption, based on the fact that you're reading this book, is that you are already part of a collaborative teacher team and have embraced a healthy, collaborative school culture as an essential component of this work. Educational consultant and author Anthony Muhammad (2018) defines a *healthy school culture* as one in which:

> Educators have an unwavering belief in the ability of all their students to achieve success, and they pass that belief on to others in overt and covert ways. Educators create policies and procedures and adopt practices that support their belief in every student's ability. (p. 20)

In many cases, the school's leadership team takes the lead responsibility in coordinating collaborative teams and addressing the school's culture. However, I've learned through first-hand experience while working with priority schools that collaborative teams can also share in or even take on the lead for teaching essential behaviors to the students they serve. In either case, the greatest level of coherence and alignment for addressing behavior occurs when there is schoolwide coordination between and among every collaborative team. To do this essential foundational work, I recommend teams utilize the following four world-class resources, which hundreds of schools have used to create, develop, and sustain a healthy school culture.

1. *Building the Resilient School: Overcoming the Effects of Poverty With a Culture of Hope* by Robert D. Barr and Emily L. Gibson (2020)

2. *Cultures Built to Last: Systemic PLCs at Work* by Richard DuFour and Michael Fullan (2013)

3. *Transforming School Culture: How to Overcome Staff Division, Second Edition* by Anthony Muhammad (2018)

4. *Time for Change: Four Essential Skills for Transformational School and District Leaders* by Anthony Muhammad and Luis F. Cruz (2019)

Remember, for the students all educators must serve, behavioral programs or interventions will never be a cure for a toxic school culture, unhealthy classroom environments, unhealthy relationships, negative language, coercive strategies, or low expectations. When collaborative teams embrace a schoolwide culture in which everyone believes that *all* students can learn, they can better focus on ensuring that learning occurs.

The Need for Clarity to Precede Competence

In the teaching profession, there's universal consensus that, when done well, implementation of the PLC process, RTI, and positive behavioral interventions and supports (PBIS) significantly improves behavior and learning for all students. Once schools commit to ensuring that *all* students learn the essential standards and behavioral skills required for success in school, in work, and in life, they can use RTI and PBIS as tools to complement the PLC process. While these terms are familiar to most educators, there is a lack of clarity on their meaning. For the sake of clarity and common language, I use the following definitions to sum up these processes.

- A PLC establishes three big ideas that both schools and districts use to improve learning for all students: (1) establish a focus on learning, (2) create a collaborative culture of collective responsibility, and (3) adhere to a results orientation in which teams gather evidence of student learning to determine future actions (DuFour et al., 2016).

- In *Taking Action*, RTI specialists Austin Buffum, Mike Mattos, and Janet Malone (2018) use an inverted pyramid (see figure 1.1) that is split to graphically organize the RTI and schoolwide positive behavior support (SWPBS) tools and processes. The following briefly explains each intervention tier.

  ‣ *Tier 1*—This tier constitute core grade-level instruction, which educators often refer to as the level of support known as *prevention*. Collaborative teams identify and teach the essential learnings (this refers to both essential academic standards and essential behavioral skills) that all students must learn at each grade level in order to be successful.

  ‣ *Tier 2*—This tier refers to *interventions*, or the additional time and support that some students will need in order to master essential learnings. For students that do show high-proficiency with Tier 1 instruction, this tier also provides support for learning extensions.

  ‣ *Tier 3*—This tier refers to the *intensive remediation* that some students need in order to learn foundational skills they lack. These are necessary skills to learn grade-level essential learnings.

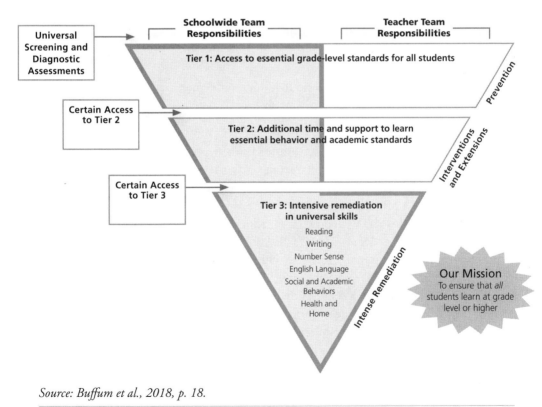

Source: Buffum et al., 2018, p. 18.

Figure 1.1: The RTI at Work inverted intervention pyramid.

In my work with priority schools across the United States, I've noticed that it is impossible to create a healthy school culture when there is ambiguity among staff and students regarding terms and concepts they use. School cultures benefit greatly when there is a common understanding of terms and concepts like PLC, RTI, and SWPBS. It is critical to devote time with staff to clarify and communicate these terms in order to lay the foundation for future competence.

The Four Critical Questions to Guide Behavioral Instruction

The four critical questions of a PLC provide a process for teams to determine essential learnings, assess whether students have learned them, and determine the need for further intervention or extension. The answers to these questions serve the needs of academic instruction; however, when students learn essential behavioral skills, they are more likely to be successful in learning academic standards. Teaching essential behavioral skills to students is especially important when serving students who come to school from home environments that are counter-productive to learning.

To support the teaching and learning of essential behavioral skills, I recommend schoolwide adoption of the following adaptations to the four critical questions (Cuddemi, 2017a, 2017b).

1. What behaviors do we expect all students to learn?
2. How will we know if they've learned the skills necessary to successfully meet behavioral expectations?
3. How will we respond when a student does not demonstrate the appropriate behaviors?
4. How will we respond when a student has learned the expected behaviors?

In effective PLC schools and districts, teams learn about behavior together. Teachers don't need to be therapists to know that students' behavior is a function of their choice and their learning environment. At Kinard Middle School in Fort Collins, Colorado, where I worked as a principal from 2003–2015, we studied the work of psychiatrist turned educational theorist William Glasser, who developed a behavioral theory based on Maslow's hierarchy of needs. Glasser's (1999) basic assumption is that people behave in order to meet their needs. There are two kinds of needs among those he posits that bear particular attention: (1) survival needs (having food, water, air, and shelter) and (2) psychological needs (having a sense of belonging, feeling valued, feeling empowered, and having variety). Students' behavior provides feedback to adults as to whether their needs are being met (Brendtro, Brokenleg, & Van Bockern, 2019; Colburn & Beggs, 2021; Jensen, 2019). For students who come to school hungry, learning arithmetic will not meet their hunger need; food will. Students who come to school without a sense of belonging will seek either positive or negative attention to meet that need. If we educators design our schools and classrooms to meet our students' needs, then students are more likely to learn to behave appropriately, and we are more likely to understand the cause of the behavior rather than punish the symptom.

Many students who attend priority schools come from home environments that are counterproductive to student learning. These students arrive at school without the behavioral skills they need to be successful in learning the academic content. In priority schools, where teacher teams struggle to manage student behavior and improve academic performance, team members need to recognize the inextricable link between behavior and academics. Unfortunately, the language teachers often use in priority schools that are struggling to make gains reflects a lack of understanding of this connection. Consider statements like the following.

- "I already have so much curriculum to cover. I don't have the time to teach the students behavioral skills; besides, I'm not a therapist."

- "Students make choices, and choices have consequences. If you want them to learn how to behave, then give them stiffer and more punitive consequences."

- "Student misbehavior is disrespectful and disruptive to the learning environment and needs to be dealt with by administrators. That's their job."

- "It's not my job to teach students how to behave. It's the parents' responsibility."

The problem with statements like these is they reflect a lack of understanding of the connection between behavior and learning. Teams that use the four critical behavior questions outlined in this section can change how they react to problematic classroom behavior and help students who are struggling with challenges outside the classroom focus on productive learning behaviors. The following sections address how teams can approach each of the four critical behavioral questions.

Identify the Essential Behaviors

The first critical behavioral question asks, What behaviors do we expect all students to learn? Buffum and colleagues (2018) suggest that teams identify a limited number of essential behavioral expectations (typically four to five). These essential behavioral expectations need to include both academic skills such as being prepared to learn, participating and being productive, and demonstrating social skills such as treating others with respect and communicating respectfully.

Teams can draw on multiple resources to help them identify essential behaviors. For example, CASEL (n.d.) has identified five social-emotional learning competencies: (1) self-awareness, (2) self-management, (3) social awareness, (4) relationship skills, and (5) responsible decision making. The Framework for 21st Century Learning further identifies four learning and innovation skills to prepare students for life in and beyond school: (1) creativity and innovation, (2) critical thinking and problem solving, (3) communication, and (4) collaboration (Battelle for Kids, 2019). In *Getting Ready for College, Careers, and the Common Core*, David T. Conley (2014) also identifies four essential skills: (1) metacognition, (2) self-regulation, (3) motivation, and (4) volition.

The research backing all the skills present in these frameworks emphasizes that social-emotional learning is an essential process for life and not a one-time event. Regardless of which framework or which combined elements of multiple frameworks a school decides to use, students will not learn these competencies and skills at any one point in time or via a single course, even one specifically dedicated to explicitly teaching the social-emotional skills. The skills require practice and reinforcement throughout students' schooling and lives.

Further, after determining essential expectations, many schools create an acronym associated with the school's name or mascot to represent the school's values and behavioral expectations. A common such acronym is ROAR (respect, outstanding citizen, attitude, responsibility). Many schools stop here. They put the acronym on a poster and then expect students to behave in accordance with expectations. The problem with this approach is that if the adults haven't clarified the meaning of the words they are using to describe these behavioral expectations, then it will be impossible for all students to learn the behavioral skills needed to be successful in school and in life. Consider the following three questions when identifying the essential behaviors.

1. Do all students and educators have the same understanding of terms the school is using?

2. How and when will students learn the skills?

3. What are the criteria for success with the skills?

Let's look at an example of how schools might determine an initial list of essential behaviors and use a protocol to achieve consensus around what they mean in terms of student behavior.

Choosing Essential Behaviors

In *School Improvement for All*, Sharon V. Kramer and Sarah Schuhl (2017) assert that having a triage plan is *critical* to the school-improvement process. Part of that triage plan is choosing essential behaviors. While leading the change process at the schoolwide level is necessary for creating schoolwide systems of support, there is nothing that prohibits a collaborative team from initiating and implementing the process for identifying the essential behavioral skills specific to their grade level or course.

At Kinard Middle School, we used the six Ps derived from Eric Larsen and William M. Timpson (2001) to begin to identify behavioral expectations.

1. **Prompt:** Be on time and where you belong.

2. **Prepared:** Have all materials and be ready to learn.

3. **Positive mental attitude:** Choose positivity.

4. **Polite:** Speak and act with dignity and respect.

5. **Participate:** Follow directions and engage in learning.

6. **Productive:** Complete your tasks with quality.

This was only a starting point, not a comprehensive list of all the skills that students need to learn. We used the terms *promptness* and *politeness* to address the social skills that students need in order to behave appropriately while interacting with others. We addressed behavioral skills for academics with the other four Ps: *preparedness* (self-monitoring), *participation* (motivation), *productivity* (volition), and *positive mental attitude* (self-concept). We quickly learned that we couldn't just teach the six Ps the first day or week of school and expect students to have the skills to successfully meet the expectations the rest of the academic school year; we needed to continuously engage students in practicing these skills. We were most effective when we established positive relationships with students and used effective communication strategies while teaching the meaning of all the expectations and their relevance to the world of work.

The lesson of this experience is that when collaborative teams of teachers are involved in identifying the essential behaviors that all students must learn, then they are more likely to be committed to the process, ensuring all students learn these behavioral skills.

Reaching Consensus

Once a collaborative team chooses a limited number of behavioral expectations, they need to reach consensus on the meaning of the words used to describe the behavioral expectations. In a collaborative culture, building consensus is critical to success, which is why DuFour and colleagues (2016) set two standards that teams must meet to find consensus about a decision and move forward: (1) All points of view have been heard and even solicited, and (2) The will of the group is evident even to those most opposed to the proposal.

To meet these standards and achieve consensus, I suggest teams use the *table-mat protocol*, which usually needs about forty-five to sixty minutes to complete. Using this protocol, a single collaborative team or teams schoolwide complete the following six-step process.

1. For each behavioral skill, the team draws a circle in the center of a large piece of chart paper and draws lines that represent the number of people in the team (four people would produce four lines, for example), as shown in figure 1.2. This step takes about two minutes.

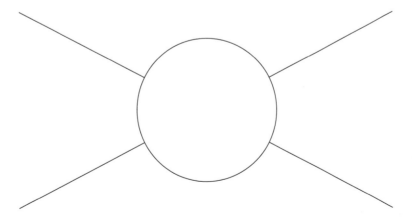

Figure 1.2: Graphic organizer for the table-mat protocol.

2. In the spaces between two adjacent lines, team members each write their understanding of the behavioral expectation. These descriptors can be words, phrases, or short sentences. This step takes about two minutes.

3. Taking turns, team members each read aloud what they wrote while everyone else in the group listens and takes notes in their chart space on the ideas, words, and concepts that resonate most with them. This step takes about three minutes.

4. Team members discuss the concepts, words, and ideas that they want to make sure get placed in the circle, which represents agreement. Using the protocol, *no one speaks twice until everyone speaks once.* This step takes about ten minutes.

5. Team members come to a consensus, using the following *fist-to-five process* to determine a short phrase that best describes the ideas or concepts from step 4. The phrase or statement should be easy for both teachers and students to remember. This step takes about five minutes.

   ‣ *Five fingers*—"I fully support this proposal."

   ‣ *Four fingers*—"I support this proposal."

   ‣ *Three fingers*—"I'll go along with the will of the group."

   ‣ *Two fingers*—"I have a concern with this proposal." (Provide the opportunity to share concerns.)

   ‣ *One finger*—"I am opposed to this proposal." (Provide the opportunity to share opposing views.)

   ‣ *Fist*—"If I were king or queen, I would veto the proposal altogether."

6. The collaborative team repeats this process for each of the behavioral skills. This step takes about twenty to thirty minutes.

At Kinard Middle School, this process yielded the results and common language I listed in the previous section. However, this represents just the start of the journey toward establishing positive classroom behaviors. In addition to setting schoolwide behavioral standards, teacher teams often need to emphasize behavioral skills that are specific for their grade or content area. For example, at Kinard Middle School, teachers had the freedom to use their professional discretion to establish safety procedures for a science lab, which looked different from the procedures for physical education or the mathematics classroom.

Determine Whether Students Have Learned the Behavioral Skills

The second critical question for teaching essential behavioral skills asks, How will we know if students have learned the skills necessary to successfully meet behavioral expectations? Teachers typically assess student behavior through observation. Schools can create a very simple rubric for this purpose by establishing the criteria for behavioral expectations (the first critical behavioral question) and then determining the criteria that define various levels of success relative to each expectation. Students can also use this rubric to self-assess their own behavior and set improvement goals. Figure 1.3 shows an example of such a rubric using the same six Ps I introduced in Choosing Essential Behaviors. (See page 29 for a reproducible version of this figure.) Every three weeks, our collaborative

Schoolwide Behavioral Expectations (Work Habits)

The Six Ps

1. **Prompt:** Be on time and where you belong.
2. **Prepared:** Bring all materials and be ready to learn.
3. **Positive mental attitude:** Choose a positive mental attitude.
4. **Polite:** Speak and act with dignity and respect.
5. **Participate:** Follow all directions and fully engage in learning.
6. **Productive:** Complete all tasks on time and with quality.

Work Habits Rubric

Behavioral Expectation	4 Consistently Exceeds Expectations	3 Frequently Meets Expectations	2 Sometimes Meets Expectations	1 Never or Rarely Meets Expectations
I am prompt.	I am consistently early or on time to class.	I am frequently early or on time to class.	Sometimes I am early or on time to class.	I am never or rarely early or on time to class.
I am prepared.	I am consistently prepared. I consistently bring needed materials to class and am consistently ready to work.	I am frequently prepared. I frequently bring needed materials to class and am frequently ready to work.	I am sometimes prepared. I sometimes bring needed materials to class and am sometimes ready to work.	I am never or rarely prepared. I never or rarely bring needed materials to class and am never or rarely ready to work.
I demonstrate a positive mental attitude.	I consistently stay focused on the task and what needs to be done. I am self-directed. I consistently have a positive attitude.	I frequently stay focused on the task and what needs to be done. I am self-directed. I frequently have a positive attitude.	I sometimes stay focused on the task and what needs to be done. I sometimes am self-directed and sometimes have a positive attitude.	I never or rarely stay focused on the task and what needs to be done. I rarely am self-directed and rarely have a positive attitude.
I am polite.	I consistently treat others respectfully in my words and actions.	I frequently treat others respectfully in my words and actions.	I sometimes treat others respectfully in my words and actions.	I never or rarely treat others respectfully in my words and actions.
I participate.	I consistently participate. I share information or ideas when participating in discussions or groups. I am a definite leader.	I frequently participate. I share information or ideas when participating in discussions or groups. I am often a leader.	I sometimes participate. I inconsistently share information or ideas when participating in discussions or groups.	I never or rarely participate. I never or rarely share information or ideas when participating in discussions or groups; I rely on the work of others.
I am productive.	I am consistently productive. I am punctual or early in turning in assignments. I exceed the stated assignment requirements.	I am frequently productive. I am punctual in turning in assignments. I meet the stated assignment requirements.	I am sometimes productive. I am sometimes punctual in turning in assignments. I sometimes meet the stated assignment requirements.	I am never or rarely productive. I am not punctual in turning in assignments. I never or rarely meet the stated assignment requirements.

Figure 1.3: Sample rubric for defining schoolwide behavioral expectations.

teams used this rubric to update our online gradebook system and communicate to both students and parents the progress that our students were making toward meeting the behavioral expectations (or, as we called them, *work habits*).

However, knowing the criteria by which teams will assess student behavior is only a first step toward answering the second critical behavioral question. Teachers must also show students how to meet those expectations. As instructional researcher and education expert Robert J. Marzano (2018) states, "Effective teaching is not a simple matter of executing specific behaviors [and] strategies, because effective teaching is grounded in human relationships. If teachers don't have sound, supportive relationships [with] their students, the effects of their instructional practices are muted."

Once collaborative teams have agreed on the behavioral expectations, a behavior leadership team needs to coordinate a schoolwide process with those teams to teach students the expectations. For example, during the first week at Kinard Middle School, our eighth-grade student leaders and sixth-grade teachers cofacilitated an activity to teach sixth-grade students the expectations. They asked the sixth graders two questions: (1) "What expectations do you, the students, have of the adults in this school?" and (2) "What expectations should the adults have of the students?" Each class recorded student responses on the board and then grouped them by color for each of the six Ps. It soon became evident that all the brainstormed expectations fell under one of the six Ps.

The students' responses gave teachers a specific understanding of what knowledge their specific students needed to acquire to behave according to the six Ps. Among the strategies our teachers adopted to teach this knowledge is one called *STEPS* (Johnson, Johnson, & Holubec, 1994), which works as follows.

1. **S**how the need for the skill.

2. Create a **T**-chart to show what the skill sounds like and looks like.

3. **E**ngage students in practicing the skill (through role playing, for example).

4. **P**rovide feedback as often as possible.

5. Continuously teach and practice the **s**kill.

After teaching students about the meaning of and expectations for meeting the six Ps, teachers facilitated with students the same *fist-to-five process* described earlier to reach consensus on the behavioral expectations. Once consensus was reached for students on the same grade level, teachers would then engage the sixth graders in a ceremony that we called *Stepping Into the Kinard Circle*. Each sixth-grade classroom went to the gymnasium, where a giant Mustang (our mascot) was painted in the circle at center court. Students stepped into the circle as a way to demonstrate their commitment to the six Ps and what it meant to be a Kinard Mustang. Through this process, which I've used successfully in dozens of schools across the United States for schoolwide coordination of behavior expectations, we built a learning community based on agreements and commitments, not a set of rules to police.

In addition to teaching the six Ps, our school also used the various content departments as a way to organize and ensure that all students were learning academic skills such as memorization, note taking, organization, and problem solving. For example, history teachers taught memorization skills, science teachers taught teamwork skills, mathematics teachers taught problem-solving skills, and the homeroom and advisory teachers taught organizational skills.

Determine Responses for When Students Do Not Learn Essential Behaviors

The third critical behavioral question asks, How will we respond when a student does not demonstrate the appropriate behaviors? There are two categories of support for which educators and teams answer this question: (1) classroom level (support within specific collaborative teams) and (2) beyond classroom level (schoolwide support). The following sections address both of these categories.

Classroom-Level Support

Classroom teacher responsibilities are multi-faceted and complex. Trying to meet the learning needs of each student is a daunting task. Effective teachers understand that students might struggle to learn academic content if they haven't learned the appropriate academic and social skills. At Kinard, we studied cognitive strategies and learned the impact that our thinking and mindset have on our behavior and professional practices. The following are a few guiding principles and mantras we used to remind ourselves and each other that our classroom culture would be defined by our relationships with students and our beliefs and expectations about student behavior.

- What you tolerate, you teach.

- What you permit, you promote.

- Silence is consent.

- The best intervention is prevention.

- Fair is not equal. Fair is meeting the individual needs of each individual student.

In addition to these expectations, our collaborative teams needed specific strategies for creating a positive classroom learning community. After all, one of the primary purposes for creating high-performing collaborative teams is for teachers to learn strategies from each other that are most effective in supporting students to learn, and classroom teachers are responsible for creating a healthy environment and positive relationships with students. Research from the Center for Educational Leadership (n.d.) at the University of Washington's College of Education characterizes the classroom environment of highly effective teachers as having the following attributes.

- The physical environment is safe and arranged to enhance learning.

- Routines and rituals are embedded for collaboration and accountability.

- Time is maximized.

- Students manage their own behavior and assist each other in managing behavior.

- Teachers respond to student misbehavior by following schoolwide agreements and by using effective communication techniques.

At the classroom level, teachers also need to provide corrective feedback when students don't behave in accordance with the expectations. Effective feedback requires that teachers use assertive communication skills that include both nonverbal and verbal components. Nonverbal communication includes tone of voice, body language, and facial expressions, while verbal communication includes the words that teachers use. Assertive communication is noncoercive. It is the ability to express ideas and feelings in an open, honest, and direct way. It honors and respects oneself and others; it is when people take responsibility for themselves. In contrast, coercive communication is aggressive, punitive, and threatening. Coercive communication is when someone raises their tone of voice, points their finger at the person being spoken to, or uses statements like "you should . . ." which can be perceived as shaming or blaming (Valdes, 2018).

After receiving effective feedback, students need the opportunity to reflect on their behavior in order to address and change their behavior. Educators get the best results in these conversations with students when they speak to the behavior, using assertive communication, instead of engaging in an escalated and emotionally charged exchange (Jensen, 2019). When speaking to the behavior, a teacher can communicate questions and statements like the following.

- "What's going on today?" (Shows interest)

- "Are you doing OK?" (Makes a connection)

- "Here's what I am seeing." (Speaks to the behavior)

- "Here's what I'm needing." (Refers to the behavioral standard the student isn't meeting)

- "Can you get there? Can you fix this?" (Provides choice and empowerment)

When in a state of panic, anxiety, or stress, we are all (adults included) susceptible of reacting with a fight, flight, or freeze response. (Brendtro, Brokenleg, & Van Bockern, 2019; Harris, 2018). We know from brain research that, when confronted, students and adults suffering from trauma will have a greater tendency to react with a fight, flight, or freeze response (limbic system; Ham, 2017). This variable shows why it is critical that adults use respectful, calm, and noncoercive communication to help students access their learning brain (neocortex). While accessing their learning brain, students are more likely to be reflective and emotionally calm when given feedback about their behavior.

While doing this work, collaborative teams not only need to discuss the progress that students are making in learning academic standards but also the progress students are making in learning behavioral skills. Collaborative teams can engage in conversations about behavior by using prompts such as: What strategies did you use to support students in successfully meeting the criteria for each of the behavioral expectations? What strategies did you use to create a positive classroom learning environment? What strategies did you use to create positive relationships with your students? What evidence do you have that these strategies are working or not working?

Schoolwide Support

The PLC process requires a collaborative culture, which means not only are teachers organized into collaborative teams but schools' resources are also coordinated to meet all students' learning needs. Collaborative teams can make a significant impact supporting one another to become more effective in teaching and monitoring student behavior; however, to address student behavior that is chronically inappropriate or severe, egregious or unsafe, there needs to be schoolwide support and coordination. To support students who chronically misbehaves or whose behavior is so severe and egregious it impacts the safety of themselves and others, schools need an all-hands-on-deck approach. This requires schools to establish a schoolwide intervention team (or behavior team) comprised of staff members ranging from school psychologists and social workers to counselors and behavior specialists. These team members are not necessarily assigned to another specific collaborative team or grade level. Although not every school has personnel who are licensed or certified in these specific areas, all schools can create an intervention team with staff members that have the strengths and expertise for dealing with difficult student behavior (Buffum et al., 2018).

The intervention team helps create a schoolwide process that helps individual teachers and collaborative teams identify students who need intensive behavioral support. The team also facilitates a problem-solving process to examine the concerns that the staff may have for a student, the possible causes of his or her misbehavior, and interventions to support behavioral change. Lastly, the intervention team leads the process to evaluate the effectiveness of interventions schoolwide. Consider using the following tools from *Taking Action* (Buffum et al., 2018). (Visit www.solutiontree.com/free-resources/rti/tarti to access free reproducible versions of these resources.)

- "The RTI at Work Pro-Solve Intervention Targeting Process: Tier 1 and Tier 2" (p. 169)
- "The RTI at Work Pro-Solve Intervention Monitoring Plan: Tier 1 and Tier 2" (p. 179)
- "Supplemental Interventions for Essential Academic and Social Behaviors: Critical Questions" (p. 215)
- "The RTI at Work Pro-Solve Intervention Targeting Process: Tier 3" (p. 244)
- "The RTI at Work Pro-Solve Intervention Monitoring Plan: Tier 3" (p. 248)

At Kinard Middle School, we used several schoolwide coordinated strategies to address the need that some students had for intensive behavioral support. Here are a few of those strategies for your consideration.

1. We engaged the entire staff in conversations with each other through the use of structured conversations or protocols and examined our mindsets and the effectiveness of our practices for meeting students' behavioral needs (Easton, 2009). One effective strategy we discovered as a staff through the use of protocols was helping students to retrace the path of their misbehavior by posing questions such as the following.

> ‣ "What did you see or hear that triggered you?"
>
> ‣ "What stories were you telling yourself?"
>
> ‣ "How were you feeling, emotionally?"
>
> ‣ "What physical feelings were you experiencing?"
>
> ‣ "What choice did you make?"
>
> ‣ "What other choices could you make the next time you feel this way?"

2. As a staff, we created an intervention that we called *Each One Reach One*. We generated a list of the fifty students who were struggling the most with their dysregulation and misbehavior. Each of our fifty staff members then chose one student from that list they had a connection with, either in a current course, from a previous school year, or with the student's family, so that each of those students had an adult advocate at our school. Each advocate would check-in and out with their selected student on a daily, weekly, or monthly basis (as needed) and then report progress to the intervention team.

3. Our intervention team created a quick-reference card, similar to the one in figure 1.4, that enabled grade-level teams to assess and report student behavioral concerns every three weeks. Once collaborative teams identified students, we enlisted the support of the intervention team to help problem solve possible causes and determine interventions to support them.

Three-Week Quick Check

Student name: _____   Date: _____

Teacher name: _____

Please circle the student's level of performance for each behavioral skill.

Politeness:	Excellent	Average	Poor	Improving
Promptness:	Excellent	Average	Poor	Improving
Participation:	Excellent	Average	Poor	Improving
Productivity:	Excellent	Average	Poor	Improving
Preparedness:	Excellent	Average	Poor	Improving
Listening Skills:	Excellent	Average	Poor	Improving
Test Performance:	Excellent	Average	Poor	Improving
Completion of Homework:	Excellent	Average	Poor	Improving
Interaction With Peers:	Excellent	Average	Poor	Improving
Interaction With Adults:	Excellent	Average	Poor	Improving
Mental Attitude:	Excellent	Average	Poor	Improving

Figure 1.4: Quick-reference card for behavior.

*Visit **go.SolutionTree.com/PLCbooks** for a free reproducible version of this figure.*

Determine Responses for When Students Learn Essential Behaviors

The fourth critical behavioral question asks, How will we respond when a student has learned the expected behaviors? Just as collaborative teams extend the learning when students have demonstrated proficiency for an essential academic standard, teams also need to respond when students have successfully demonstrated the expected essential behaviors. Teams reinforce positive behaviors by celebrating those behaviors with students and, importantly, within the team. By celebrating successes with each other, team members fortify their commitments to each other and strengthen the health of both their classroom culture and school culture.

Reinforcing positive behavior need not be a complicated process. For example, PBIS Rewards (n.d.) provides free examples of incentives that schools can use for reinforcing positive behavior without a cumbersome record-keeping system that keeps track of points. Primarily, it's important for teams to foster a balance between external rewards, which produce compliance and cooperation, and strategies that intrinsically motivate positive behaviors.

Schools committed to learning for all develop learning communities where students care about each other's success. When students are already demonstrating the appropriate behavioral skills, teams can extend the students' learning through the development of leadership skills. The leadership model organizational leadership experts and authors James M. Kouzes and Barry Z. Posner (2017) propose has five leadership traits collaborative teams and students can apply.

1. Model expected behaviors to other students.

2. Empower other students to act; don't do for others what they can do for themselves.

3. Respectfully challenge other students when their behaviors are inappropriate.

4. Use words of encouragement with other students, especially when they are struggling.

5. Inspire other students with a vision for what they could become.

When students demonstrate these traits while modeling for their peers, they help inspire a vision for the future of the school, challenge the status quo when examining the school's practices and procedures, encourage each other from the heart, and help empower their peers to learn. Further, collaborative teams can use these five leadership strategies not only with their students but also with each other.

Conclusion

The mission of a school with a healthy culture is to ensure high levels of learning for all students. We know that some students will struggle in school because they lack essential behavioral skills. We also know that each day, thousands of interactions occur between students and educators and define the culture of the school, and we know that the health of the relationships among adults and students is critical to students' learning the essential behavioral skills. Because students are excellent observers and terrible interpreters, educators need to model the behaviors that they expect from students and be willing to examine their own behaviors in light of their impact on student behavior. Students and teachers alike can learn new behaviors, but remember: it takes ten minutes to learn a behavior but a lifetime to practice it. Use the following key actions, in sequence, to remember this chapter's key concepts.

1. Staff need to create and sustain a healthy school culture.

2. School leadership needs to lead, coordinate, and design a schoolwide process for students to learn the essential behaviors.

3. Teams need to use the four critical behavioral questions to ensure that all students are learning the essential behaviors.

4. All staff must commit to a culture of continuous improvement.

Simplistic as it may sound, remember that the difference between those who do (establish, model, and encourage positive behaviors) and those who don't is those who do, *do*, and those who don't, *don't*.

References and Resources

Barr, R. D., & Gibson, E. L. (2020). *Building the resilient school: Overcoming the effects of poverty with a culture of hope*. Bloomington, IN: Solution Tree Press.

Battelle for Kids. (2019). *Framework for 21st century learning: A unified vision for learning to ensure student success in a world where change is constant and learning never stops*. Accessed at http://static.battelleforkids.org/documents/p21/P21_Framework_Brief.pdf on October 12, 2020.

Brendtro, L. K., Brokenleg, M., & Van Bockern, S. (2019). *Reclaiming youth at risk: Futures of promise* (3rd ed.). Bloomington, IN: Solution Tree Press.

Buffum, A., Mattos, M., & Malone, J. (2018). *Taking action: A handbook for RTI at Work*. Bloomington, IN: Solution Tree Press.

Center for Educational Leadership. (n.d.). *Five dimensions of teaching and learning*. Accessed at https://info.k-12leadership.org/5-dimensions-of-teaching-and-learning?_ga=2.10877874.761693058.1608766917-1250493070.1608766917 on January 19, 2021.

Colburn, L., & Beggs, L. (2021). *The wraparound guide: How to gather student voice, build community partnerships, and cultivate hope*. Bloomington, IN: Solution Tree Press.

Collaborative for Academic, Social, and Emotional Learning. (n.d.). *SEL: What are the core competence areas and where are they promoted?* Accessed at https://casel.org/sel-framework on October 12, 2020.

Conley, D. T. (2014). *Getting ready for college, careers, and the Common Core: What every educator needs to know*. San Francisco: Jossey-Bass.

Cuddemi, J. (2017a, August 30). *Creating a culture of commitment* [Blog post]. Accessed at www .allthingsplc.info/blog/view/354/creating-a-culture-of-commitment on September 28, 2020.

Cuddemi, J. (2017b, June 20). *Decision making: "How can we get on the same page?"* [Blog post]. Accessed at www.solutiontree.com/blog/decision-making-getting-on-the-same-page on September 28, 2020.

DuFour, R., DuFour, R., Eaker, R., Many, T. W., & Mattos, M. (2016). *Learning by doing: A handbook for Professional Learning Communities at Work* (3rd ed.). Bloomington, IN: Solution Tree Press.

DuFour, R., & Fullan, M. (2013). *Cultures built to last: Systemic PLCs at Work*. Bloomington, IN: Solution Tree Press.

Easton, L. B. (2009). *Protocols for professional learning*. Alexandria, VA: Association for Supervision and Curriculum Development.

Glasser, W. (1999). *Choice theory: A new psychology of personal freedom*. New York: HarperPerennial.

Ham, J. (2017, July 25). *Understanding trauma: Learning brain vs survival brain* [Video file]. Accessed at www.youtube.com/watch?v=KoqaUANGvpA on November 2, 2020.

Harris, N. B. (2018). *The deepest well: Healing the long-term effects of childhood adversity*. Boston: Houghton Mifflin Harcourt.

Jensen, E. (2019). *Poor students, rich teaching: Seven high-impact mindsets for students from poverty* (Rev. ed.). Bloomington, IN: Solution Tree Press.

Johnson, D. W., Johnson, R. T., & Holubec, E. J. (1994). *Cooperative learning in the classroom*. Alexandria, VA: Association for Supervision and Curriculum Development.

Kouzes, J. M., & Posner, B. Z. (2017). *The leadership challenge: How to make extraordinary things happen in organizations* (6th ed.). Hoboken, NJ: John Wiley & Sons.

Kramer, S. V., & Schuhl, S. (2017). *School improvement for all: A how-to guide for doing the right work*. Bloomington, IN: Solution Tree Press.

Larsen, E., & Timpson, W. M. (2001). *The discovery program: Essential skills for teachers and students*. Longmont, CO: Sopris West Educational Services.

Lezotte, L. W., & Snyder, K. M. (2011). *What effective schools do: Re-envisioning the correlates*. Bloomington, IN: Solution Tree Press.

Marzano, R. J. [@robertjmarzano]. (2018, July 24). Effective teaching is not a simple matter of executing specific behaviors & strategies, because effective teaching is grounded in human relationships. If teachers don't have sound, supportive relationships w/ their students, the effects of their instructional practices are muted [Tweet]. *Twitter*. Accessed at https:// twitter.com/robertjmarzano/status/1021943141816041473 on September 28, 2020.

Muhammad, A. (2018). *Transforming school culture: How to overcome staff division* (2nd ed.). Bloomington, IN: Solution Tree Press.

Muhammad, A., & Cruz, L. F. (2019). *Time for change: Four essential skills for transformational school and district leaders*. Bloomington, IN: Solution Tree Press.

PBIS Rewards (n.d.). The ultimate list of PBIS incentives. Accessed at www.pbisrewards.com /pbis-incentives on December 24, 2020.

Peterson, K. D. (2002). Positive or negative. *Journal of Staff Development, 23*(3), 10–15.

Valdes, K. S. (2018). *Modeling assertiveness with students: Simple role-playing exercises can show students how to stand up for themselves without being unkind to others.* Accessed at www .edutopia.org/article/modeling-assertiveness-students on December 23, 2020.

Weber, C. (2018). *Behavior: The forgotten curriculum—An RTI approach for nurturing essential life skills.* Bloomington, IN: Solution Tree Press.

Rubric for Defining Schoolwide Behavioral Expectations

List Schoolwide Behavioral Expectations (Work Habits)

Work Habits Rubric

Behavioral Expectation	4 Consistently Exceeds Expectations	3 Frequently Meets Expectations	2 Sometimes Meets Expectations	1 Never or Rarely Meets Expectations

 **Gerry Petersen-Incorvaia, PhD,** is assistant superintendent for educational services at Glendale Elementary School District in Arizona. He has served as a teacher, principal, university professor, and director for curriculum and instruction. He has worked at both school sites and district offices while implementing professional learning communities (PLCs). In the time that Gerry has worked as director for curriculum and instruction and as assistant superintendent at Glendale Elementary School District, the district has become a model PLC, implementing best practices of the PLC process.

In addition to working with Solution Tree and PLCs, Gerry has trained and presented with Rick Stiggins and Jan Chappuis regarding assessment, presented with the State Collaborative on Assessment and Student Standards, and written curriculum and presented with Jay and Daisy McTighe regarding Understanding by Design. The diverse experiences he has had in schools and school districts have invigorated his philosophy that all students should have equity of access to a rigorous education.

Gerry earned his bachelor's degree from Luther College in elementary education and music and his master's and doctoral degrees from the University of Arizona in music education, with post-doctoral work in educational leadership.

To learn more about Gerry's work, follow @DrGerryPI on Twitter.

To book Gerry Petersen-Incorvaia for professional development, contact pd@SolutionTree.com.

Rethinking SMART Goals to Accelerate Learning

Gerry Petersen-Incorvaia

As collaborative teams focus on program-
improvement goals, they should expect to get better
results every year because they are learning more
about what works and what needs improvement in
instruction, curriculum, and assessment practices.

—Sharon V. Kramer and Sarah Schuhl

In the fall of 2015, I was the director for curriculum and instruction at Glendale Elementary School District in Arizona. We had just begun our work as a PLC with the support of Sharon V. Kramer, who helped our teams realize it would not take years to feel like we were making progress toward student achievement. With a focus on creating SMART goals (goals that are strategic and specific, measurable, attainable, results oriented, and time bound; Conzemius & O'Neill, 2014), Sharon introduced the *zone of opportunity* as part of the SMART goal creation process. This thinking, which focuses on helping students whose assessment scores mark them just below proficiency, helped teachers and students realize the opportunity to move more students to proficiency. Our focus on zones of opportunity shifted our teachers' conversations with students from "Look how far away you are from proficiency" to "Look how close you are." Adding the zone of opportunity remains an automatic part of our school's annual creation of SMART goals as well as its creation of intermittent goals.

Priority schools need to accelerate achievement; however, they can have difficulty breaking through the feeling of failure that is often in place during both in-person and especially distance learning. As Sharon Kramer (2015) puts it in *How to Leverage PLCs for School Improvement*, "When these circumstances persist over years, a culture of failure exists that is difficult to overcome" (p. 7). Part of achieving necessary acceleration is giving school staff a carrot of sorts that allows them to see that more students achieving proficiency is possible. This process starts with the yearlong SMART goal.

In this chapter, I will cover the concept of SMART goals in more detail, offer a rethinking of the concept that focuses on accelerating learning, apply this rethinking to zones of opportunity, show how data boards can support this work, and show how to use this accumulated knowledge to increase student self-efficacy.

Understanding SMART Goals

Business and educational organizations have created and implemented SMART goals for quite some time (Conzemius & O'Neill, 2014). SMART goals around student achievement on site-based, district-level, and state or provincial assessments has helped learning organizations focus their work on each aspect of the acronym. Having collaborative teacher teams create, implement, monitor, and evaluate SMART goals has further proven to be an effective strategy for increasing achievement (DuFour, DuFour, Eaker, Many, & Mattos, 2016). Kramer and Schuhl (2017) add that collaborative teams "know they are making a difference in student learning when they establish SMART goals" (p. 141).

Given the importance of SMART goals to collaborative teams and the PLC process, it's critical that teams well understand each of the following components.

- **Strategic and specific:** SMART goals have a tight focus on what they are assessing. Collaborative teams use prior data to identify a leverageable target that is clear to the team and has the power to move student achievement forward.

- **Measurable:** To ensure the goal has a positive trajectory, there must be a measure of quantitative (measurable) data.

- **Attainable:** SMART goals are not set out of reach. Teams can achieve them. It is important to strike a balance of attainable yet ensuring a positive trajectory with regard to student achievement.

- **Results oriented:** Teams must be accountable to the goal through the data they collect. In this way, they assess whether the results they achieve are in line with the goal.

- **Time bound:** The goal itself has a deadline, which helps to create a definitive timeline for the work. SMART goals can be month-long, quarter-long, or even yearlong. The important thing to remember is that they work in cooperation with the other parts of a SMART goal.

Figure 2.1 shows nonexamples and examples of yearlong SMART goals. Note that SMART goals must meet all components of the acronym.

If you review the nonexamples in figure 2.1, you can see there are no time-bound or measurable criteria. When do students need to reach a proficiency percentage? How will we know they have reached it? With the other nonexamples, who is increasing proficiency? How is it results-oriented? How is it strategic and specific?

Nonexample of a Yearlong SMART Goal	Example of a Yearlong SMART Goal
Tenth-grade students will increase their proficiency to 80 percent.	During the 2020–2021 school year, tenth-grade students will increase their proficiency on the state assessment by 15 percent, from 65 percent to 80 percent.
Third-grade students will increase their proficiency by 10 percent.	During the 2020–2021 school year, third-grade students will increase their proficiency on the state reading assessment by 10 percent, from 45 percent to 55 percent.
Band students will play their scales.	By the spring of 2021, the percentage of band students who can play all their major and minor scales will increase from 45 percent to 100 percent.
Fifth-grade teams will increase student achievement.	By the spring of 2021, the number of fifth-grade students will increase their proficiency on the district benchmark from 10 percent (on a universal screener) to at least 80 percent (on the final benchmark).
Ninth-grade students will increase their writing proficiency.	By the spring of 2021, the number of ninth-grade students writing a proficient five-paragraph argumentative essay will increase from 25 percent (pre-test) to at least 85 percent (post-test).

Figure 2.1: SMART goal nonexamples and examples.

Collaborative teacher teams and students alike become hyperfocused on increasing student achievement when they know exactly where they are going and then, with an action plan to reach SMART goals, how they will get there. This is a necessary first step in ensuring collaborative teams are on the right path. The next step is to rethink the process of creating SMART goals.

Rethinking SMART Goals

All SMART goal components are important to the power and success of the school-improvement process, but the attainable portion necessitates a deeper and more targeted approach when it comes to transforming priority schools into performing schools. Sometimes teams set goals so attainable it leads to micro-results that don't lead to the accelerated improvement these schools and students need. If teams set their goals out of reach, it can lead to dismay. Balance is critical.

Finding balance is further complicated because schools that are underperforming may have a high number of students in poverty or face challenges related to accessible distanced learning. Such schools are frequently part of Title I, which makes it paramount that teachers close achievement gaps by ensuring equity of learning opportunities for all students, regardless of the setting. Many times, students in these schools need diverse supports to ensure achievement growth. Collaborative teams work hard, and when low achievement occurs among their students, team members may become despondent. Avoiding this outcome requires a shift in mindset. To start to think differently about students in need at your school, Sharon V. Kramer (personal communication, August 19, 2019) states team members must remember, "Title I describes how a student eats, not how they learn." Removing this mindset and other excuses for students' growing and learning is important to this work. Ensuring school staff have a growth mindset helps transfer a similar mindset to students (Dweck, 2016).

In priority schools, the *attainable* in the SMART acronym may not allow schools to immediately get out of the failing percentages at a rate that helps school improvement in terms of state or provincial accountability. Attainability requires that collaborative teams have a more realistic goal to work toward. As a result, collaborative teams tend to consider what they can attain for certain. This desire for certainty is also an anathema to accelerating learning. To accelerate learning and foster school improvement, teams need a mindset that focuses on the achievable while not limiting the idea of what they *can* achieve. If teams also think of the *A* in *SMART* as standing for *audacious*, it can allow team members to consider higher goals that will have an accelerated impact on student achievement. For the purposes of priority schools, setting audacious goals is vital, but at the same time, teachers need to feel capable of attaining those goals.

Learning by Doing (DuFour, DuFour, Eaker, Many, & Mattos, 2016), the best guide and resource about the work of a PLC, clarifies the balance between audacious goals (what it calls *stretch goals*) and attainable goals:

> Attainable goals are intended to document incremental progress and build momentum and self-efficacy through short-term wins. Stretch goals are intended to inspire, to capture the imagination of people within the organization, to stimulate creativity and innovation, and to serve as a unifying focal point of effort. (p. 92)

A collaborative team's current reality in terms of student achievement is important to consider when discussing a realistic and attainable goal versus a stretch or audacious goal. Attainability requires context. Even though educators should strive for 100 percent learning, it may be unattainable within specific restraints, such as a single school year (DuFour, 2014; Martin & Rains, 2018).

Most state (or provincial) and local assessments provide four proficiency levels when reporting student achievement. Figure 2.2 shows an example. The data in this figure represent the division of third-grade students who tested to the various proficiency levels on a state assessment.

Reading	Falls Far Below Proficiency	Approaching Proficiency	Proficient	Exceeds Proficiency
Third Grade	45%	25%	23%	7%

Figure 2.2: Sample state assessment data.

Historically, to create, implement, monitor, and evaluate attainable goals, collaborative teams have written goals similar to the following example. This example is based on the achievement data listed in figure 2.2.

SMART goal: *For the current school year, third-grade students will increase proficiency by 10 percent on the state reading assessment, improving from 30 percent to 40 percent.*

I created this sample SMART goal by adding together the Proficient and Exceeds Proficiency percentages and adding 10 percent on top. The issue with setting goals this way is that, although it may feel attainable and show some progress, the goal isn't *accelerating* the third-grade students as a whole out of the underperforming categories. In fact, at this pace, it may take quite a few years to move the majority of students into proficiency.

Setting a SMART goal that is audacious and actually accelerates learning is critical in school improvement. In the Glendale Elementary School District, I have seen first-hand how acceleration has not only lifted student achievement but improved school climate and team collaboration. However, to maintain a growth mindset, collaborative teams need to feel that an audacious goal is still attainable. This is where the zone of opportunity comes in.

Creating a Zone of Opportunity

A zone of opportunity groups the students listed as approaching proficiency in figure 2.2. These are the students who might be a concept away or a skill away from being proficient. To move a SMART goal from only attainable to both audacious and attainable, it is important to focus on the students in this zone.

Conventional SMART goals are generally based on the following formula: the percentage of students exceeding proficiency plus the percentage who are proficient plus an additional reasonable and attainable percentage (typically about 10 percent) equals the new goal. For example:

10 percent (exceeds proficiency) + 40 percent (proficient) + 10 percent (a reasonable, attainable increase) = 60 percent (goal for students who will be proficient or better)

Creating a zone of opportunity using SMART goals involves replacing the third metric (the additional reasonable and attainable percentage) with a concrete number based on the percentage of students approaching proficiency. For example:

10 percent (exceeds proficiency) + 40 percent (proficient) + 18 percent (approaching proficiency) = 68 percent (goal for students who will be proficient or better)

Based on a zone of opportunity, collaborative teams rethink SMART goals in ways that are both attainable *and* audacious. Consider the example SMART goal I provided based on data from figure 2.2. It states:

For the current school year, third-grade students will increase proficiency by 10 percent on the state reading assessment, improving from 30 percent to 40 percent.

If teams instead think of their students approaching proficiency as their zone of opportunity, that SMART goal turns into this.

For the current school year, third-grade students will increase proficiency by 25 percent on the state reading assessment, improving from 30 percent to 55 percent.

This calculation of a yearlong SMART goal not only helps collaborative teams realize they may get over the 50 percent mark for student reading proficiency but also crystallizes the reality that many students are not that far from proficiency. It helps highlight that this seemingly audacious goal for student improvement is also *attainable*. However, teams have a further metric they must consider. If the sum of the top three quartiles *does not* equal or is below the 50 percent mark, teams must still write the goal at 50 percent. This is arbitrary but necessary. Establishing a goal of half the students' reaching proficiency is important not just for accelerating achievement but also for instilling a growth mindset and high expectations with teachers and students.

Now, this does not mean that collaborative teams do not focus on the students in the Falls Far Below Proficiency group. All students need to show growth. When teams raise the bar for one group, they raise the bar for all students. Using a zone of opportunity also helps more students in the bottom quartile grow to at least become part of the zone of opportunity. Also, using the zone of opportunity as part of SMART goal calculation is something teams can apply to all forms of assessment-based data analysis, whether based on all students or the grade or course level, demographic subgroups, and so on.

So far, I have focused on using SMART goals to address yearlong efforts regarding state- or province-wide assessment results. However, a struggle that may arise when implementing this strategy is creating incremental goals after an end-of-unit summative assessment or benchmark type of assessment. This same process for rethinking yearlong SMART goals also works to ensure students stay in the grade- or course-level curriculum. Teams can track this interim progress using data boards.

Utilizing Data Boards

Data boards give collaborative teams a visual way to track schoolwide data and rethink SMART goals; they can be as comprehensive as teams need them to be. For example, data boards often come in the form of a graphic organizer to organize schoolwide data and ensure goals appear are at the forefront of the work. In this way, data boards help drive the work while showcasing summative data that helps to benchmark where teams are at with their goals. Some examples of summative data teams include in a data board are state assessment results, end-of-course or end-of-year assessments, benchmark assessments, or more general performance tasks throughout the school year.

I recommend that teams track at least benchmark and state or provincial assessment data using a data board. A key reason why teams should have access to these data is this access helps all schoolwide and collaborative team members take ownership of the data and their students. Also, in schools that are on a continuous school-improvement journey and need to accelerate proficiency, a data board for reading and mathematics is a good place to start because it shows progress toward the overall goal and monitors growth.

Oftentimes, schools may not look at K–2 data, as many states and provinces measure student benchmark data for only third grade and higher. As a result, schools frequently omit K–2 teachers from the school-improvement process, and hence, the PLC process. However, early childhood experts Diane Kerr, Tracey A. Hulen, Jacqueline Heller, and Brian K. Butler (2021) explain in detail that collaboration among early childhood educators is vital to laying a foundation of learning all throughout students' schooling. Further, the lack of state and provincial testing in grades K–2 does not mean early childhood teams can't issue their own benchmark assessments to fill a data board. For these teams, identifying assessments to ensure grade-level readiness is necessary to prompt the vertical articulation and alignment discussions and decisions that occur in a PLC. The following are some examples of K–2 skills to collect data about to determine grade-level readiness.

- Knowing letter names and sounds
- Reading consonant-vowel-consonant (CVC) and vowel-consonant-vowel (VCV) words
- Counting one to one hundred
- Skip counting by twos, fives, and tens
- Printing one's first and last name
- Adding and reading prefixes and suffixes
- Identifying shapes and rotations
- Telling time on analog and digital clocks
- Counting money
- Adding and subtracting within twenty
- Reading one hundred sight words
- Writing uppercase and lowercase letters
- Dividing partition circles and rectangles into two and four equal parts
- Writing four connected sentences with an introduction and details

Some examples of upper-elementary and secondary are more standard-based and perhaps less foundational, including the following.

- Citing textual evidence using informational text
- Writing a coherent, five-paragraph argumentative essay
- Solving equations and inequalities with two variables
- Constructing and comparing linear, quadratic, and exponential models
- Developing claims and counterclaims with evidence to analyze information
- Analyzing multiple complex causes and effects of past and present events
- Developing and using models to analyze forces of nature

Regardless of grade or course level and regardless of whether students are learning in the school building or virtually, the construction of a data board is straightforward. Figure 2.3 presents an example of a schoolwide data board for grades 3–5. (See page 48 for a reproducible version of this figure.)

Content area: Reading			
Grade	3	4	5
Prior-Year State Assessment Results	n/a	56%	75%
Yearlong SMART Goal	80%	85%	80%
Benchmark 1 Results	23%	42%	34%
Intermittent Goal	50%	65%	50%
Benchmark 2 Results	45%	67%	52%
Intermittent Goal	60%	80%	75%
Benchmark 3 Results	58%	83%	75%
Current-Year State Assessment Results	62%	89%	72%

Figure 2.3: Schoolwide data board.

To increase the depth of data on a board, teams may divide each cell into quadrants aligned to proficiency levels, providing even more detailed information. Figure 2.4 shows an example of this. (See page 49 for a reproducible version of this figure.)

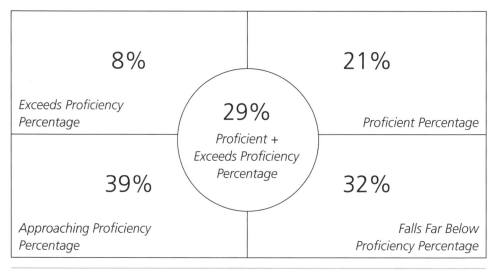

Figure 2.4: Data board by proficiency level.

The depth to which a data board can go doesn't stop here. In the Creating a Zone of Opportunity section (page 35), I noted teams can gather and report data to include various subgroups. Figure 2.5 shows what this looks like based on a variety of diverse student

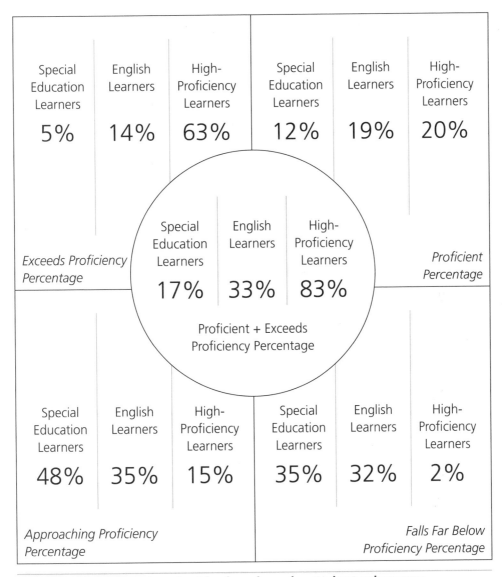

Figure 2.5: Data board content broken down by student subgroups.

populations. Think about the crucial data for your school and its students. How might you customize a data board to best reflect the data your collaborative team needs to focus on to achieve a SMART goal?

In addition to reviewing their own data with the school leadership team, teacher teams should review the data for vertically adjacent teams and the schoolwide data. This ensures all team members understand the big picture for student learning beyond their grade or course level. Further, reviewing data with the school leadership team after each benchmark assessment is important to not only monitor progress toward SMART goals but also reflect on lessons learned throughout the process. Some example reflective questions for celebrating progress toward SMART goals and pondering lessons learned within collaborative teams are listed in table 2.1. Collaborative team members should ask each other these reflective questions throughout the entire collaborative process. More specifically, when looking at common formative assessment data and benchmark data, it is important to ensure proficiency levels are consistently aligned with the year-long goal. This alignment ensures teams meet or even exceed their goals.

Table 2.1: Reflective Questions About SMART Goals

Examples of Reflective Questions for Progress Toward Yearlong SMART Goals	Examples of Reflective Questions for Lessons Learned
What is the percentage of current grade-level students in each proficiency quartile?	Did our pacing of the learning targets and standards align with what was assessed on the summative assessment?
What is the percentage of students who are proficient?	Were our common formative assessments aligned with the summative assessment?
Are we moving students out of the lowest quartile?	Did our common formative assessments predict the summative assessment results?
What is our zone of opportunity?	Is our response to intervention supports and structure working?
What is the proficiency of the cohorts of students from year to year?	What may need adjusting to ensure a tighter alignment of curriculum, instruction, and assessment?
What standards need more support for the grade level?	Is there anything we need to revise or change in our collaboration to have even better results?
What standards does each student need support with?	Did we include students in the data-analysis and goal-creation process?
How did cohort groups of students grow from the end of the prior year? Are students growing?	If we are on track for goal attainment, can we use what we have learned and stretch our goal even higher?

When implementing these audacious yet attainable goals, teams may have a hard time transitioning from small incremental goals for small wins to larger acceleration goals that support student achievement movement. Teams may have trepidation regarding these types of goals, as they may feel they cannot attain them, and therefore, they go further down the spiral of underperformance and feelings of failure. For these teacher teams, this rethinking of SMART goals automatically begs the question, "But, how do we move the partially proficient student to proficiency?" The short answer is teams must try everything. They must look under every rock for options to ensure students reach proficiency and grade-level readiness. Part of your success in this endeavor will involve increasing student self-efficacy.

Increasing Student Self-Efficacy

Just as collaborative teams use SMART goals to accelerate learning based on data, so too can students. Having students build their own data board that is specific by standard, learning target, and grade- or course-level expectation will help students monitor their progress toward their goals regardless of whether they are learning in the classroom or at home. Team members can facilitate this with the students in their classrooms or online via a video-conferencing platform such as Zoom, and they can do so either as a whole-class activity, individually, or both.

Nancy Frey, John Hattie, and Douglas Fisher (2018) share Hattie's meta-analysis that shows students' self-reporting grades has an effect size of 1.44. This effect size represents approximately three years of growth in a single school year, making self-reporting a tremendously high-leverage strategy for accelerating student growth. About this, Frey and colleagues (2018) write:

> In order for students to understand where they're going, they need to have an accurate sense of where they currently stand. . . . The evidence clearly suggests that students are acutely aware of their performance and understand their achievement levels. But if they have to rely on their teacher (and their grades) to tell them where they are and when they have learned something, they become dependent on adults, and they don't develop that internal compass they need to drive their own learning. (p. 17)

Kramer (2015) further shares that when students know their current reality and "determine the gap between where they are now and where they need to be . . . [it] allows them to set goals and monitor their progress toward achieving the goals" (p. 51).

Students should write their personal SMART goals with the support of the teacher; these goals also easily become their own data boards, or more specifically, their own data tracker. In the following sections, I explore how collaborative teams can support students in this work at the primary (grades K–5) and secondary (grades 6–12) levels.

Primary Students

In the primary years, learning and becoming proficient with foundational skills are important to the future success of the student. These foundational skills usually fall into the content areas of reading, writing, and mathematics and include the following.

- Writing your name
- Recognizing and verbalizing letter names and sounds
- Recognizing and verbalizing numbers
- Skip counting by fives and tens
- Recognizing and verbalizing CVC (consonant-vowel-consonant) words
- Telling time on digital and analog clocks
- Recognizing two-dimensional shapes

These foundational skills are usually identified in state and provincial standards as year-long standards but are often separated from standards related to computation reading for information or reading literature.

Let's consider a yearlong SMART goal for a kindergarten team's students: *By May, I will read one hundred sight words.* An incremental goal toward the yearlong goal might be this: *By October, I will read twenty-five sight words.* (Remember to use age-appropriate, student-friendly language when helping students determine their personal goals.) These SMART goals can be tracked on a data board but also with a student's own data tracker. Figure 2.6 shows an example of what a data tracker for these goals might look like. In this example, teachers would have students color in the sight words they know at the end of each quarter or throughout the quarter in order to complete the assessment when the student is ready.

Figure 2.7 (page 44) shows another example tracker that teachers might use with students at the primary level. This example derives from an actual form the kindergarten collaborative team used with Desert Garden Elementary School students in Glendale, Arizona. The tracker allows students to think about and engage with a goal in a fun way and identify when they have met one. The learning goal is listed at the top of the page, and for every piece of that goal, the student can add a chocolate chip or even cut away a piece of the cookie.

For primary students, using a data tracker that engages the student in tracking their own data in a meaningful way is important in increasing their self-confidence and self-efficacy. I have seen students in both in-person and distance learning show their teachers their tracker, stating, "I want to show you what I know," and proceeding to check off another goal or color in another sight word.

Secondary Students

Tracking personal and, perhaps, grade-level or class-level data is not just for primary students. With student efficacy being important at all ages, secondary students should track their data as well. Instead of tracking foundational skills, tracking secondary learning targets and more complex standards against a summative assessment can help improve student success at this level. This can happen in every content area or course, regardless of whether students are learning in person or remotely.

For secondary students in grades 6–12, a semester-long strong SMART goal might be this: *By May, I will increase my mastery of all standards on the semester exam from 50 percent to 75 percent.* To measure progress toward this goal, a student might use a bar or line graph that shows the changes in mastery based on a rubric (scoring levels 1–4). The data are derived from his or her common formative assessments, summative end-of-unit assessments, and semester exam (by standard). Figure 2.8 (page 45) shows a simplified bar-graph example. A full-semester version of this chart might include several additional common formative assessments and end-of-unit assessments. Figure 2.9 (page 45) shows what this might look like arranged by assessment.

Sight Words I Know			
all	was	make	her
be	do	well	open
black	our	must	most
blue	what	saw	home
brown	five	take	any
come	ran	new	in
you	will	there	mall
did	from	who	ask
of	she	out	it
here	yes	please	he
good	four	again	fly
look	that	old	no
green	so	word	very
me	get	eats	let
on	three	put	thing
see	ate	stop	now
they	this	food	may
white	too	just	or
with	pretty	thank	once
yellow	came	going	round
are	under	know	his
go	eat	walk	many
two	ride	went	about
but	want	think	people
one	into	back	day
First Quarter	**Second Quarter**	**Third Quarter**	**Fourth Quarter**

Figure 2.6: Data board for kindergarten-level student goals.

Source: Adapted from Desert Garden Elementary School, Glendale, Arizona.

Figure 2.7: Primary-level student achievement tracker.

Figure 2.8: Student data board on multiple semester assessments—By standard.

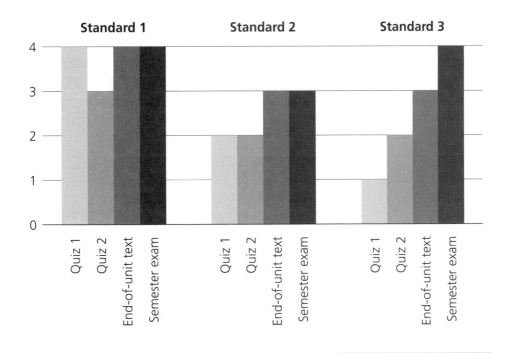

Figure 2.9: Student data board on multiple semester assessments—By assessment.

A meta-analysis of strategies that increase student achievement reflects that the effect size of students' self-reporting grades and self-efficacy is quite high at 1.33, which represents more than three years' growth in a year's time (Hattie, 2017). When upper elementary and secondary students learn to assess their own learning against success criteria, the self-reporting of their grades is a powerful means of taking ownership of their learning. Teams might use the following three strategies to increase upper-elementary and secondary students' self-efficacy.

1. Having a plan or tools for success (such as using graphic organizers, close-reading strategies, and annotation strategies)

2. Simulating the task of assessment prior to high-stakes assessments (that is, ensuring common formative assessments and summative assessments align with state or provincial assessment blueprints and item specifications, and simulating assessment conditions)

3. Tracking personal achievement data as a passport to success

Using SMART goals will specifically help students with the third strategy. Also, if students have tools for success, those tools can transfer to their future years in school and beyond.

Conclusion

Collaborative teams have utilized SMART goals at grade, school, and district levels to provide an understandable direction and pathway for student achievement. Oftentimes, when a school or district does not meet its academic goals or is slow to reach the desired achievement, there is a sense of despair. For this reason, teams typically create SMART goals by taking the percentage of students who are proficient and highly proficient and adding about 10 percent to that number. For a team that is underperforming or is part of an underperforming school or district, it is important and advantageous to use zones of opportunity to build a culture of success and accelerate student achievement. When teacher teams realize there is opportunity instead of deficiency, there is hope. Although hope is not a specific strategy, it is a mindset that is needed to move the work and achievement forward (Jensen, 2019). In the end, students win when learning goals are met.

Collaborative teams can rethink their approach to SMART goals schoolwide and districtwide regardless of geography or student demographics. Most accountability systems and assessments divide student data into quartiles using labels such as (1) highly proficient, (2) proficient, (3) partially proficient, and (4) minimally proficient. If teams can understand that sometimes just one skill, one assessment question, or one concept places some students into that third quartile, it will help teams realize that accelerating achievement to meet an audacious goal is doable. This can and does work.

References and Resources

Conzemius, A. E., & O'Neill, J. (2014). *The handbook for SMART school teams: Revitalizing best practices for collaboration* (2nd ed.). Bloomington, IN: Solution Tree Press.

DuFour, R. (2014, April 2). *Realistic SMART goals* [Blog post]. Accessed at www.allthingsplc.info/blog/view/244/realistic-smart-goals on September 28, 2020.

DuFour, R., DuFour, R., Eaker, R., Many, T. W., & Mattos, M. (2016). *Learning by doing: A handbook for Professional Learning Communities at Work* (3rd ed.). Bloomington, IN: Solution Tree Press.

Dweck, C. S. (2016). *Mindset: The new psychology of success* (Updated ed.). New York: Random House.

Frey, N., Hattie, J., & Fisher, D. (2018). *Developing assessment-capable visible learners, grades K–12: Maximizing skill, will, and thrill.* Thousand Oaks, CA: Corwin Press.

Hattie, J. (2017). *Visible Learning plus: 250+ influences on student achievement.* Accessed at https://visible-learning.org/wp-content/uploads/2018/03/VLPLUS-252-Influences-Hattie -ranking-DEC-2017.pdf on September 28, 2020.

Jensen, E. (2019). *Poor students, rich teaching: Seven high-impact mindsets for students from poverty* (Rev. ed.). Bloomington, IN: Solution Tree Press.

Kerr, D., Hulen, T. A., Heller, J., & Butler, B. K. (2021). *What about us? The PLC at Work process for grades preK–2 teams.* Bloomington, IN: Solution Tree Press.

Kramer, S. V. (2015). *How to leverage PLCs for school improvement.* Bloomington, IN: Solution Tree Press.

Kramer, S. V., & Schuhl, S. (2017). *School improvement for all: A how-to guide for doing the right work.* Bloomington, IN: Solution Tree Press.

Martin, T. L., & Rains, C. L. (2018). *Stronger together: Answering the questions of collaborative leadership.* Bloomington, IN: Solution Tree Press.

Schoolwide Data Board

Content area:				
Grade or Course				
Prior-Year State Assessment Results				
Yearlong SMART Goal				
Benchmark 1 Results				
Intermittent Goal				
Benchmark 2 Results				
Intermittent Goal				
Benchmark 3 Results				
Current-Year State Assessment Results				

Data Board Organized by Proficiency Level

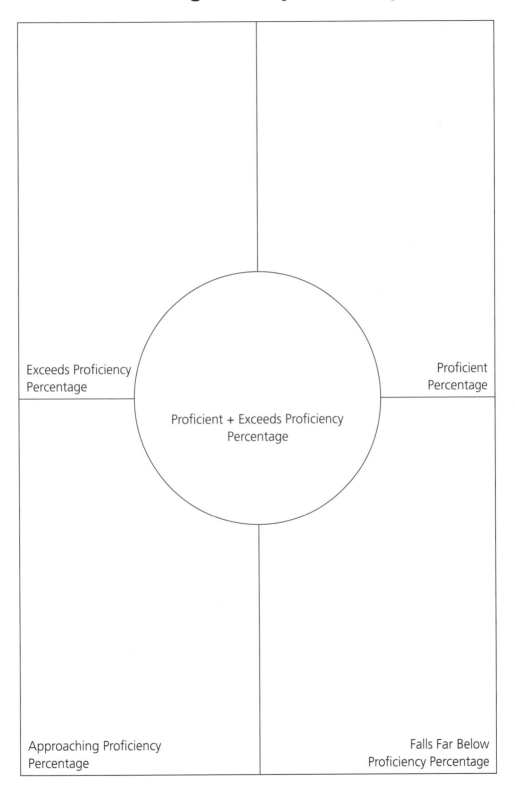

Exceeds Proficiency Percentage

Proficient Percentage

Proficient + Exceeds Proficiency Percentage

Approaching Proficiency Percentage

Falls Far Below Proficiency Percentage

Tamie Sanders has worked in education for over thirty years as a teacher and administrator. She is known for her ability to facilitate implementation of successful professional learning communities (PLCs) and to utilize the school-improvement process to increase student achievement. Through her leadership as a principal and district executive director of secondary schools, she has proven that school and district turnaround is eminently achievable.

Tamie has presented research about U.S. Grant High School to the Oklahoma City Public School District and the Oklahoma State Department of Education and presented to educators at Vision 2020 Institutes offered by the Oklahoma State Department of Education. She received a citation for exemplary academic performance from Oklahoma state senator Al McAffrey and was featured in *Stars of Education* magazine, published by the Foundation for Oklahoma City Public Schools.

Tamie earned a bachelor's degree in secondary education from Oklahoma State University and a master of education in administration, curriculum, and supervision from the University of Oklahoma.

Dana Renner is assistant superintendent of Stillwater Public Schools in Stillwater, Oklahoma. She has more than twenty-five years of experience in education as a teacher, instructional facilitator, assistant principal, head principal, and director of human resources. Dana has extensive experience in large urban and suburban districts and has worked at all levels of education.

As principal, Dana led Central Middle School, in Edmond Public Schools, Edmond, Oklahoma to model PLC status. As principal of the Freshman Academy at U.S. Grant High School, she was part of an administrative team that led the school to become the first model PLC in the state of Oklahoma. Dana has extensive experience in continuous school improvement and school turnaround, the PLC at Work process, common formative assessments, data-analysis protocols, diverse student populations and student achievement.

Dana was recognized as the Oklahoma State Middle School Principal of the Year for 2015–2016 and was a representative at the National Association of Secondary School Principals Leadership Institute in Washington, DC. She was selected by the Oklahoma state superintendent of public instruction to serve on the Principal's Advisory Committee and Teacher Leader Effectiveness Advisory Committee.

Dana has a bachelor's degree in secondary education from Oklahoma State University and a master's degree in school administration from the University of Central Oklahoma. Dana is pursuing her doctorate in curriculum and leadership at Oklahoma State University.

To book Tamie Sanders or Dana Renner for professional development, contact pd@ SolutionTree.com.

Adopting the Ten-Day Collaborative Cycle

Tamie Sanders and Dana Renner

> I believe this anonymous quote describes what it takes to improve schools: "In the end, real school improvement requires us to . . . risk more than others think is safe . . . dream more than others think is practical . . . expect more than others think is possible.
>
> —*Sharon V. Kramer*

In 2011, when given the task of leading U.S. Grant High School in Oklahoma City, Oklahoma, through school improvement, Tamie was the school principal and highest-ranking school officer. She gathered her leadership team to discuss the plans for the day and to walk through the logistics of initiating a school-improvement effort.

As a state-designated turnaround school, the team was in uncharted territory, and if it failed to improve, no one was quite certain what the outcome might be, and so the principal's office at U.S. Grant High School had come to resemble the Situation Room at the White House. There was a conference table with chairs around it, where the leadership team gathered regularly with the latest information about students' needs. There were bullet points and notes on the whiteboard, with inspirational sayings to motivate the team. Despite how hard the leadership team was working to lead the school's collaborative teacher teams in the right direction, teachers struggled to grasp many aspects of the PLC process.

In a desperate move to refine the collaborative process and focus on the four critical questions of a PLC (see page 3), the leadership team came up with an out-of-the-box idea to specifically encourage teachers to more quickly assess and respond to student data. Team members called it *the cycle*. To help teacher teams better understand the need for timely data, the leadership team put the cycle into a ten-day framework, defining each day within it, making it a *ten-day cycle*. This premise supported teachers in sustaining PLC big idea 3 (a focus on results) by gathering and responding to data with intentionality (DuFour, DuFour, Eaker, Many, & Mattos, 2016), from start to finish, within ten days.

It is difficult to monitor and adjust learning and instruction without timely data, and the ten-day cycle allows teams to answer all four critical questions of a PLC over and over again, refining their work as they go. Figure 3.1 shows an example of the planning, actions, and products that comprise the ten-day cycle. You'll note two columns related to enhancement in this figure. The students in this example were enrolled in both an algebra class and an algebra enhancement class. The purpose of the enhancement class was to preteach prerequisite skills for each unit and engage in reteaching as needed, utilizing course-level data as the guide. This highlights the flexibility of the ten-day cycle. If your collaborative team uses this or similar class structures or formats, you simply adjust the columns as needed to plan content and products for each associated class.

At U.S. Grant High School, the ten-day cycle would become the platform that propelled teacher teams to do the work of a PLC, and work they did. During the 2012–2013 school year, having demonstrated a sustained commitment to the PLC process for three years running and having gained clear evidence of increased student learning and achievement, U.S. Grant High School became the first model PLC school in the state of Oklahoma. Throughout this chapter, you'll learn more about the work highlighted in figure 3.1 and how it supports teams in answering all four critical questions of a PLC. We write about the following ten steps that our school's collaborative teams took as part of the ten-day cycle. (Note that, although there are ten tasks in this list, the tasks do not align to each day of the ten-day cycle; they overlap and spread across it based on need.)

1. State the problem.
2. Bring focus to the work.
3. Identify essential skills.
4. Unpack learning standards.
5. Establish learning targets.
6. Write common formative assessments.
7. Plan daily lessons.
8. Give common formative assessments.
9. Analyze data.
10. Respond to data.

Just as U.S. Grant High School did, your school's collaborative teams can follow these steps to fulfill their ongoing mission to increase student achievement.

State the Problem

Schools in similar positions to U.S. Grant High School face the same pressure we did to achieve a turnaround. All eyes are on them, often at the federal, state or provincial, and district levels, and there is no time to waste, not a second to spare in achieving learning for all. When collaborative teams struggle to achieve success, the leadership team must

	Collaborative Team Meeting Actions	Products Needed for Collaborative Team Meeting	Lesson Content	Lesson Products	Enhancement and Enrichment Content	Enhancement and Enrichment Products	Artifacts
Day 1	Review data from the previous common assessment. Discuss instructional strategies for the current ten-day cycle.	A printed list of student proficiency levels and the associated common assessment Note: Enhancement teachers must understand individual student levels by the end of the team meeting.	Cover objectives for the upcoming common assessment in alignment with the curriculum pacing guide.	Instructional materials for the day's lesson Note: These should be handed out before the day of the lesson.	Conduct a spiral review based on essential standards. Note: This review ensures students gain or extend proficiency with previously taught essential standards.	An enhancement and enrichment plan derived from the spiral review	Year-at-a-glance unit guide Team norms Team roles Team-meeting agenda List of essential standards Data-analysis protocol Lesson-planning template
Day 2					Review differentiated instruction options based on common assessment data discussed in the previous day's team meeting.	Three levels of instructional materials for differentiated instruction with students at different proficiency levels	
Day 3	Discuss what will be in the next common assessment and who will make it. Note: The assessment should be completed no later than day 7 of the cycle. Creating the common assessment for *this* cycle (not the next one) will guide the associated lesson plans.	Any necessary materials to determine what will be on the common assessment					

Figure 3.1: The ten-day cycle.

continued →

	Collaborative Team Meeting Actions	Products Needed for Collaborative Team Meeting	Lesson Content	Lesson Products	Enhancement and Enrichment Content	Enhancement and Enrichment Products	Artifacts
Day 4	→	→					
Day 5	Map out lesson plans for the next cycle. Note: Lesson plans should be based on the common assessment and pacing guide. Assign tasks and complete them no later than day 7 of the cycle.	A complete lesson-planning template for the next two weeks of instruction	→	→	→	→	→
Day 6	Grade- and course-level and enhancement and enrichment teachers assign and share responsibility for making instructional materials as needed. Everyone should have an assigned task.	Instructional materials for the grade- or course-level class, including materials for enhancement and enrichment Note: These should be materials for the upcoming cycle, not the current cycle.	Cover objectives for the upcoming common assessment in alignment with the unit-pacing guide.	Instructional materials for the day's lesson (Do not hand these out the day of the lesson.)	Provide support for the objectives for the upcoming common assessment in the current cycle.	Instructional materials needed for support	
Day 7	→	→	→	→	→	→	→

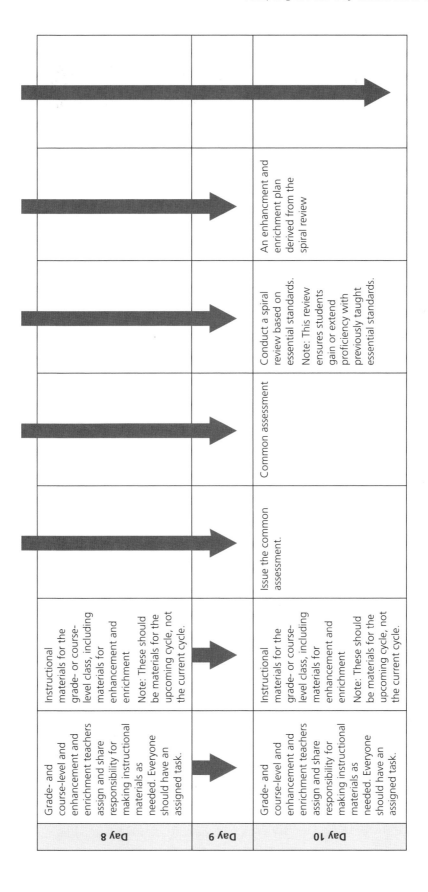

Day 8	Grade- and course-level and enhancement and enrichment teachers assign and share responsibility for making instructional materials as needed. Everyone should have an assigned task.	Instructional materials for the grade- or course-level class, including materials for enhancement and enrichment Note: These should be materials for the upcoming cycle, not the current cycle.		
Day 9			Issue the common assessment.	Common assessment
Day 10	Grade- and course-level and enhancement and enrichment teachers assign and share responsibility for making instructional materials as needed. Everyone should have an assigned task.	Instructional materials for the grade- or course-level class, including materials for enhancement and enrichment Note: These should be materials for the upcoming cycle, not the current cycle.	Conduct a spiral review based on essential standards. Note: This review ensures students gain or extend proficiency with previously taught essential standards.	An enhancment and enrichment plan derived from the spiral review

remind them of their purpose, their why, and their mission. If a problem presents itself within the work, it is through collaboration that teams clarify the problem, what team members are involved, what they need, when they need it, and where and how the work will ensue. Your team's achievement results will tell you if your team has solved the problem or if it's necessary to try something else.

Our leadership team developed the ten-day learning cycle and other artifacts to ensure our school's collaborative teams had answers to their questions and access to an accountability system they knew we monitored. In our case, it was easy to identify the problem. Students weren't learning. We knew this because our data from end-of-year assessments showed little to no growth after a year of instruction. What essential content standards weren't our students learning? We had no idea. More important, what were we doing about the lack of learning we identified?

Notice how these questions align to the four critical questions of a PLC (DuFour et al., 2016). Our teams had essential standards they knew they wanted students to learn (the first critical question); however, they needed the means to determine what standards students weren't learning (the second critical question) and then how to respond to that information (the third critical question). (To learn more about responding to the fourth critical question, see chapter 9, page 189.) We knew that establishing a framework where interventions could happen in close proximity to grade-level instruction was critical. By understanding and stating the problem via the ten-day learning cycle, our collaborative teams had the map and supporting products they needed to guide them to our ultimate schoolwide goal of filling in gaps in learning. Put simply, when it comes to interventions, X (the learning problem) marks the spot.

Bring Focus to the Work

By the 2010–2011 school year, U.S. Grant High School had been on Oklahoma's Needs Improvement list for six consecutive years. To help break this unfortunate streak, in March 2010, the Oklahoma City Public Schools Board of Education supported the school with a *Turnaround School* designation, which ensured it would receive additional funding. With this funding, the school administrative team collaborated with district leaders to select the PLC process as the vehicle for school improvement. This decision was the beginning for how the school could reshape the makeup and culture of collaborative teams.

The culture and media surrounding U.S. Grant High School, the largest school in Oklahoma City Public Schools, has historically been negative. Many in the state and community referred to it as a "dropout factory" and "ground zero of education reform in Oklahoma." Further, many of the gangs in Oklahoma City resided within U.S. Grant High School boundaries. As a result, the school focused on compliance and order instead of student achievement. To change this culture to one dedicated to improving learning required every stakeholder to focus on improving both learning and culture.

Before the start of the 2011–2012 school year, 204 seniors (83 percent) had not met the state testing requirements for graduation (a specific number of course credits and a passing result on four of seven end-of-instruction exams). Teams knew the problem, but they needed a point of focus. So, at the start of that year, administrators, counselors, and teachers analyzed each senior's data to ensure every student would have maximum opportunities and resources to meet the state requirements. Using PLC concepts and processes as a foundation, collaborative teams focused on analyzing data that would help them simultaneously improve student learning toward graduation requirements and improve the school's culture. This improvement didn't happen overnight, but by the 2013–2014 school year, U.S. Grant High School became a B+ school, earning eighty-nine points on a one hundred–point scale in which a ninety-point rating qualifies as an A. Further, of the three schools in the Oklahoma City Public School District that received an A or B rating, U.S. Grant High School was the only comprehensive high school to rate so high. With a focus on learning and a new, higher bar for academic growth established for all students, the school moved from thirty-three seniors receiving the Super 7 Seniors designation (having passed all seven end-of-instruction state-mandated tests as opposed to the required four) in the 2011–2012 school year to more than half the senior class receiving the designation in the 2013–2014 school year.

No matter where it's starting from, your school can also find this kind of success. However, doing so requires both understanding and stating the problem *and* sustaining focus from all teacher teams. Building that focus has three components, which we explore in the following sections: (1) determine your reality, (2) plan to answer the four critical questions of a PLC, and (3) establish next steps.

Determine Your Reality

Even if they understand their school's problems, it's fair for collaborative teams to ask, "Where does our work begin when everything is a need?" That's why conducting an autopsy around student-learning data is so important. In conjunction with school leadership, teams must critically examine the situation at hand. Triage the needs, addressing the critical (most emergent) needs first, followed by urgent needs and then non-urgent needs. Use a resource on backward planning, such as *Leading Modern Learning* (McTighe & Curtis, 2019), so that your team plans with the end in mind, beginning with assessing where the team is in its improvement journey. Be thorough, and use relevant data—such as school report cards, dissected into content area and grade level—to inform the process.

To accomplish this task, collaborative team members should ask the following questions and then work with school leadership to determine answers.

- "What is our current reality?"
- "Where do we want to be?"
- "How are we going to get there?"
- "What needs to happen first?"
- "What is our plan?"

- "What is our timeline?"
- "How will we know if we are moving in the right direction?"

At U.S. Grant High School, the turnaround process toward increasing student achievement focused on creating an atmosphere of shared leadership (ensuring every teacher had a voice, listening to ideas, and building consensus) and building expertise through job-embedded professional development for collaborative teams. As part of the PLC process, collaborative teams met for a minimum of ninety minutes each week with an emphasis on seeking out best practices, assessing student achievement, improving current instructional methods, and getting results. The key attributes influencing U.S. Grant High School's success included the following.

- A highly dedicated, driven, and caring staff
- A supportive and dedicated principal with a laser-sharp focus on measurable results
- A structured approach to implementing the PLC process
- Daily teacher collaboration during the regular school day
- A flexible master schedule the leadership team developed and updated as needed to support student and teacher success
- The development of authentic common formative and common summative assessments
- The use of data to drive instruction
- A focus on student-specific data and achievement
- The establishment of a Freshman Academy that implemented the rules and routines for incoming students to support a culture of success
- The creation of a culture of success by engaging students in monitoring their own learning (which developed students' desire for success inside and outside the classroom)
- Ongoing professional development provided by education experts

Achieving success with each of these attributes requires schools to answer the four critical questions of a PLC (DuFour et al., 2016).

Plan to Answer the Four Critical Questions of a PLC

The purpose of the four critical questions of a PLC is for all school stakeholders, from school leadership to individual collaborative teams, to understand what they want all students to know and be able to do, to ensure a means for determining whether that learning is happening, and to know how they should respond when that learning does or does not happen (DuFour et al., 2016). The following list explains how we at U.S. Grant High School approached each question.

- **What do we want students to learn?** This question focuses on teacher teams' knowing what they should teach, maintaining vertical and horizontal alignment between and among grade levels, understanding Norman L. Webb's Depth of Knowledge (DOK; Francis, 2017; Webb, 1997), and understanding essential standards (also called *power standards*). In addition to teams ensuring they understood what standards students should master, the U.S. Grant High School teachers also showed students how to track their progress toward those standards. Students and teachers worked together to create meaningful word walls and data walls to allow for strong connections between students and content. Each word wall reflected three to five academic vocabulary words derived from their repeated appearances in essential standards within a unit. It ensured teachers focused on the actions and criteria students needed to know and understand. Data walls served as a real-time measure of students' progress toward mastering standards.

- **How will we know if they have learned it?** This question is ultimately about teams' establishing a guaranteed and viable curriculum (Eaker & Marzano, 2020). At U.S. Grant High School, teams accomplished this by creating common formative assessments, common summative assessments, and benchmark assessments with at least one writing component, regardless of the course. Because data are the best way to determine whether learning is happening, our teams relentlessly analyzed continuous streams of incoming data to reveal curricular issues, highlight individual and collective student strengths and weaknesses, and determine future lesson-planning decisions.

Because assessments were based on standards, and teachers provided students with student-friendly versions of those standards, students knew what skills they needed proficiency in. This engaged them in their own learning process. In addition, the school's leadership conducted quarterly data reviews with Oklahoma State Department of Education members, district-level administrators, site-level administrators, and department chairs. The leadership team then shared all findings and action steps with the entire staff.

- **What will we do if they don't learn it?** This question provides the intervention piece for students. (See chapter 8, page 171.) At U.S. Grant High School, teacher teams made a positive impact by creating and implementing differentiated, student-centered lessons based on what specific learning data said students knew or did not know. For students who hadn't met proficiency on essential standards, teams utilized leadership-provided break periods to hold boot camps and intercessions to remediate the students quickly. These remediation sessions occurred during breaks (fall, winter, and spring) to ensure students had multiple opportunities for success.

- **What will we do if they already know it?** Teams' use of differentiated lessons also served as extension opportunities for students and a means for teams to answer this question. Honor the learning of students who have mastered content by challenging them beyond the standard's rigor.

Establish Next Steps

Answering the critical questions is only one piece of the PLC journey. To help set a focused direction, leadership teams in priority schools must also work with collaborative teams to accomplish the following.

1. **Conduct an autopsy:** Gather state or provincial achievement data, and examine it thoroughly to discover the cause of students' low achievement.

2. **Triage the needs:** Assign urgency within the improvement areas to decide the order of action from critical to urgent to not urgent.

3. **Establish a plan with the highest-yielding learning outcomes:** Once you have clarified your emergent needs, working with the end in mind, how might your action plan align with those outcomes? Say, "This is where we are. This is where we need to be. How are we going to get there?"

4. **Set goals:** To ensure you can reach the desired outcomes, teams should set goals. We recommend using SMART goals, goals that are strategic and specific, measurable, attainable, results oriented, and time bound (Conzemius & O'Neill, 2014). (See chapter 2, page 31, to learn more about SMART goals.)

5. **Build teacher capacity:** For a PLC to function, teachers must be able to work as members of high-performing collaborative teams that focus their efforts on improving learning for all students.

At U.S. Grant High School, the principal strategically selected department chairs and collaborative team leaders based on each individual's collaborative leadership skills, not based on seniority or years of experience. These leaders participated in professional development and received coaching to further develop their facilitation skills. With school administrators, they also participated as members of the schoolwide leadership team and monitored *grant expectations*, the protocols leadership expected departmental teacher teams use in their collaborative work. The protocols included the following.

1. **Establish SMART goals:** Each collaborative team should have SMART goals that align to and support the schoolwide SMART goals.

2. **Review SMART goals:** As teams gather common formative and summative assessment achievement data within each instructional unit, they should review those data within the SMART goal's context to see if the results align with the intended outcomes.

3. **Develop and review norms:** Each collaborative team should develop and follow meeting norms, such as what days and times the team will meet, where it will meet, how long it will meet for. All team members should know their attendance requirements, what tasks they will share or are assigned to specific members, how they will communicate, and so on. Teams should periodically review norms for refinement, as needed. At a minimum, teams should review norms at the start of each school year.

4. **Use team agendas and record minutes:** Team agendas determine the focus of any particular meeting, who is involved, what products are needed, and so on.

Recording minutes from each meeting ensures there is a record of any decisions the team has made, actions team members will take prior to a subsequent meeting, and so on.

5. **Effectively and efficiently focus on the four critical questions of a PLC:** Use the results of the common assessments to assist each other in building on strengths and weaknesses as part of an ongoing process of continuous improvement designed to help students achieve at higher levels, and use the results to identify students who need additional time and support to master essential learning.

6. **Utilize authentic and frequent common assessments that genuinely measure and monitor learning:** Whether creating new assessments or modifying or repurposing existing assessments, teams must continually review their assessments to ensure they generate accurate data about student proficiency with the standards the assessments measure.

7. **Engage in data analysis to the student level:** With data derived from assessments, teams engage in data analysis, standard by standard and student by student, to determine who has gained proficiency and who requires additional support.

8. **Use data to drive instruction:** After analyzing data, teams determine what story those data tell. They ask, "How will we respond to these data to meet the needs of every student?" Subsequent actions should reflect both intervention and extension opportunities based on each student's needs.

9. **Monitor for conflicts and barriers that get in the way of student learning:** When students don't learn, there are always barriers at work. It may be as simple as misunderstanding a core concept or lack of proficiency in a single foundational skill. Sometimes barriers are larger or reflect factors from outside the classroom (problems at home, social problems, and so on). Teams must meet students where they are, determining and addressing barriers as best they can. There are numerous ways to proceed with this work and many resources teams can tap; one such resource is *The Wraparound Guide* (Colburn & Beggs, 2021), which shows how to engage in a schoolwide effort to determine barriers to learning that come from outside the classroom and help students overcome them.

These team processes allow for collaboration as opposed to teachers working in isolation. As teachers work within these expectations, it brings clarity to the work and begins to build efficacy.

Identify Essential Skills

Defining essential skills students need to know (answering the first critical question of a PLC) is interwoven into the entirety of the ten-day collaborative cycle. It is not a linear process because, in a priority school, you are defining the work at the same time you are doing the work. To determine what students need to know and be able to do, teacher teams must identify which skills are essential for students to show proficiency in.

Essential skills define knowledge or skills that (1) endure beyond a single test, (2) are of value in multiple disciplines, and (3) are necessary for success in the next grade level (DuFour et al., 2016). This is straightforward. However, teams must come to a consensus as to which skills are essential. At U.S. Grant High School, we developed the following three-step process for every collaborative team member to complete.

1. List five to seven essential skills and understandings you would like every student to know before the start of your course.

2. List five to seven essential skills and understandings you could commit to ensuring that all your students master for your course.

3. Determine which content standards you would identify as the essential (power) standards for your content area, and specify why these are essential.

Figure 3.2 provides an example of how an individual algebra 1 teacher, and then the full algebra 1 team, identified essential skills for the course. (See page 78 for a reproducible version of this figure.) Note that the standards involved reflect Oklahoma state standards in use at the time but have since been updated.

To help identify the essential skills, teacher teams analyze state or provincial testing data and make connections to the content standards. Again, working with the end in mind, the teachers at U.S. Grant High School accomplished this work through a process called *year at a glance* (see figure 3.3, page 64).

Once teams have established which essential standards they will teach in each quarter, they should drill down deeper into the essential components of each standard using a tool like the one shown in figure 3.4 (page 65). Because this process occurs quarterly, this drill down into essential components is not a thorough unpacking of standards as described in the next section.

Essential Standards for Algebra 1
Guiding Questions
• Will these skills provide value that endures beyond a single test?
• Will these skills be of value in multiple disciplines?
• Are these skills or knowledge items necessary for success in the next grade level or beyond?
1. List five to seven essential skills or understandings you would like every student to know when they come to you.   • Solve one-step equations.   • Understand order of operations.   • Be proficient with the distributive property.   • Understand number sense (positive, negative, integers, and decimals).   • Be able to plot points.

2. List five to seven essential skills or understandings you could commit to ensuring that all your students have mastered.

- *Solve multistep equations.*
- *Solve equations with the variable on both sides.*
- *Find the slope of a line.*
- *Graph a line.*
- *Write the equation of a line.*

3. Determine which essential skills the team has consensus on, and list the essential standards that specify those skills along with the DOK required.

Students will:

- *Simplify and evaluate linear, absolute value, rational and radical expressions (A1.1.2.a) — DOK 2*
- *Solve linear equations by graphing or using properties of equality (A1.2.2.a) — DOK 2*
- *Recognize the parent graph of the functions $y = k$, $y = x$, $y = |x|$, and predict the effects of transformations on the parent graph (A1.2.2.b) — DOK 1*
- *Calculate the slope of a line using a graph, an equation, two points, or a set of data points (A1.2.2.c.i) — DOK 2*
- *Use the slope to differentiate between lines that are parallel, perpendicular, horizontal, or vertical (A1.2.2.c.ii) — DOK 3*
- *Interpret the slope and intercepts within the context of everyday life (A1.2.2.c.iii) — DOK 2*
- *Make valid inferences, predictions, and/or arguments based on data from graphs, tables, and charts (A1.3.1.b) — DOK 2*
- *Translate word phrases and sentences into expressions and equations and vice versa (A1.1.1.a) — DOK 1*
- *Develop the equation of a line and graph linear relationships given the following: slope and y-intercept, slope and one point on the line, two points on the line, x-intercept and y-intercept, a set of data points (A1.2.2.d) — DOK 3*
- *Simplify polynomials by adding, subtracting, or multiplying (A1.1.2.b) — DOK 2*

Source for standards: Oklahoma State Department of Education, n.d.

Figure 3.2: Individual and team identification of essential skills.

School Year: _____   Course: _____

Directions: Within each box, divide and distribute the essential standards according to which standards should be covered within each quarter of instruction.

First Quarter	Third Quarter
Second Quarter	**Fourth Quarter**

Figure 3.3: Year-at-a-glance planning tool.

*Visit **go.SolutionTree.com/PLCbooks** for a free reproducible version of this figure.*

Quarter _____		
Content and Concept Focus	**Essential Questions**	**Reading Components**
Examples of Rigor	**Writing Components**	**Vocabulary Components**
	.	
Assignments and Activities	**Study Skills and Research Components**	**Grammar Components**
Assessments	**Differentiated Instruction Components**	**Resources**

Figure 3.4: Tool to determine components of essential standards.

*Visit **go.SolutionTree.com/PLCbooks** for a free reproducible version of this figure.*

Once teachers have identified the essential components of each essential standard, they pace the number of days needed to cover the content within each quarter. As part of this process, they build in opportunities for timely common formative assessment of learning, intervention, and extension. Figure 3.5 shows an example of this process, using bold to indicate the assessment opportunities. Note that the third column, Driver, refers to the teacher best associated with teaching to the listed skill or standard. Teams typically determine a teacher based on the highest-yielding results on common assessments based on the previous year's data.

Quarter 1

Day	Daily Plan or Standard Taught	Driver
Days 1–14	Beginning-of-year rituals and routines	
Day 15	Two-step equations	
Day 16	Two-step equations	
Day 17	**Issue common assessment, and plan learning interventions and extensions.**	
Day 18	Two-step equations with word problems	
Day 19	Two-step equations with word problems	
Day 20	Multistep equations with variables on both sides and word problems	
Day 21	Multistep equations with variables on both sides and word problems	
Day 22	Multistep equations with variables on both sides and word problems	
Day 23	Literal equations	
Day 24	Literal equations	
Day 25	Literal equations using word problems	
Day 26	**Review.**	
Day 27	**Issue common assessment, and plan learning interventions and extensions.**	
Day 28	Plotting points, coordinate graph	
Day 29	Plotting points, coordinate graph	
Day 30	Two-variable equations; graph lines using points and tables (build on review of plotting and solving literals)	
Day 31	Characteristics of lines (positive or negative slopes, intercepts)	

Day 32	Slope in the context of everyday life	
Day 33	Slope from two points	
Day 34	Slope from two points	
Day 35	Graphing with $y = mx + b$	
Day 36	Open day (Having an open day allows for adjustments to the instructional cycle based on frequent checks for understanding.)	
Day 37	Graphing with $y = mx + b$	
Day 38	Graphing with $y = mx + b$	
Day 39	Open day	
Day 40	Flex day (Teams allot five flex days at the end of the unit to use for reteaching, if needed, and extensions. If not needed, teams can omit these days.	
Day 41	Flex day	
Day 42	Flex day	
Day 43	Flex day	
Day 44	Flex day	
Day 45	**Issue common assessment, and plan learning interventions and extensions**	

Figure 3.5: Example of planning instruction and assessments for a quarter.

In this way, planning instruction over multiple ten-day learning cycles ensures teams can pace units appropriately while providing flex days teachers can use to ensure students master essential standards.

Unpack Essential Standards

After identifying essential standards, determining their components, and planning for a full quarter of instruction, teams are prepared to unpack the standards into learning targets (components of standards) and learning progressions (the sequences of targets that build up to the full standards). This action ensures that, as teams proceed through each day of the ten-day cycle, they know and have consensus around the standards they are prioritizing.

Unpacking standards and drilling down to essential content (learning targets) is vital, and teacher teams may need more in-depth guidance to lead them through it. In *School Improvement for All*, Sharon V. Kramer and Sarah Schuhl (2017) write about the significance of unpacking standards into learning progressions and student learning targets:

> Five different teachers can read a standard and interpret it five different ways. To have a guaranteed and viable curriculum that is equitable for all students, teachers on a collaborative team must share an understanding as to the content and skills students must demonstrate to be proficient with the standard. (p. 63)

As when determining which learning standards are essential, teams must have consensus around the learning targets that make up a standard. To create effective learning targets (as we describe in the next section), teams need to agree about the specific content and skills a standard asks students to master. Without this deep understanding, the quality of the work to follow will be insufficient to achieve learning for all.

Fortunately, teams can do the following exercise to help all team members understand the importance and the significance of knowing what a standard asks of students.

1. Without setting aside any time for preparation, a leadership team member or a teacher team leader (for this purpose, we refer to this person as the *facilitator*) pulls together a full collaborative team and asks each team member to create an assessment on two to three standards with a maximum of ten questions. Team members should do this without talking or collaborating with each other.

2. When team members finish the task, they turn in their assessment to the facilitator (still without talking).

3. The facilitator chooses two to three questions from each assessment and combines those into a new ten-question assessment.

4. The facilitator shares the new assessment with the team and asks team members to take that assessment, independent of each other.

5. Team members grade the assessments together (each marking their own assessment) and walk through the team's data-analysis protocol using teachers' scores. The facilitator can anonymously gather the results from the teachers if he or she does not want to openly share their scores.

6. The facilitator asks the teachers what they thought about the test. He or she listens closely as team members begin to dissect each question, justify their answers, talk through their thinking, and lament about the questions they answered incorrectly. The facilitator should expect to hear teachers say things like, "Oh, I thought this question was about _____," or "I assumed this answer was correct because _____," or "I didn't include this as a question on my assessment because _____."

Having a facilitator dedicated to asking probing questions of everyone in the room helps the whole team understand the thinking behind every team member's actions. It deepens collective understanding about standards and brings to light questions or misconceptions teachers may have. Such reflection consistently leads to proactive adjustments that improve teaching and learning.

In addition to conducting this exercise, teams can use a variety of tools to help them unpack standards. Figure 3.6 features an adapted version of the tool Kramer and Schuhl (2017) provide in *School Improvement for All*.

Standard:

Annotate this standard by doing the following.

- **Content**—Underline nouns within the standard.
- **Skills**—Circle verbs within the standard.
- **Context**—Place brackets around words that contextualize students' use of content and skills.

Use the following columns to break down the standard.

Content (Nouns) What do students need to know? Include the DOK level associated with each content item.	Skills (Verbs) What do students need to be able to do? Include the DOK level associated with each skill.	Context What is the context for students' use of these content and skills.

Source: Adapted from Kramer & Schuhl, 2017.

Figure 3.6: Unpacking essential standards to determine core content items and skills.

*Visit **go.SolutionTree.com/PLCbooks** for a free reproducible version of this figure.*

Once teacher teams identify the content and the skills inherent within a standard, they assess the proficiency level students need to reach with that content and those skills. This is where depth of knowledge comes in (Francis, 2017; Webb, 1997). Team members need to know to what DOK level students must demonstrate a content item or skill. With this knowledge, teams can align assessment questions' DOK levels to gauge student proficiency with content items, skills, and the overall standard. This becomes a guide throughout the unit and course.

Establish Learning Targets

Teacher teams and students must know what proficiency looks like; that is, what it looks like to be proficient with each of an essential standard's components. With this knowledge, teachers can synthesize the content and skills into learning targets that can be converted to numbers and used with a proficiency scale like the one in figure 3.7. Use this tool on the first day of each ten-day learning cycle to help students set achievable target goals within each standard. Then, challenge students to know their number. This helps students structure their thinking, plan their learning, set goals, monitor progress, make adjustments, and evaluate their learning regarding the outcomes.

Once teams know what they want students to know and be able to do, the next step is to write an assessment that reflects that.

Write Common Formative Assessments

When writing a common assessment, a team uses the DOK level defined when unpacking the standard (see figure 3.6, page 69) to ensure that the assessment correlates with any end-of-year class or state or provincial test students must take. The team members use curriculum resources, state or provincial resources, and released test items to create questions for the unpacked content items and skills that the team will assess throughout the year. These are items the team knows students must master to score proficient or above on an end-of-year assessment. Common assessment questions should mirror end-of-instruction questions, with the same format, common language, length of passages, and so on. Also, one constructed-response question per assessment should require students to justify their answer as a means to enhance writing and stimulate critical thinking.

Plan Daily Lessons

Once collaborative teams write an assessment, the next day in the ten-day cycle involves planning lessons that will enable students to be proficient with the assessed standards. Figure 3.8 (page 72) provides an example of a weekly lesson-planning template teams can use to plan lessons for each day of the week.

My target number is _____.

Each layer of the target represents a performance band. The further away a student is from the target, the further away the student is from mastery.

My performance band result is (circle one):
Below standard   Approaching standard   Met standard   Exceeds standard
Strengths:
Areas for improvement:
List the interventions or extensions that will be in place for the student to meet his or her target.   **Student:** What will I do to hit or extend beyond my target goal?   **Teacher:** What will I do to help this student reach or extend beyond his or her target?

Figure 3.7: Using a proficiency scale to determine next steps.

*Visit **go.SolutionTree.com/PLCbooks** for a free reproducible version of this figure.*

Lesson Plan

Week: _____ Course: _____ Teacher: _____

	1. **What do we want students to learn?**	2. **How will we know if they have learned it?** (Include the context of any formative or summative objectives.)	3. **What will we do if they don't learn it?** (Describe intervention measures.)	4. **What will we do if they already know it?** (Describe extension measures.)
Monday	Academic standard: Student-friendly objectives:			
Tuesday	Academic standard: Student-friendly objectives:			
Wednesday	Academic standard: Student-friendly objectives:			

	Thursday			
	Academic standard:			
	Student-friendly objectives:			
	Friday			
	Academic standard:			
	Student-friendly objectives:			

Fill out the following for the unit as a whole. You may or may not need to utilize each section daily.

List real-world connections:
List collaboration opportunities:
List options for student choice:
Describe options to elevate the DOK to reach the synthesize level.

Figure 3.8: Lesson-planning template.

*Visit **go.SolutionTree.com/PLCbooks** for a free reproducible version of this figure.*

In addition to completing the lesson-planning template, teams should keep in mind the following considerations as they work to plan instruction, regardless of content area.

- Incorporate a writing component into each assessment (effective writing prompts to increase the DOK and rigor level required of students).

- Consult with the leadership team about creating a schoolwide writing rubric shared across all content areas. This rubric should reflect state or provincial standards that provide accuracy and consistency about writing standards within the learning. Nontested subjects (content not tested on end-of-year state or provincial exams) should focus on and assess interdisciplinary literacy standards (not English language standards, specifically).

Additionally, when planning lessons, remember the following.

- Establish the number of days for the unit. Because units can not all be taught in ten-day chunks, they will often span across iterations of the ten-day cycle.

- Backward plan from the end of the unit, leaving time to issue a common formative assessment and intervene or extend learning as each student needs.

- Use a tiered lesson-plan design with an emphasis on first-time delivery. That is, have a plan to address core grade- or course-level instruction, a plan to help scaffold learning for students struggling to reach grade- or course-level proficiency with standards, and a plan to ensure students who lack foundational knowledge for meeting grade- or course-level standards receive the necessary support to bring them up to grade- or course-level learning.

- Determine the structure and parts of the lesson (its beginning, middle, and end).

- Write the learning target in student-friendly terms.

- Predetermine questions for discourse with and among students during the lesson that mirror the content's level of rigor. This helps students move from merely recalling information to building conceptual understanding.

- Identify what modifications might be necessary to support all learning levels.

- Determine an approach to instruction that helps students grow toward proficiency. For this purpose, we recommend the use of gradual release of responsibility (Fisher & Frey, 2014), which consists of direct instruction by the teacher (*I do*), student activity with teacher support (*we do*), and independent student learning (*you do*).

- Plan ways to assess for learning throughout, not just utilizing a common formative assessment. Use exit ticket questions or prompts to gauge students' understanding of daily lessons.

- Engage in instruction. The number of days required for instruction will vary for each unit and depend on what was established during the year-at-a-glance plan.

Once teams plan and give their daily lessons, it will inevitably be time to assess students' learning of those lessons.

Give Common Formative Assessments

Once teams have developed common formative assessments and established lesson plans, they will be ready to execute those lessons and, as part of that process, issue common formative assessments. To achieve a constant stream of incoming data, we suggest teams administer these assessments a minimum of every two weeks, again ensuring that each assessment includes at least one writing prompt. Team members should all give the assessment in the same manner and, during their collaboration time, analyze the results to determine which instructional strategies have been effective, any needs or improvements for the curriculum, and specific student-level strengths and weaknesses the team can match to interventions or extensions. The results drive the upcoming instruction with a team approach for extension and remediation.

Analyze Data

After giving assessments, teams gather to analyze the resulting data and determine the need for intervention and extension groups. To accomplish this, use a data-analysis protocol, like the one featured in An Intentional Data-Analysis Protocol (page 153 in chapter 7), to do the following.

- Analyze data by team (the overall pass rate per class).

- Analyze data by teacher (the overall pass rate per hour, or individual student scores per question or per standard).

- Determine the appropriate intervention strategy based on the number of students needing it.

- Plan for intervention or remediation.

- Plan for reassessment at the same rigor level.

You will find more details about collaborative data analysis in chapter 7 (page 149).

Respond to Data

In responding to data, teams create systems of intervention to provide students with additional time and support for learning. These systems constitute action plans for the team to deliver; after all, without action on the data, teams cannot maximize learning. Students who are struggling will continue to struggle, and students showing high-level proficiency won't receive the kind of extensions that build on that learning. Teams at U.S. Grant High School used the following interventions and extensions to ensure all students learned at grade or course level or higher levels.

- Create differentiated and tiered lessons to allow maximum student-centered learning in each classroom.

- Provide flexible grouping among the teachers in which students go to different rooms and work with specific teachers to focus on weaknesses or strengths determined from initial Tier 1 instruction and assessment.

- Establish enhancement courses focused primarily on individual student needs. Schools can provide an enhancement class in addition to the regular course in the content area. For example, highly proficient students might do coursework in both algebra 1 and algebra 1 enhancement as an elective course.

- Provide additional instructional time before and after school.

- Create intersession opportunities during school breaks (fall, winter, and spring) to remediate and allow students additional opportunities for success.

- Spiral standards through bell work and exit tickets.

- Provide intense boot camp sessions before each state assessment, during the regular school day.

- Create and monitor a plan for each senior to meet graduation requirements.

- Reflect on instructional practices

See chapter 8 (page 171) for more information on intervention and chapter 9 (page 189) for support with providing extensions.

Conclusion

At U.S. Grant High School, leadership and teacher teams enhanced their adoption of the PLC process by developing a structured ten-day learning cycle. Teams repeated this cycle over and over and over again, progressing through course content during the school year. Each time, teams refined their work, and teachers became comfortable and more confident. After years of failure, this work helped turn a dire situation at the school (a state grade of F) into a statewide success story (a state grade of B+), and it can help improve outcomes at your priority school. Through the power of collaboration, teams will see continuous and motivating improvement and sustainability as the collective focus on results shifts the work from teaching to learning.

References and Resources

Colburn, L., & Beggs, L. (2021). *The wraparound guide: How to gather student voice, build community partnerships, and cultivate hope.* Bloomington, IN: Solution Tree Press.

Conzemius, A. E., & O'Neill, J. (2014). *The handbook for SMART school teams: Revitalizing best practices for collaboration* (2nd ed.). Bloomington, IN: Solution Tree Press.

DuFour, R., DuFour, R., Eaker, R., Many, T. W., & Mattos, M. (2016). *Learning by doing: A handbook for Professional Learning Communities at Work* (3rd ed.). Bloomington, IN: Solution Tree Press.

Eaker, R., & Marzano, R. J. (Eds.). (2020). *Professional Learning Communities at Work and High Reliability Schools: Cultures of continuous learning.* Bloomington, IN: Solution Tree Press.

Fisher, D., & Frey, N. (2014). *Better learning through structured teaching: A framework for the gradual release of responsibility* (2nd ed.). Alexandria, VA: Association for Supervision and Curriculum Development.

Francis, E. M. (2017, May 9). *What is depth of knowledge?* [Blog post]. Accessed at https://inservice.ascd.org/what-exactly-is-depth-of-knowledge-hint-its-not-a-wheel on May 4, 2020.

Kramer, S. V. (2015). *How to leverage PLCs for school improvement.* Bloomington, IN: Solution Tree Press.

Kramer, S. V., & Schuhl, S. (2017). *School improvement for all: A how-to guide for doing the right work.* Bloomington, IN: Solution Tree Press.

McTighe, J., & Curtis, G. (2019). *Leading modern learning: A blueprint for vision-driven schools* (2nd ed.). Bloomington, IN: Solution Tree Press.

Oklahoma State Department of Education. (n.d.). *Oklahoma state standards for mathematics.* Accessed at www.perma-bound.com/state-standards.do?state=OK&subject=mathematics on October 13, 2020.

Oklahoma State Department of Education. (2016). *Oklahoma academic standards for mathematics.* Accessed at https://sde.ok.gov/sites/ok.gov.sde/files/OAS-Math-Final%20Version_3.pdf on October 13, 2020.

Webb, N. L. (1997, April). *Criteria for alignment of expectations and assessments in mathematics and science education* (Research Monograph No. 8). Washington, DC: Council of Chief State School Officers.

Individual and Team Identification
of Essential Skills

Essential Standards for _____
Guiding Questions
1. List five to seven essential skills or understandings you would like every student to know when they come to you.
2. List five to seven essential skills or understandings you could commit to ensuring that all your students have mastered.
3. Determine which essential skills the team has consensus on, and list the essential standards that specify those skills along with the DOK required. Students will:

Diane Kerr is an educational consultant and former assistant principal at Mason Crest Elementary School in Fairfax County Public Schools (FCPS) of Virginia. She supports schools on their journey to become high-functioning professional learning communities (PLCs) and especially enjoys working with schools with diverse student populations. During her tenure as a coprincipal at Mason Crest, the school earned the distinction of becoming the very first recipient of the coveted DuFour Award, which recognizes top-performing PLCs around the world.

Before joining the Mason Crest team in 2012, Diane was one of two coordinators of English for speakers of other languages in FCPS, which has more than 180,000 students. She supervised and led multiple teams that provided services to schools, parents, and students, and she was a sought-after resource about other central office programs. Working in Connecticut, Bahrain, and Virginia, Diane focuses her career on collaboratively supporting students with diverse needs and specifically teaching English to speakers of other languages of all ages.

Throughout her career in education, Diane has provided professional development in many venues, including presenting to large groups of school leaders, school board members, teachers, and teacher teams. She has taught university-level classes on differentiation and meeting the needs of diverse learners. She presented at the 2018 and 2019 Solution Tree Soluciones Institutes and at select PLC at Work® Institutes in 2018 and 2019. She also presented at the first-ever Culture Keepers Institute in 2018.

Diane coauthored *What About Us? The PLC at Work Process for PreK–2 Teams* and was part of a team that helped contributing author Brian K. Butler write chapter 3, "Collaborating in the Core," of *It's About Time: Planning Interventions and Extensions in Elementary School.*

Diane earned an education specialist degree and a preK–12 administration and supervision endorsement from the University of Virginia, and she holds a master's degree in teaching with an endorsement in teaching English to speakers of other languages from Sacred Heart University. She also has a bachelor of science in economics from the College of Charleston.

To learn more about Diane's work, follow @diane_KerrWerx on Twitter.

To book Diane Kerr for professional development, contact pd@SolutionTree.com.

Answering the First Critical Question From an English Learner's Point of View

Diane Kerr

> In a healthy [school] culture . . . educators believe
> that the same expectations and desires they hold for
> the future of their own children and grandchildren
> are the norm for the students who they serve.
> This moral imperative underpins their efforts
> and drives each instructional decision.
>
> —*Sharon V. Kramer and Sarah Schuhl*

During my career as an educational consultant, I've supported a number of schools in their PLC journey. The following scenario represents an amalgamation of that experience and the many commonalities I've encountered in my work when it comes to helping schools better and more equitably support their populations of English learners (ELs).

On a warm August morning, I enter the front doors of Sunshine Elementary School. It's my first day meeting the administrators and staff of this state-identified priority school, and I will be coaching its staff on their school-improvement journey. I know that the school has a wonderfully diverse student body with many students learning English, and it is situated in a neighborhood with significant socioeconomic diversity.

My first goal is to learn about the school, the people who make up the community, and the successes and challenges of the entire school community. Unsurprisingly, one of the first things I learn is that the educators are working *really* hard and care deeply about their work. They are tired. They are also frustrated with the lack of progress of the students they serve. I ask a series of questions that elicit responses, including the following.

- "Well, if only they spoke English."
- "If only their parents were involved."

- "They can't learn grade-level content because they can't read on grade level."
- "Their English language development teacher only takes them for thirty minutes a day."

Statements such as these give me the sense that the teachers feel defeated before they even begin teaching because they think there are factors out of their control that are greater than the things they can control. There is a sense of hopelessness and helplessness in the air. This hopelessness is rooted in a culture of low expectations. The school is hyperfocused on what the students can't do instead of what the teachers can do, and the result an inequitable learning environment. The teachers have yet to develop collective team efficacy, a belief that together, they can ensure *all* students learn (DuFour, DuFour, Eaker, Many, & Mattos, 2016).

As is true of other schools struggling with student achievement, the school doesn't know where to start to turn the tide and to have educators think and act differently. If and when schools such as this do attempt to push for school improvement, they often leave specific student groups completely out of the discussion, which perpetuates the inequities that exist in our traditional system of education. In particular, educators can't even begin to imagine how they could have the same expectations for their EL students as they have for students (including their own children and grandchildren) who are native language speakers.

With a specific focus on ELs, this chapter offers collaborative teams strategies for building efficacy so they have only the highest expectations for every student's learning, as though every student were their own child or grandchild. Further, this chapter will assist teams to better understand and support a growing population of students who are learning grade-level content while simultaneously acquiring English language skills. *English as a second language (ESL) students, English language learners (ELLs), limited English proficient (LEP) students, students with interrupted formal education (SIFE)*, and *language minority students (LMS)* are all terms educators use to describe subcategories of students on the journey to becoming bi- or multilingual. Other nations may use other terms, but while these terms are prevalent in North American schools, I recommend that educators refrain from labeling students with these terms or acronyms, as they often carry with them a negative connotation. *English learners* is the preferred term for referring to this group of students and is the term I use in this chapter.

The ideas in this chapter supplement the work found in Sharon Kramer and Sarah Schuhl's (2017) book *School Improvement for All*, filtering it through the lens of English learners. This chapter is not meant to go into depth on the stages of second-language acquisition or to delve into the multifaceted challenges that EL populations face. Instead, I designed this chapter to provide collaborative teams with ideas to add to their current practices and approach to planning, as well as resources to deepen their understanding of how they can learn together about these special students' needs. I know from experience that the strategies in this chapter not only support the needs of English learners but also benefit all other students in the classroom and assist in providing equitable access to grade-level learning.

The following sections will help you understand who your team's English learners are, what EL-related problems of practice your team faces and how to address them, and how to more deeply understand your EL students' needs. The chapter ends with some closing advice and extra resources for getting started with this work.

Who Your English Learners Are

According to the U.S. Department of Education's National Center for English Language Acquisition (NCELA, 2021), during the 2017–2018 school year, more than five million English learners were enrolled in U.S. schools. This represents over 12 percent of the total student population. A similar report from the NCELA (2020a) explains that Spanish is the primary spoken language for nearly 75 percent of EL students. Although the next-largest groups of ELs speak Arabic, Chinese, Vietnamese, and Somali (NCELA, 2020b), ELs in U.S. public schools speak over four hundred different languages. Additionally, it is interesting to note that students who are designated as *homeless*, *Title I*, or *migrant* are more likely to also be emerging bilinguals and ELs.

In schools, it is common to find educators discussing their ELs as "a problem" or "at a deficit" because of ELs' need to develop their English skills. But many researchers, including Judith F. Kroll of the University of California at Irvine, and Paola E. Dussias of Pennsylvania State University, disprove such labels through their elaboration of the benefits of multilingualism (Kroll & Dussias, 2017). Becoming bi- or multilingual is actually an asset that will greatly benefit these students and their communities. Neel Burton (2018), a professor at the University of Oxford, explains the benefits of being bilingual in his *Psychology Today* blog post "Beyond Words":

> According to several studies, people who learn another language do significantly better on standardized tests. Language management calls upon executive functions such as attention control, cognitive inhibition, and working memory, and there is mounting evidence that bi- and multi-lingual people are better at analyzing their surroundings, multitasking, and problem solving. They also have a larger working memory, including for tasks that do not involve language. In terms of brain structure, they have more grey matter (and associated activity) in the dorsal anterior cingulate cortex, a locus for language control and broader executive function. Superior executive function is, in turn, a strong predictor of academic success.

Viorica Marian and Anthony Shook (2012), researchers of bilingualism and the brain, find that bilingual experiences have cognitive benefits for young learners. They state that babies as young as seven months old show "bilingualism to positively influence attention and conflict management" (Marian & Shook, 2012). They go on to conclude that "even for very young children, navigating a multilingual environment imparts advantages that transfer beyond language" (Marian & Shook, 2012).

The critical takeaway from these numerous findings is that your team's EL students provide diversity and bring to your classrooms a wealth of strengths that are waiting to be built on, shared, and celebrated. While it is impossible to define a "typical" English learner due to their diversity of experience and many countries of origin, the shared backdrop of multilingualism puts ELs in a beneficial position for tackling content. Team members must see EL students as an asset to the classroom and the community at large. Understanding the benefits of multilingualism is the first step to separating the negative impressions gained through disadvantaged socio-economic status from their cognitive and linguistic strengths.

A Problem of Practice

Although many English-speaking countries have federal mandates for supporting language acquisition and content learning, the reality is most teachers do not receive adequate professional development, strategies, and techniques to meet English learners' needs. For example, U.S. requirements for preservice teachers vary from state to state. In a report on preparing all teachers to meet EL students' needs, researchers Jennifer F. Samson and Brian A. Collins state:

> There are further inconsistencies across states in the required knowledge and skills regarding ELLs for all teachers as part of initial certification. While some states require specific coursework (Arizona, California, Florida, Pennsylvania, and New York) and others make a general reference to the special needs of ELLs (17 states), several states (15) have no requirement whatsoever. (p. 8)

Once teachers are in the classroom, professional development is provided at the local level to varying degrees of intensity. As a result, the instructional programs that teachers and their schools implement to meet federal requirements often fall short, as evidenced by a lack of grade- or course-level academic achievement and often a lack of growth in English language proficiency. NCELA (2021) data show that ELs continue to lag behind their monolingual peers in mathematics, reading and English language arts, and science, even four years after they stop receiving support for language acquisition. Further, many teachers struggle to effectively and efficiently support the needs of this specific group of students outside of mandated English language development time. Clearly, experience and research show it is not enough that EL students go to their ESL class or that the English language development paraprofessional pulls EL students out of grade- or course-level instruction in favor of language instruction. If English learners are going to meet the challenge of simultaneously learning grade- or course-level content *and* English, they will need equitable and explicit instruction all day and in all content classes. A PLC culture, with collaborative teams emphasizing collective responsibility for all their students, is the answer to this challenge!

Educators in schools that operate as a PLC understand that three big ideas guide their work: (1) a focus on learning, (2) a collaborative culture and collective responsibility, and (3) a results orientation (DuFour et al., 2016). If you review additional literature about PLCs and the three big ideas, you will notice the words *each* and *all* used throughout them (Kramer & Schuhl, 2017; Buffum, Mattos, & Malone, 2018; Spiller & Power, 2019).

Nowhere do the authors and researchers exclude English learners or say, "All students except English learners." You will hear them say, "All means *all*," and this includes emerging bilingual students, ELs. Schoolwide collaborative teams must have a system for planning for their English learners' specific needs, and they must integrate their resulting plan into the team cycle such that it ultimately becomes a habit of mind (Costa, n.d.), a natural part of a team's work. This work begins with understanding.

How to Plan for Your English Learners' Needs

Non-native language learners and their families, regardless of their spoken language or cultural background, are an integral part of their resident nation's fabric and future. This is true regardless of whether we're talking about the United States, Canada, or any other nation. ELs enter their schools and classrooms with varying strengths, backgrounds, language proficiencies, academic experiences, hopes, and dreams. Their academic, social, and emotional needs vary just as the needs of any other students entering the classroom do. The first step for teacher teams is to get to know their students as individuals—to learn their strengths, interests, and goals. Teams need to learn about their ELs' academic experiences *before* the students enter the school. They should build relationships with these ELs and their families. Then, teams should dig deeper to discover more about their ELs' language proficiency and how that knowledge can support the teams' approach to instruction and assessment.

ELs' language needs are much more than an English language proficiency (ELP) score. To summarize my AllThingsPLC blog post "'But They Don't Speak English!'" (Kerr, 2020), every U.S. state has a federally required ELP assessment that assesses the four domains of English: (1) reading, (2) writing, (3) speaking, and (4) listening (NCELA, 2017). Each student receives an overall score that combines the individual scores of the four language domains. A student's overall score places him or her on a continuum of language proficiency, which in most assessment systems is on a scale of 1–5 or 1–6. For example, a student at ELP level 1 is likely at the beginning levels of acquiring English language skills. An ELP level of 5 or 6 indicates the student has neared English language proficiency. ELP levels 2–4 show that the student is progressing and needs additional time and support to acquire more advanced skills in each of the English language domains.

It is important to avoid the trap of assuming that prescribing an approach based on your students' *overall* ELP score will meet their needs. Very often, I hear teams say, "Oh, this student is a level 3; this is what he needs." Instead, consider the example shown in table 4.1 (page 86). Two students, both Spanish speakers, have an overall ELP level of 3; however, their scores differ in three domains. (Note that a student's overall ELP score is not necessarily an average of the four individual domain scores. These scores are often slightly weighted to emphasize reading and writing skills.)

Table 4.1: Comparing ELP Scores for Two EL Students

Student	Overall ELP Level	Listening	Speaking	Reading	Writing
Student 1	3.3	5.0	4.2	2.8	2.8
Student 2	3.8	3.2	4.2	4.8	2.1

Source: Kerr, 2020.

In this example, the students are likely to present as having very similar needs due to the similarity in their speaking scores. However, if you look closer, you'll discover distinct differences that will impact and guide instructional decisions. These students can do very different things in listening and reading. One student has a listening score of 5.0, and the other 3.2. One student has a reading score of 2.8, and the other 4.8. If teams assume that these two students require the same instruction in listening and reading, they will not be targeting the appropriate language needs for the students to move forward in both their language acquisition and their content learning. (Visit https://wida.wisc.edu/teach /can-do/descriptors [WIDA, n.d.] to learn more about these differences.) This ELP information serves as a baseline for understanding each student's language needs.

Once teacher teams get better acquainted with the English learners' language strengths in the domains of reading, writing, listening, and speaking, they can then begin the work of planning for the students' specific needs. This work includes establishing academic language and academic vocabulary, determining essential standards and a content vocabulary, building in language objectives, planning for instruction and differentiation according to each student's proficiency level, and engaging in vocabulary instruction.

Establishing Academic Language and Academic Vocabulary

It is important that teams understand the role academic language and academic vocabulary plays in English learners' success and that they learn how to use that knowledge to plan instruction.

Simply stated, *academic language* is the language and discourse of school, as compared to the social language that English learners need to communicate their everyday wants and needs. In his book *Building Academic Language*, Jeff Zwiers (2014) further defines academic language as "the set of words, grammar, and discourse strategies used to describe complex ideas, higher-order thinking processes, and abstract concepts" (p. 22). A simpler way to think of this term comes from the Colorín Colorado (2012) video "Vocabulary: Bricks and Mortar," in which English language development specialist Cynthia Lundgren describes academic language as "the mortar that holds the brick wall of vocabulary together." The bricks of the wall represent the content vocabulary, and the mortar is the language that pulls the vocabulary together, holds it in place, and communicates a more complex and sometimes more abstract idea or concept than the meaning of the individual words.

So, what differentiates academic language from academic vocabulary? James F. Baumann and Michael F. Graves (2010), in their article "What Is Academic Vocabulary?" define *academic vocabulary* in this way: "General academic vocabulary is used to refer to words that appear in texts across several disciplines or academic domains" (p. 6). They add that general academic vocabulary is challenging to master because the words often have abstract definitions, and the words' meaning can change in different content areas. Academic vocabulary that routinely crosses content areas includes the verbs found in U.S. state standards (for example, *explain, identify, describe, sequence, interpret, compare, predict, identify, cause,* and *effect*) and also words that have multiple meanings across content areas (for example, *table, plot, process, power,* and *value*).

Teacher teams must stop and closely analyze common vocabulary and determine whether the words' meanings differ across the content areas students will study. If so, teams *must* make these differences explicit to all students, including ELs. For example, as part of a reading standard for literature (National Governors Association [NGA] & Council of Chief State School Officers [CCSSO], 2010a), a team may be teaching students about prediction and its ability to help readers comprehend what they are reading. The team has incorporated vocabulary instruction into the unit plan that includes defining the words *prediction, character, problem,* and *solution,* as well as additional vocabulary the team agreed are integral to students' learning. In a subsequent literature lesson, when the teachers on the team ask students to predict what a character in a story will do next, they might receive the following answers.

- **Student 1:** "She will go a different way."

- **Student 2:** "Because she was scared, I think she will go somewhere else."

- **Student 3:** "I predict that the mother will go somewhere else because Rosa said that the original plan was dangerous."

- **Student 4:** "As a result of the main character's response, I predict that the mother will choose a different route."

The response from student 1 is typical of how many students, including native English speakers, respond, *regardless* of their English proficiency level. Many teachers are excited when students show a general understanding of the text and the question and may actually praise this student for his or her participation and response. Student 2 adds reasoning behind the response. Both responses are very simple and are great examples of social language. These responses are informal, and their vocabulary is not specific or technical. Note also that the use of pronouns instead of the character names lacks precision and clarity.

Now, let's look closely at the responses of student 3 and student 4. These students are applying their understanding of the academic language required to communicate in a more formal, academic manner. They are not only using the content and academic vocabulary (*character* and *prediction*) but also demonstrating that they understand how to put the words together to communicate what they predict will happen next. The ability to put the individual vocabulary words together using a precise sentence structure signifies that these two students have built a strong wall of academic understanding and they can communicate more complex ideas and thoughts using the language of the standard. In their response, both students use the phrase *I predict that* along with an explanation of why they made their prediction. They signal this explanation using the words *because* and *as a result*. When readers encounter this academic language in a text, these specific words, when found together, signal a prediction is being made along with a reason for that thinking. This supports reading comprehension.

To obtain responses like those of students 3 and 4, teacher teams need to plan for and provide opportunities for students to learn the vocabulary *and* the associated academic language function (that is, the verbs of the standard that determine the academic language). They must then have students practice and use them in multiple ways. In *Practical Guidelines for the Education of English Language Learners*, David J. Francis, Mabel Rivera, Nonie Lesaux, Michael Kieffer, and Hector Rivera (2006) stress that:

> Academic language is an area of weakness for many ELLs, and their difficulties are known to persist over time. Moreover, native English speakers from all ethnic and socioeconomic backgrounds benefit from explicit instruction to develop academic language. Therefore, targeted, class-wide instruction in this area is warranted to augment the skills of learners in the overall population, and possibly prevent some of the difficulties ELLs have in this area. (p. 16)

Building your awareness and understanding of academic language not only benefits English learners but provides a system for all students to better utilize and build on their understanding of how words work together to communicate more complex academic topics. Team members should see this not as something more to do but as a way to deepen understanding of standards and a vital strategy to support student learning and more equitable access to content.

Determining Essential Standards and Content Vocabulary

I advise teacher teams to approach learning about and planning for academic language as part of their team's daily work. Start with answering the first critical question of a PLC, "What do we want our students to learn?" (DuFour et al., 2016). Teams begin answering this question by identifying the essential standards for their grade level or course. This process is beyond the scope of this chapter, but you can learn more about it in chapter 3 (page 51) and in Kramer and Schuhl's (2017) *School Improvement for All*, which clearly outlines the process. Once teams identify essential standards, they can move forward in building a common understanding of each standard through the process of unpacking (also called *unwrapping*) the essential standards. This unpacking process breaks an individual standard into its component learning targets. As Kramer and Schuhl (2017) explain:

> Five different teachers can read a standard and interpret it five different ways. To have a guaranteed and viable curriculum that is equitable for all students, teachers on a collaborative team must share an understanding as to the content and skills students must demonstrate to be proficient with the standard. (p. 63)

Once teams identify and build consensus around learning targets, they then identify the *content vocabulary*. This is the vocabulary unique to the content area. Content vocabulary for mathematics would include words like *factor, product, dividend, perimeter, angle,* and *sum.* Science and social studies vocabulary would include words like *experiment, energy, cells, hypothesis, civilizations, political, ancient,* and *civics.* The specific vocabulary for the content area is easy for teams to identify, as it is often highlighted in curriculum resources and guides. It is through this process of unpacking the essential standards into learning targets and identifying content vocabulary that teams also dig deeper to discover the academic language embedded in the standards. The academic language associated with the content takes more analysis and conversation within teams.

Let's use the science practice of generating a hypothesis as an example. Teams will likely identify *hypothesis* as a word to explicitly teach at some point in the lesson, along with content-specific terminology that form the appropriate content vocabulary. The next step is to discuss the academic language necessary for students to make a hypothesis. Asking the following questions will help teams hone in on the academic language of that standard and practice.

- What is the language you would want to hear students use in conversations or see them use in their writing?
- What are the sentence structures students need to learn?
- Is there a unique order of words that will help students be successful?
- Are there signal words that are associated with making a hypothesis?

Teacher team members might develop the following conclusions as they discuss the answers to these questions.

> We want students to be able to understand that a hypothesis is an answer to the question, "What do you think will happen?" and that the response (the hypothesis) is based on a reason. Students need to be able to explain the rationale behind their reason.

> We want to hear students using sentences similar to the following, applying these structures and key words (signal words).

> - "I hypothesize that _____ because _____."
> - "Based on _____, I hypothesize that _____."
> - "If we _____, then maybe _____ will happen because _____."
> - "The hypothesis was [or was not] confirmed by _____."

As a result of their conversation, the team members agree that they would all use these team-created sentence frames and sentence starters to help students learn the expected academic language.

Continuing with this example, the team's conversation about how the vocabulary is used in scientific discourse will help teachers plan instruction for teaching their English learners. Sentence starters and sentence frames are not the only tools that teams have to support the complicated task of teaching academic language. However, they are an easy starting point for teams beginning this work. Sentence frames encourage language production and peer interaction. They also provide students the language support they need to communicate effectively in oral and written language for higher-level thinking. Additionally, all students will benefit from having a model for the expected academic language to be used in classrooms.

Remember, to ensure students achieve the desired results, teams must explicitly teach the language of the different content areas, and students must have multiple opportunities to use the language in authentic ways. Capturing the team decisions around the academic language of a standard is important, and the team can do it by adapting team templates already used for unpacking essential standards. Consider the following English language arts (ELA) example.

A teacher team has unpacked and discussed the Common Core ELA standard RL.3.9 (NGA & CCSSO, 2010a), and team members have filled in the template shown in figure 4.1. (See page 103 for a reproducible version of this figure.)

Standard: RL.3.9 Compare and contrast the themes, settings, and plots of [stories written by the same author about the same or similar characters] (e.g., in books from a series).

Content (Nouns) _What Students Need to Know_	Skills (Verbs) _What Students Need to Be Able to Do_	Depth of Knowledge Level
Themes Settings Plots	Compare Contrast	DOK 2–3

Vocabulary Specific to the Content	Academic Language _Language Function, Text Structure, and Signal Words_	
Theme Main idea Plot Setting Character	Compare Similar "Have in common" <ul><li>_____ is _similar to_ _____ because _____.</li><li>The _similarities between_ _____ and _____ are _____.</li><li>Contrast</li><li>Different</li><li>_____ is _different from_ _____ because _____.</li><li>_____ is like _____, _whereas_ _____ is like _____.</li></ul>	

Learning Targets
I can identify the theme.
I can identify the plot.

I can identify the setting.

I can determine the difference between comparing and contrasting.

I can compare and contrast the themes of stories written by the same author about the same or similar characters.

I can compare and contrast the plots of stories written by the same author about the same or similar characters.

I can compare and contrast the settings of stories written by the same author about the same or similar characters.

Student Language Objectives (Reading, Writing, Listening, Speaking)

Students will be able to *write* about the similarities and differences between themes, settings, and plots using specific content vocabulary. (Writing)

Students will *explain* to a partner how themes, settings, and plots are similar and different using at least one sentence frame for comparing and one for contrasting. (Speaking)

- _____ is *similar to* _____ because _____.
- The *similarities between* _____ and _____ are _____.
- _____ is *different from* _____ because _____.
- _____ is like _____, *whereas* _____ is like _____.

Source for standard: NGA & CCSSO, 2010a.

Source: Adapted from Kramer & Schuhl, 2017.

Figure 4.1: Sample filled-in template to unpack essential standards.

I've adapted the template in figure 4.1 from *School Improvement for All* (Kramer & Schuhl, 2017) to include vocabulary, academic language, and language objectives. Teams follow the steps in the unpacking process as outlined in *School Improvement for All* (Kramer & Schuhl, 2017) to fill in the template and to gain clarity around the essential standard. Those steps include the following.

1. Circle the verbs and underline the nouns and noun phrases of the standard. Put brackets around the context.

2. Transfer the nouns and noun phrases to the section labeled What Students Need to Know.

3. Transfer the verbs to the section labeled What Students Need to Be Able to Do.

4. Determine the level of rigor required of each learning target. This example uses Norman Webb's Depth of Knowledge (DOK) levels (Francis, 2017).

5. Identify key vocabulary.

6. Capture the academic language of the standard. Use the preceding questions (page 89) to guide your conversations.

7. Write student-friendly learning targets.

8. Create language objectives that support the standard's academic language. (I write more about these objectives in the next section.)

The most important part of taking these steps is that all team members are discussing the standard and developing a common, deep understanding of what they want all students to learn and be able to do. With an added focus on the standard's academic language, they are keeping the needs of English learner's language acquisition a part of the conversation. The last step, creating language objectives, ensures that all team members focus on strengthening at least one of the four language domains (reading, writing, listening, and speaking), which assists their students' progression along the language-acquisition continuum. Read on to learn more about language objectives.

Building in Language Objectives

The last section of the template in figure 4.1 (page 91) asks teacher teams to add language objectives. Earlier in this chapter, I stressed that English learners must *simultaneously* learn content objectives *and* develop their English language proficiency. When teacher teams systematically include a language objective in their lessons, they are taking an important step toward supporting their English learners' language needs. A *language objective* focuses on one of the four language domains (reading, writing, listening, or speaking) and states how the students will demonstrate their learning through the domain. In the previous section's ELA example, the team chose the domains of writing and speaking for its language objectives, as they are a natural fit for that content standard and are areas of need for the team's students.

Teams need to consider the English proficiency levels of their students when deciding on language objectives that satisfy the need to develop students' academic language. Not every unit needs a language objective for each domain, but teams should be mindful of developing all four language domains and choosing language objectives that best fit with the units and lessons they are developing. As an example, figure 4.2 shows language objectives for a mathematics standard.

The mathematics team that created the four language objectives in figure 4.2 did so as a result of the discussion team members had about the featured standard. The team discussed what they wanted students to be able to do and how that fit into developing the domains of speaking, reading, writing, and listening. During such a conversation, a teacher says something like, "I think we would want students to be able to compare data with a partner and hear them use the terms *more than, less than.* We can provide them with differentiated sentence frames to help them with this task." As the conversation naturally progresses, another teacher might say, "I think that we would also want them to be able to write their own problems or questions about two different graphs using the same terms, *more than* and *less than.*" This conversation would continue to build to include expectations around reading and listening skills. As a result, the team creates more specificity around supporting the language needs of their students and a common approach across the team and fosters an overarching goal of ensuring equitable access to essential standards for all students.

Standard: 3.MD.B.3. Draw a scaled picture graph and a scaled bar graph to represent a data set with several categories. Solve one- and two-step "how many more" and "how many less" problems using information presented in scaled bar graphs. *For example, draw a bar graph in which each square in the bar graph might represent 5 pets.*

Language Objectives

- Explain to peers how the different data categories compare using the terms *more than* and *less than*. (Speaking)

- Read mathematics problems and identify the important information and appropriate algorithms to use to solve the problems. (Reading)

- Write mathematics problems that correspond to a given graph using the phrases *how many more* and *how many less*. (Writing)

- Answer questions posed by the teacher or peers about the graphed data. (Listening)

Source for standard: NGA & CCSSO, 2010b.

Figure 4.2: Language objectives for a mathematics standard.

Planning for Instruction and Differentiating According to English Proficiency Level

Once teams have done the work of identifying and unpacking essential standards, determining content vocabulary, and developing academic language objectives, they are ready to move to the next steps of the team learning cycle of discussing proficiency and creating common assessments which, in turn, informs planning for and differentiating instruction. Teams can easily incorporate the academic language objectives into assessment and instructional decisions. Team members must agree that they will hold all students accountable for the academic discourse in their classrooms. In mathematics classrooms, teachers ask students to speak and write like mathematicians, and in other content areas, like scientists, authors, or historians.

As teams plan for assessment and instruction, they should go back to their students' English language proficiency levels *in each domain*. (See How to Plan for Your English Learners' Needs, page 85.) If an EL has a lower score in the writing domain, teams need to explore what the student *can do* in writing and scaffold their support accordingly. For example, some ELs may need a word bank to help them focus on the vocabulary they are expected to use. Others may need images to help them identify vocabulary and language to use.

Let's look at another example. Figure 4.3 (page 94) shows how a team can differentiate a compare-and-contrast writing activity for the Virginia Department of Education (2015) social studies standards so the activity supports all learners while also providing English learners a much-needed scaffold. Some students may need the word bank shown in the figure, while others may not. Some students may need a picture added to their graphic organizer to remind them of abolitionism and women's suffrage movements. Notice how important it is to reinforce that many students know the meaning of the prepositions *to* and *from* but, in this instance, they combine with the words *similar* and *different* to introduce comparisons.

Standards

- **USI.1e:** The student will demonstrate skills for historical thinking, geographical analysis, economic decision making, and responsible citizenship by comparing and contrasting historical, cultural, and political perspectives in United States history.

- **USI.8e:** The student will apply social science skills to understand westward expansion and reform in America from 1801 to 1861 by explaining the main ideas of the abolitionist and women's suffrage movements.

Word Bank	
Movement	Sojourner Truth
Equal Rights	Harriet Tubman
Emancipation	William Lloyd Garrison
Slavery	Frederick Douglass
Civil War	Susan B. Anthony
	Elizabeth Cady Stanton
	Declaration of Sentiments

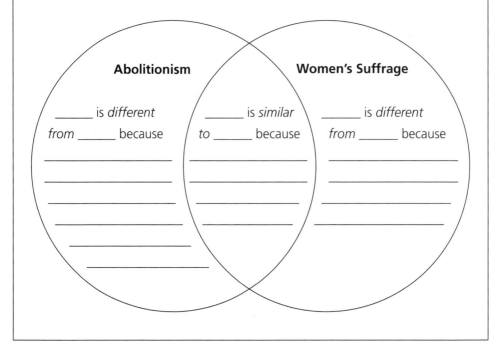

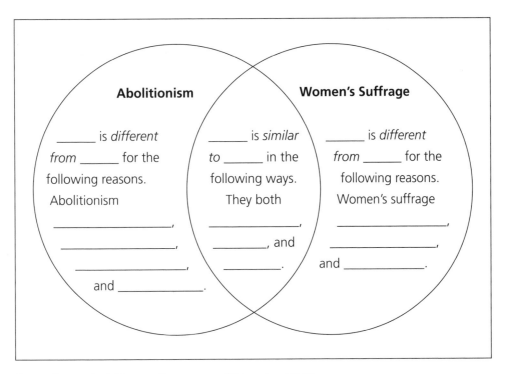

Source for standard: Virginia Department of Education, 2015.

Figure 4.3: Differentiating a compare-and-contrast writing activity.

Teams need to understand that they can adapt the sentence frames featured in figure 4.3 for any content area and differentiate them for English learners at different proficiency levels.

1. A _____ *has* _____.

2. A _____ *has* _____, but a _____ *has* _____. Both *have* _____.

3. *While* a _____ and a _____ both *have* _____, they are different because _____.

Consider how teams might use these differentiated sentence frames across content areas. For example, although figure 4.3 uses these core frames for a social studies lesson, a team could adapt the same sentence frames for a mathematics lesson to explain how shapes are similar and different. Consider the following.

1. A <u>triangle</u> *has* <u>three sides</u>.

2. A <u>triangle</u> *has* <u>three sides</u>, but a <u>rectangle</u> *has* <u>four sides</u>. <u>Both</u> *have* <u>angles</u>.

3. *While* a <u>triangle</u> and a <u>rectangle</u> both *have* <u>angles</u>, they are different because <u>a triangle</u> *has* <u>three sides and a rectangle</u> *has* <u>four sides</u>.

Additionally, these scaffolded frames give teachers the chance to highlight several grammatical nuances of the English language about which English learners require explicit teaching. In sentence frame 2, teachers can highlight the verb *to have* and its correct use. Sentence frame 3 adds the word *while*. Many students, including English learners, would benefit from understanding that the word *while* can be a noun, a conjunction, and a verb, and the word *awhile* is an adverb. It is important to use these opportunities to point out differing meanings in a real-life context where students can practice using the words in a meaningful way. Native English speakers will understand these differences and will explain that a correct usage "just sounds right." English learners do not yet have that internal understanding of the English language to know how to use these structures, and therefore must learn them. You'll find additional sentence frame examples in a reproducible at the end of this chapter (see page 104).

While doing this work in differentiation, teacher teams can benefit from remembering why teaching academic language is so important and why there is an urgency to include this in their instructional practices. In a Colorín Colorado (2014) webcast titled *Academic Language and English Language Learners*, Robin Scarcella, director of the Program in Academic English and ESL at the University of California, Irvine, shares the following: "Students who master academic language are more likely to be successful in academic and professional settings. Students who do not learn academic language may struggle and drop out of school." Don't underestimate the importance of this. Teams must move toward understanding and teaching academic language and building systematic vocabulary instruction into their instructional practices for the success of all students.

Engaging in Vocabulary Instruction

There are a plethora of excellent books on the market that provide strategies for teaching vocabulary. The message for teams in this chapter is that *planning for vocabulary instruction must be part of their work*. In *Teaching Reading and Comprehension to English Learners, K–5*, Margarita Calderón (2011) explains:

> To effectively teach vocabulary, educators must provide explicit instruction, which entails: presenting both student-friendly and formal definitions; offering multiple exposures to a word in multiple forms; ensuring understanding of meaning(s); providing examples of a word's use in phrases, idioms, and usual contexts; highlighting characteristics or word parts; ensuring proper pronunciation and spelling; and, when possible, teaching a word's cognate or false cognate in the student's primary language. (p. 67)

For the instruction to be meaningful for English learners (and all students), teacher teams must embed the learning into content units that provide context and authentic opportunities for students to use the words and the academic language associated with those words. Vocabulary instruction must revolve around activities where the students (not the teacher) explore and manipulate the language. Robert Marzano has done extensive work in the area of vocabulary instruction and has written many books that address this topic (Marzano, 2018, 2020; Marzano & Simms, 2013). You can also access a summary of vocabulary tips, including the following six steps for vocabulary instruction, on the Marzano Resources website (Marzano, n.d.). I've provided notes in this list to aid teacher teams in applying the steps.

1. **Provide a description, explanation, or example of the new term:** This step is the *only* step where the focus is on the teacher. It can be very brief, providing

students with an understanding of the word through an explanation or story. If possible, accompany this with a visual or video.

2. **Ask students to restate the description, explanation, or example in their own words:** Teams can easily do this using a cooperative learning structure like turn and talk, where all students get an equal opportunity to share their example.

3. **Ask students to construct a picture, symbol, or graphic representing the term or phrase:** Marzano (2020) asserts that people store knowledge of words in a filing system that is labeled or accessed with visual representations of the words. Providing students with the opportunity to draw a visual representation is a critical step. They can do this in a vocabulary section of a notebook or on a whiteboard.

4. **Engage students in activities that help them add to their knowledge of the terms in their vocabulary notebooks:** Provide students with a notebook in which they can record and discuss vocabulary-related examples and nonexamples and create metaphors, analogies, synonyms, and antonyms of the terms.

5. **Periodically ask students to discuss the terms with one another:** Plan for authentic opportunities for students to discuss vocabulary words with one another. Students must practice using the vocabulary and the academic language in order to internalize it.

6. **Involve students in games that allow them to play with terms:** There are numerous vocabulary games to include: matching games, guess the word, and $50,000 pyramid, to name a few. You can find even more in *Vocabulary Games for the Classroom* (Carleton & Marzano, 2010).

To reiterate, teacher teams should always keep in mind that students require multiple opportunities to use and practice the academic language to make it part of their lexicon. The U.S. Department of Education's report *Teaching Academic Content and Literacy to English Learners in Elementary and Middle School* (Baker et al., 2014) provides an excellent summary of this concept. The report recommends and discusses how educators need to choose a small set of academic vocabulary words to explicitly and intensively teach over several days. The report also explains that educators should engage students in a variety of instructional activities that go into depth and include the modalities of speaking, writing, and listening. Students then practice reading and discussing the vocabulary using grade-level texts. (The full report goes into depth on each of these suggestions; Baker et al., 2014.) Therefore, teams should consider these components of vocabulary instruction and embed them in unit plans and lessons.

Advice and Resources for Teams on Getting Started

Teams that are successful start small and grow with practice and experience. In answering the first critical question of a PLC with your ELs in mind, I suggest you follow these eight steps to ensure you take advantage of all the information this chapter has presented.

1. Learn more about your English learners and their English language proficiency by language domain.

2. Choose one content area or one course on which to focus.

3. Choose one essential standard to unpack into learning targets and language objectives.

4. Agree on and start to use a template to unpack the standard, record the academic vocabulary, and record the language objectives.

5. Write one language objective.

6. Identify and learn about one strategy for explicitly teaching the academic language of the standard.

7. Plan for and provide vocabulary and language instruction.

8. Celebrate your successes and adjust your approaches at a team meeting.

As teacher teams get more comfortable and start to see results with their students, they will be able to expand their work to other courses or content areas. However, sometimes teams believe that they may not have the expertise or knowledge to do this work. As individuals, team members may struggle, but together, they can do great things! Reach out for resources to assist you and your team in learning more about supporting your English learners. The following resources are at your fingertips.

- If your school has an English language development specialist or coordinator, invite this specialist to your team meetings, and ask him or her for resources.

- Read articles and books as a team. See the References and Resources section at the end of this chapter (page 99) for a few ideas.

- Join a social media teacher's group. ELL Teachers in the U.S. (www.facebook .com/groups/1618995185073060) and Colorín Colorado's ELL Educator Group (https://bit.ly/3npJ8T6) are both supportive Facebook groups.

- Visit https://bit.ly/3lchabE to access the U.S. Department of Education's (2016) *English Learner Toolkit for State and Local Education Agencies (SEAs and LEAs)*.

- Explore the resources on Colorín Colorado (www.colorincolorado.org), a bilingual site for English learners.

- Discover the National Clearinghouse for English Language Acquisition's resources (https://ncela.ed.gov).

- Explore the resources for supporting English learners found on your state's or province's department of education website.

- Access the *Academic Language Function Toolkit* available from Sweetwater Union High School District (2010; https://bit.ly/2F4T8zW). Teams can use this resource to develop academic language skills for students at all grade levels and in all content areas.

- For information about supporting English Learners in a virtual learning environment, see "English Learners and Distance Learning: Five Essentials for Success" (Anderson, Mathews, Park, Padilla, & Kerr, 2020).

Conclusion

The ideas and strategies in this chapter are best practices teams can utilize no matter the model of instruction: in-person, virtual, or hybrid. All teams can succeed at providing equal opportunities for *all* students to learn at high levels, regardless of the resources available in their school. The key is to start now. Together with your team members, start to learn about your students who are on their way to becoming bi- or multilingual. Ask them about their life stories, build relationships, and learn about their strengths and areas of need. Dig into your essential standards, think about the academic language necessary for all students to be successful, and create a plan for systematically embedding strategies and tools into your unit plans and instruction. Choose an area for your team to tackle first, and use the resources in your school, your district, and this chapter to help you on your way. You will have successes and failures, but that's part of the process. Use the following reproducible tools to help your team in doing its work, and embrace the bumps in the road as learning opportunities. As a result, your team will grow stronger, and most importantly, your students will benefit.

References and Resources

Anderson, B., Mathews, K., Park, D., Padilla, K., & Kerr, D. (2020, Fall). English learners and distance learning: 5 Essentials for success. *AllThingsPLC Magazine*, 12–20.

Baker, S., Lesaux, N., Jayanthi, M., Dimino, J., Proctor, C. P., Morris, J., et al. (2014, April). *Teaching academic content and literacy to English learners in elementary and middle school* (NCEE 2014-4012). Washington, DC: National Center for Education Evaluation and Regional Assistance, Institute of Education Sciences, U.S. Department of Education. Accessed at https://ies.ed.gov/ncee/wwc/Docs/PracticeGuide/english_learners_pg_040114 .pdf on September 17, 2020.

Baumann, J. F., & Graves, M. F. (2010). What is academic vocabulary? *Journal of Adolescent and Adult Literacy, 54*(1), 4–12.

Bresser, R., Melanese, K., & Sphar, C. (2009). *Supporting English language learners in math class, grades 3–5.* Sausalito, CA: Math Solutions.

Buffum, A., Mattos, M., & Malone, J. (2018). *Taking action: A handbook for RTI at Work.* Bloomington, IN: Solution Tree Press.

Burton, N. (2018, July 28). Beyond words: The benefits of being bilingual [Blog post]. *Psychology Today.* Accessed at www.psychologytoday.com/us/blog/hide-and-seek/201807 /beyond-words-the-benefits-being-bilingual on September 17, 2020.

Calderón, M. (2011). *Teaching reading and comprehension to English learners, K–5.* Bloomington, IN: Solution Tree Press.

Carleton, L., & Marzano, R. J. (2010). *Vocabulary games for the classroom.* Bloomington, IN: Marzano Resources.

Colorín Colorado. (2012, December 4). *Vocabulary: Bricks and mortar* [Video file]. Accessed at www.colorincolorado.org/video/vocabulary-bricks-and-mortar on September 17, 2020.

Colorín Colorado. (2014, March 14). *Academic language and English language learners* [Video file]. Accessed at www.colorincolorado.org/webcast/academic-language-and-english -language-learners on September 17, 2020.

Costa, A. L. (n.d.). *What are habits of mind?* Accessed at www.habitsofmindinstitute.org/what -are-habits-of-mind on December 7, 2020.

DuFour, R., DuFour, R., Eaker, R., Many, T. W., & Mattos, M. (2016). *Learning by doing: A handbook for Professional Learning Communities at Work* (3rd ed.). Bloomington, IN: Solution Tree Press.

Fillmore, L. W., & Fillmore, C. J. (2012). *What does text complexity mean for English learners and language minority students?* Accessed at https://ell.stanford.edu/sites/default/files/pdf /academic-papers/06-LWF%20CJF%20Text%20Complexity%20FINAL_0.pdf on September 17, 2020.

Francis, D. J., Rivera, M., Lesaux, N., Kieffer, M., & Rivera, H. (2006). *Practical guidelines for the education of English language learners: Research-based recommendations for instruction and academic interventions.* Portsmouth, NH: RMC Research Corporation, Center on Instruction. Accessed at www.centeroninstruction.org/files/ELL1-Interventions.pdf on September 17, 2020.

Francis, E. M. (2017, May 9). *What is depth of knowledge?* [Blog post]. Accessed at https://inservice .ascd.org/what-exactly-is-depth-of-knowledge-hint-its-not-a-wheel on October 6, 2020.

Kerr, D. (2020, February 26). *"But they don't speak English!"* [Blog post]. Accessed at www .allthingsplc.info/blog/view/411/but-they-dont-speak-english on September 17, 2020.

Kramer, S. V., & Schuhl, S. (2017). *School improvement for all: A how-to guide for doing the right work.* Bloomington, IN: Solution Tree Press.

Kroll, J., & Dussias, P. (2017). The benefits of multilingualism to the personal and professional development of residents of the US. *Foreign Language Annals, 50*(2), 248–259. Accessed at https://www.ncbi.nlm.nih.gov/pmc/articles/PMC5662126 on December 29, 2020.

Marian, V., & Shook, A. (2012). The cognitive benefits of being bilingual. *Cerebrum, 13.* Accessed at www.ncbi.nlm.nih.gov/pmc/articles/PMC3583091 on September 17, 2020.

Marzano, R. J. (n.d.). *Tips from Dr. Marzano: Vocabulary for the Common Core.* Accessed at www.marzanoresources.com/resources/tips/vcc_tips_archive on September 17, 2020.

Marzano, R. J. (2018). *Building basic vocabulary: Tracking my progress.* Bloomington, IN: Marzano Resources.

Marzano, R. J. (2020). *Teaching basic, advanced, and academic vocabulary: A comprehensive framework for elementary instruction*. Bloomington, IN: Marzano Resources.

Marzano, R. J., & Simms, J. A. (2013). *Vocabulary for the Common Core*. Bloomington, IN: Marzano Resources.

National Center for English Language Acquisition. (2017, October). *English learner toolkit for state and local education agencies (SEAs and LEAs)*. Accessed at https://ncela.ed.gov/files /english_learner_toolkit/OELA_2017_ELsToolkit_508C.pdf on January 27, 2021.

National Center for English Language Acquisition. (2020a, September). *English learners who speak Spanish as a home language*. Accessed at https://ncela.ed.gov/files/fast_facts/20200915 -Del4-4%20SpanishELs-508.pdf on January 2, 2021.

National Center for English Language Acquisition. (2020b, November). *English learners who speak Vietnamese as a home language*. Accessed at https://ncela.ed.gov/files/fast_facts/20201102 -Vietnamese-FactSheet-508-OELA.pdf on January 2, 2021.

National Center for English Language Acquisition. (2021, January). *Profile of English learners in the United States*. Accessed at https://ncela.ed.gov/sites/default/files/fast_facts/DEL4.4 _ELProfile_508_1.4.2021_OELA.pdf on January 27, 2021.

National Governors Association Center for Best Practices & Council of Chief State School Officers. (2010a). *Common Core State Standards for English language arts and literacy in history/social studies, science, and technical subjects*. Washington, DC: Authors. Accessed at www.corestandards.org/assets/CCSSI_ELA%20Standards.pdf on October 1, 2020.

National Governors Association Center for Best Practices & Council of Chief State School Officers. (2010b). *Common Core State Standards for mathematics*. Washington, DC: Authors. Accessed at www.corestandards.org/assets/CCSSI_Math%20Standards.pdf on October 1, 2020.

Samson, J. F., & Collins, B. A. (2012, April). *Preparing all teachers to meet the needs of English language learners: Applying research to policy and practice for teacher effectiveness*. Accessed at https://cdn.americanprogress.org/wp-content/uploads/issues/2012/04/pdf/ell_report.pdf? _ga=2.48811439.826011842.1609530462-767625493.1609530462 on January 1, 2021.

Spiller, J., & Power, K. (2019). *Leading with intention: Eight areas for reflection and planning in your PLC at Work*. Bloomington, IN: Solution Tree Press.

Sweetwater Union High School District. (2010, October). *Academic language function toolkit: A resource for developing academic language for all students in all content areas*. Accessed at https:// sweetwaterschools.instructure.com/courses/1080113/files/31344925 on December 1, 2020.

U.S. Department of Education. (n.d.a). *Part A: Improving basic programs operated by local educational agencies*. Accessed at https://www2.ed.gov/policy/elsec/leg/esea02/pg2.html on January 1, 2021.

U.S. Department of Education. (n.d.b). *Our nation's English learners*. Accessed at www2.ed.gov /datastory/el-characteristics/index.html on September 17, 2020.

U.S. Department of Education. (2016, November). *English learner toolkit for state and local education agencies (SEAs and LEAs)*. Washington, DC: Author. Accessed at www2.ed.gov /about/offices/list/oela/english-learner-toolkit/eltoolkit.pdf on December 1, 2020.

Virginia Department of Education. (2015). *History and social science standards of learning for Virginia public schools*. Accessed at www.doe.virginia.gov/testing/sol/standards_docs /history_socialscience/#sol2015 on October 6, 2020.

WIDA. (n.d.). *Can do descriptors*. Accessed at https://wida.wisc.edu/teach/can-do/descriptors on December 1, 2020.

Zwiers, J. (2014). *Building academic language: Meeting Common Core standards across disciplines, grades 5–12* (2nd ed.). San Francisco: Jossey-Bass.

Template to Unpack Essential Standards

Standard:		
Content (Nouns) *What Students Need to Know*	**Skills (Verbs)** *What Students Need to Be Able to Do*	**DOK Level**
Vocabulary Specific to the Content	**Academic Language** *Language Function, Text Structure, and Signal Words*	

Learning Targets

Student Language Objectives (Reading, Writing, Listening, Speaking)

Source: Adapted from Kramer, S. V., & Schuhl, S. (2017). School improvement for all: A how-to guide for doing the right work. *Bloomington, IN: Solution Tree Press.*

Sentence Frames and Sentence Starters

Language Function	Example Sentence Frames and Sentence Starters
Seek Information Inform Identify Recognize Explain Examine Analyze Evaluate	The meaning of _____ is _____. The reasons for _____ are _____. The role of _____ is _____. The relationship between _____ and _____ is _____. The author's viewpoint is _____. This passage shows or illustrates that _____. I believe that the main idea of the story is _____ because _____. The _____ process involves _____. The reason for doing it this way is _____. My two supporting reasons are _____ and _____. My first supporting reason can be found on page _____ because _____.
Compare and Contrast Distinguish Attributes Distinguish Commonalities Differentiate	_____ is different from _____ because _____. _____ is like _____, whereas _____ is like _____. The advantages of _____ are _____. The disadvantages of _____ are _____. _____ is similar to _____ because _____. The similarities between _____ and _____ are _____.
Order Sequence Outline Organize Summarize	At the beginning, _____. In the middle, _____, and at the end, _____. The sequence for answering this mathematics problem is _____. First, _____; second, _____; and third, _____. After that, _____. The transition between stages _____ and _____ can be described as _____. According to _____, _____. In conclusion, _____. In summary, _____.

Charting the Course for Collaborative Teams © 2021 Solution Tree Press • SolutionTree.com
Visit **go.SolutionTree.com/PLCbooks** to download this free reproducible.

Classify Observe	The characteristics of _____ are _____. _____ is organized by [or into] _____. These _____ are sorted by _____ characteristics. These _____ are arranged according to _____. This _____ is larger than [or smaller than, longer than, shorter than, heavier than, or lighter than] _____.
Infer Synthesize Predict Interpret	I predict that _____ because _____. Based on _____, I think _____. I think that the answer is _____ because _____. I conclude that _____ because _____. From _____, I infer _____. When _____ increases [or decreases], _____ increases [or decreases]. One way to interpret this event is _____. The author is trying to teach us _____.
Justify Persuade Verify Solve Estimate	To verify _____, use _____. To solve _____, first _____, and then _____. The best solution is _____ because _____. Estimate _____ by _____. I believe _____ is important because _____. The evidenced that supports my point of view is _____. The advantages of _____ outweigh the disadvantages of _____.
Solve Problems Hypothesize Interpret Ascertain Cause and Effect	To solve _____, first _____, and then _____. The data do [or do not] show _____. Based on _____, I predict that _____. If we had _____, then _____ might have been _____. The hypothesis was [or was not] confirmed by _____. The most likely reason for _____ was _____. Each _____ played a key role. First . . . One reason for _____ was _____. Even though many people thought the cause was _____, I believe it was _____. It was due to the reaction between _____.

page 2 of 3

Synthesize Evaluate Integrate	The impact of _____ is _____ because _____.
	The effect of _____ is _____.
	The significance of _____ is _____.
	The growth of _____ is due to _____.
	The reasons for doing it this way are _____.
	_____ was effective [or ineffective] because _____.
	Had the author _____, it would have _____.
	The argument was persuasive because _____.
	My favorite part was _____ because _____.
	From his [or her] perspective, I think he [or she] was thinking _____.
	I evaluated _____ on the following criteria: _____.

Guiding Questions

Can we use this sentence frame across content or contexts?

Can we differentiate the sentence frame by vocabulary needs?

Can we differentiate the sentence frame by grammar needs?

page 3 of 3

 **Tammy Miller** has served as a principal, director of elementary education, director of alternative education, and Indiana University adjunct professor, and is currently a Solution Tree professional learning community (PLC) and priority schools coach. Her passion is to assist schools in improving student achievement, and this work has resulted in schools' achieving gains as high as 20 percent in one year. Additionally, she has a deep commitment to literacy and has systematically tackled and redefined literacy-based challenges. Her leadership in this area has led to innovative approaches that produce results with students.

When Tammy served as director of elementary education for the Monroe County Community School Corporation in Bloomington, Indiana, she led administrators and teaching staff in a districtwide strategic plan that moved the school district from the letter grade of D to an A, a status that the district has sustained. Tammy has supported schools in all regions of the United States that have overcome the failure cycle and are now receiving awards for their increased student achievement.

Tammy holds a bachelor of science in elementary education from Indiana University and a reading certification and a master of science in administration from Butler University.

To learn more about Tammy Miller's work, follow @edvisetammymil1 on Twitter.

To book Tammy Miller for professional development, contact pd@SolutionTree.com.

Getting Students to Grade-Level Reading Fast

Tammy Miller

> Gaps in achievement are a major equity concern and occur as a direct result of eliminating opportunities for success.
>
> —*Sharon V. Kramer and Sarah Schuhl*

In the fall of 2017, during my first visit as a coach at Bragg Elementary School in West Memphis, Arkansas, I could see from teachers a culture of deep commitment to students. Bragg Elementary participated in the first cohort of the Arkansas schools for their ongoing program to develop and expand the PLC process across the state, and walking through the front doors was like a warm hug. As the staff and I discussed the needs of the school and reviewed data, the issue of reading proficiency continually came back to the center of the conversation. The principal was forthright in stating her concerns that a high percentage of students were not reading at grade level. We began discussing the possibilities for closing the reading gap, and it became clear that students needed to quickly accelerate in applying foundational reading skills with automaticity to achieve grade-level comprehension skills. This is an enormous task at the kindergarten through second-grade levels, considering that a classroom can be full of students in very different developmental stages with these skills.

Compounding the issue is the fact that reading deficits in the upper grades are also impacted when students haven't secured foundational reading skills. As a staff, identifying the guaranteed and viable foundational reading skills students require for future academic success allows for successful intervention in grade levels beyond second grade. It is this reading deficit that is at the core of equity in education. Reading is a fundamental human right that all children deserve to access. Equitable access to literacy instruction is even enumerated in the International Reading Association's (2019) *Children's Rights to Excellent Literacy Instruction*. With this firmly in mind, Cassie Adams, the Bragg Elementary principal and I began to formulate a plan to address the literacy deficit among the school's students.

Ms. Adams and I began by forming a literacy task force to address this complex challenge that included representation from the West Memphis district administration, an outside literacy consultant, Bragg instructional coaches, and other literacy specialists from nearby Harding University. The task force's members analyzed the reading data collected from several assessments, and they began to see that none of the assessments teachers used fully examined students' foundational reading skills in a way that would inform explicit classroom instruction. The misaligned assessments revealed a schoolwide lack of understanding of how to answer the first critical question of a PLC, "What do we want students to learn?" (DuFour, DuFour, Eaker, Many, & Mattos, 2016). More specifically, "What do we want students to know and be able to do in relation to foundational reading skills?"

Once we realized teacher teams lacked clarity about this question and the identified guaranteed curriculum for foundational reading skills, the work of creating systems to improve literacy achievement began. The school's literacy coach, Candace Zachary, went to work with teacher teams to build the K–2 continuum of foundational reading skills, which was composed of the most critical phonemic-awareness, phonological-awareness, and phonics skills. The literacy coach was a champion in this effort. In a short time, an entire continuum emerged with essential reading skills organized into a sequence that allowed teachers to assess mastery of each skill for each student. In other words, *student by student and skill by skill* became the mode of operation.

Prior to this work, educators taught foundational reading skills, but no one really knew which students had learned which skills. By identifying skills, educators simply needed to organize them into an appropriate sequence to establish a reading journey for students and develop better tools to assess their progress. This exemplifies how the first critical question of a PLC leads to the second. This work created the entire basis of the school's revised approach to intervention (the third critical question) and acceleration (the fourth critical question). When collaborative teams can identify exactly which skills students need in order to show proficiency, they can more quickly move students into each subsequent skill and accelerate their growth.

Once the school's collaborative teams implemented this approach, the teachers saw immediate results. During the first two weeks of implementation, my phone blew up with text messages from teachers about how quickly students were growing now that the teachers could focus attention on specific skills for students to master and could assess those skills after reteaching. As a result, students made gains. Students who were behind grade level caught up quickly, and students who were on grade level continued to move forward in their reading development. Three other priority or underperforming schools in Arkansas have since implemented this approach with the same positive results. This indicates that this targeted and specific method closes the reading gap and restores the opportunity to succeed in reading for all students, regardless of their skin color, special education labels, or socioeconomic status.

In this chapter, I describe my collective experiences at Bragg Elementary, James Matthew Elementary, and Wonderview Elementary to illustrate how your school's collaborative teams can accelerate student reading skills. Success with this approach requires understanding the reading crisis in the United States, Canada, and around the world and how this crisis indicates a problem of practice. You will find the evidence supporting this approach to reading instruction and how to implement it step-by-step throughout this chapter. By reading this chapter, your collaborative team will have the knowledge and practices it needs to accelerate student reading.

A Reading Crisis

There is a reading crisis in the United States and around the world. In fact, according to new estimates from the United Nations Educational, Scientific and Cultural Organization (UNESCO, 2017) Institute for Statistics, more than 617 million children and adolescents are not achieving minimum proficiency levels in reading and mathematics. According to the National Center for Education Statistics (2019), 65 percent of U.S. fourth graders cannot read at a proficient level. These data have not changed in three decades and could lead to a conclusion that poor student achievement in failing schools can be traced to a reading deficit. Learning to read the English language is so challenging that only 35 percent of students can read English accurately after one year, compared to an 80–90 percent accuracy rate for thirteen of the most common languages (Seymour, Aro, & Erskine, 2003).

A lack of student mastery of explicit foundational reading skills—including print concepts, phonological awareness, phonics and word recognition, and fluency—most commonly ignites this problem. This lack of foundational reading skills leads to difficulties with comprehension because the cognitive load to decode with automaticity is so great that students do not have enough working memory available to understand a text (Sweller, 2010). In other words, students are simultaneously struggling with decoding and fluency. This causes a huge cognitive demand that, in turn, slows or prevents comprehension. As students progress to higher grade levels, text complexity increases, but schools do not always have a targeted plan to attack the missing foundational reading skills students need for comprehension, including fluency.

A contributing factor to the reading crisis is programmatic in nature. Schools and districts make teachers accountable for implementing reading and phonics programs as well as multiple reading assessments. As district and school leaders strive to improve reading achievement, enhancing the programming and assessments appears to them to be the answer. Unfortunately, without identifying the most critical foundational reading skills and guaranteeing that these skills are learned (not just taught), this approach has not proven effective.

Teachers express concern that they are not meeting the moral imperative with reading and they feel trapped in a vacuum. They face a decision of whether they will follow a directive to adhere to a purchased program page by page or alter that program to provide what each student needs to become an independent reader. Teachers recognize that skills are missing in most published materials, but the pacing layout is usually designed for coverage, not mastery using a cycle of continuous improvement (Kramer & Schuhl, 2017). Students need foundational skills in reading to access text and comprehend it. If they learn these skills explicitly, they acquire the ability to read with automaticity. The focus then shifts from *teaching* the skills to students demonstrating they have learned the foundational reading skills and used them with automaticity.

Further complicating the reading crisis are the myriad literacy assessments teachers administer to kindergarten through second-grade students. Both states and districts often require teachers in these early elementary grades to give multiple benchmark assessments, such as DIBELS, DSA, DRA, PSI, and STAR Early Literacy. These assessments can serve to inform instruction, but unfortunately, not one of them provides all the information teachers need. Certainly, it is useful to gain insight into a student's understanding of these early reading skills; yet having too many benchmark assessments results in data overload that is overwhelming for teachers to apply student by student and skill by skill in an intervention or extension program.

In an effort to use the data, teams often summarize them by randomly selecting a skill that many students lack and then grouping students holistically, not by individual need. This is inefficient, as the skills are somewhat hierarchical in nature, and one cannot assume that just because a group of students have a common deficit, each student has the building blocks of previous skills. It creates a scattered approach that becomes futile and discouraging for both teachers and students. Teachers end up focusing on coverage and assessing with tools that are not completely aligned to measure mastery of the foundational reading skills as teams teach them. This results in a compliance exercise in which, rather than helping students *read to learn*, teachers lose precious time helping students *learn to read* in order to improve the priority school's test scores. As a result, students who have not broken the code, the ability to decode words in a systematic way (not by guessing), are unable to independently access text. This limitation prevents them from focusing on learning the grade-level content and comprehension that states and districts heavily assess.

A gap in achievement, particularly a gap in reading skills, creates an educational inequity that diminishes students' futures (Kramer & Schuhl, 2017). For students with a reading deficit to have the same opportunities as their peers who can read at grade level, instruction and intervention must provide students with the missing foundational reading skills while the students also access grade-level content to build comprehension. Collaborative teams must therefore consider the essential standards at grade level as the core of a guaranteed and viable curriculum (Eaker & Marzano, 2020). However, teachers must also provide an accelerated student-by-student and skill-by-skill approach to develop essential reading skills in students who are unable to decode with automaticity and read fluently to comprehend text. Students can receive this intensive remediation using the same system I described in the introduction to this chapter without sacrificing their access to grade-level instruction.

A Foundation for Accelerating Reading Instruction

In a PLC, every school-improvement journey begins with developing urgency and a collective vision for change. This means schools must examine their current reality and confront the brutal facts before they can take meaningful action (Collins, 2001; DuFour et al., 2016). This is an especially difficult task for underperforming schools because they often have extremely negative or stagnant data. Facing the current reality is a critical first step in attacking the reading deficit. As Kramer and Schuhl (2017) point out, underperforming schools "must be willing to look at the good, the bad, and the ugly, no matter how uncomfortable that may be" (p. 12).

Understanding the current reality provides the leverage for a sense of urgency and builds the momentum for a collective plan to accelerate students to grade-level reading. The continuous learning cycle that benefits all PLC work is the same for enhancing learning of foundational reading skills. The plan should utilize the first critical question of a PLC (What do we want students to know and be able to do?) to identify the foundational reading skills that must be part of a guaranteed and viable curriculum. This includes teams creating tightly aligned common assessments they will use to see the correlation between their reading-acceleration plan and the continuous learning cycle. (You can learn more about learning cycles in chapter 3, page 51.) Table 5.1 shows the correlation between the learning cycle for foundational reading skills and the learning of grade-level essential standards.

Table 5.1: Correlation Between Foundational Reading Skills and Essential Standards

Learning Cycle for Foundational Skill Sets	Learning of Essential Standards
A learning continuum (a structured plan for learning a particular set of reading foundational skills through a specified sequence)	A proficiency map (a list of essential standards organized into units with a timeline for mastery)
Learning targets to be mastered for each skill set	Learning targets to be mastered for each essential standard
Common assessments by learning target for each skill set	Common assessments by learning target for each essential standard
A plan to reteach and reassess	A plan to reteach and reassess
Data tracking	Data tracking

For teams to accelerate reading progress in the classroom, they must first determine what students must know, assess students' learning progress toward essential reading standards, and then use the resulting data to determine next steps. These steps all align with answering the four critical questions of a PLC (DuFour et al., 2016).

Determine What Students Must Know

Teams begin building a learning cycle for foundational skills by determining what students need to know and be able to do; teams need to answer the first critical question of a PLC (DuFour et al., 2016). To read complex texts with automaticity, students must achieve integration of foundational reading skills, including print concepts, phonological awareness, phonics and word recognition, and fluency. The science of reading indicates that all the most critical foundational reading skills require explicit teaching (Connor, Alberto, Compton, & O'Connor, 2014). For students to access text independently, they need mastery of foundational reading standards and not just instruction about them.

A solution is for teams to create a foundational reading skill continuum of all basic decoding skills needed for grades K–2 that will become part of the guaranteed and viable curriculum for students to learn to read independently (DuFour et al., 2016). To build a continuum, teams must engage in collaborative inquiry, utilizing research and professional knowledge to identify these skills and their sequencing. Sequencing is key; for example, teachers need to ensure students can identify letters before learning to decode vowel teams. This inquiry process becomes enlightening for team members as they define the skills and pace necessary for a student to demonstrate proficiency. They engage in powerful conversations as they gain a deeper understanding of and reach consensus on the meaning of foundational reading skills. Most critically, the outcome ensures that students learn the skills, not just that they are exposed to them.

The continuum creates clarity for both intervention and acceleration of foundational decoding skills by providing a road map of grade-level instruction, intervention, and extension that clarifies the skill sets students must learn to a proficient level. Teachers establish the foundational reading skill sets by grade level in a K–2 sequence. In struggling schools, students can be several years behind by the time teachers identify and attempt to address the deficit, so teams must move quickly to accelerate learning of the skills. One year of growth in a school year is not enough for students who are two to three years behind grade level.

Assess Reading Progress

Each school that I have worked with, including Bragg Elementary, James Matthews Elementary in Pine Bluff, Arkansas, and Wonderview Elementary in Hattieville, Arkansas, have each implemented a continuum-based acceleration model and have successfully built upon the work of one another. Collaboration between schools and educators in different districts supporting one another is to be celebrated and was always a goal of PLC architects Rick and Rebecca DuFour. For example, Wonderview Elementary stood on the work of Bragg Elementary. Eventually, James Matthews Elementary and 34th Avenue Elementary (also in Pine Bluff, Arkansas) furthered the work. These schools have all continued to refine their structure and have added specific learning targets for students to master within each skill set.

Students prove mastery of a series of foundational reading skill sets through team-created common assessments to move up to the next skill set. Students accelerate through the skills until they have mastered all skills on the continuum. Figure 5.1 shows an excerpt from the foundational reading skill continuum used for grades K–2 at James Matthews Elementary, where Leondra Williams serves as the principal. The continuum is a sequence of kindergarten through second-grade foundational skills in which teachers each list their names in the first row and list the names of students who have reached proficiency in the second row.

Skill Set: Show proficiency in spelling CVC words.

Teacher Names				
Student Names				

Skill Set: Show proficiency in identifying the short sounds with the five major vowel graphemes orally (a, e, i, o, and u—open syllables).

Teacher Names				
Student Names				

Skill Set: Show proficiency in identifying the long sounds with the five major vowel graphemes orally (a, e, i, o, and u—closed syllables).

Teacher Names				
Student Names				

Skill Set: Show proficiency in reading fluently in level aa in reading A to Z.

Teacher Names				
Student Names				

Skill Set: Show proficiency with CVC words with closed syllables (a, e, i, o, and u).

Teacher Names				
Student Names				

Skill Set: Show proficiency in applying S blends with short vowels (a, e, i, o, and u).

Teacher Names				
Student Names				

Skill Set: Show proficiency in applying L blends with short vowels (a, e, i, o, and u).

Teacher Names				
Student Names				

Skill Set: Show proficiency in applying R blends with short vowels (a, e, i, o, and u).

Teacher Names				
Student Names				

Skill Set: Show proficiency in applying final consonant blends (ft, mp, nd, nt, ng, and nk).

Teacher Names				
Student Names				

Skill Set: Show proficiency in applying consonant digraphs with short vowels (ch, sh, th, wh, ph, and ck).

Teacher Names				
Student Names				

Source: © 2019 James Matthews Elementary, Pine Bluff, Arkansas.

Figure 5.1: Excerpt from a foundational reading skill continuum.

Visit **go.SolutionTree.com/PLCbooks** for a free reproducible version of this figure.

Using this continuum, James Matthews kindergarten teachers determined that only 26 percent of their students were ready to move into first-grade skills in February of the school year. This allowed the teachers to identify that there was an urgency for the remaining 74 percent of kindergarten students and would require a restructuring of instruction, personnel, and allocation of time to get students prepared. Using the continuum and checking for mastery allowed them to adjust their instructional plan for pacing the teaching and re-teaching of skills to get the students to mastery of all kindergarten-level reading-comprehension skills by the end of the school year. In all the schools using this acceleration continuum, teachers and administrators use data derived from rolling assessments on the continuum skill sets to determine students' progress and to problem solve when mastery of grade-level skills isn't happening fast enough. This attention to pacing with mastery is necessary to prevent sending students along to the next grade level without the prerequisite skill sets.

Use Data to Determine Next Steps

With continuum-derived data, teams can begin to decide how to adjust instruction to support students who have struggled to learn and to extend learning for those who show proficiency. For example, K–2 teacher teams I worked with at Wonderview Elementary identified eighty-two skill sets for students to master between kindergarten and the end of second grade. Teams at that school support students in moving up the continuum as fast as they show mastery. So, if a student behind grade level for foundational reading shows mastery working on skill set 32, he or she can move up to skill set 33 the next day. This provides the opportunity for students who are behind to catch up quickly and have evidence that they have secured the skills. Simultaneously, a student who is ready to move ahead of grade level can do so as well. In other words, a kindergarten student could begin working on first-grade foundational reading skills if evidence shows the student has mastered the kindergarten foundational reading skills.

Similarly, the kindergarten students at James Matthews who were ready to move up to first-grade skills in February of the school year could do so. In this school, teams implement the foundational reading skill set continuum alongside instruction on essential standards for reading comprehension and writing. The work includes fluency practice and students' tracking their own accuracy rates using a fluency check. As students improve in their acquisition of foundational reading skills, their fluency rate increases, leading to more accurate comprehension. Originally, James Matthews teachers included some foundational reading standards in the proficiency map with the comprehension and writing essential standards, but they found that the foundational reading skills were all essential. The acquisition of breaking the code in reading occurs in a sequence and requires mastery of many learning targets.

The most daunting aspect of implementing the foundational reading skill continuum is getting started. It can seem overwhelming at first and create analysis paralysis. As you know, learning by doing is the best way to ensure the fastest results (DuFour et al., 2016). Waiting until the continuum is perfect or until teams give and analyze every possible assessment is not an option. If students are even one semester behind in reading, it is a crisis to handle with extreme urgency. The cumulative impact of falling behind is devastating, and in many cases, students do not recover and get back on grade level because their schools have no systems in place to truly accelerate them to a proficient level.

The direct benefit of implementing the foundational reading skill continuum is that students do learn the skills, and they do become readers who can access grade-level texts. Teams can then implement a learning continuum focused on foundational comprehension skills and a plan to guarantee accelerated learning to bridge the achievement gap for students who are far behind grade-level content. You will know the strategy has worked as your team collects and analyzes the common assessment data and use it to inform intervention.

Each skill set requires students to master specific targets in order to provide evidence of mastery. For this to happen, teachers must have consensus on what it is students must demonstrate for each skill and how the team will assess it. Using a rolling assessment approach allows teachers and administrators to quickly check for mastery of these most critical foundational reading skills. They record the data in a spreadsheet or simple table that allows team members to glean an understanding of individual student and group progress at a glance. Acceleration is truly possible when teachers and administrators can access this information quickly and move students immediately. Students should not be stuck in a skill set group if they are ready to move up to the next skill set. The strategy is to move them as quickly as possible when they demonstrate proficiency, which aligns with a PLC's go-slow-to-go-fast philosophy (DuFour et al., 2016).

In the early stages of this work at Bragg Elementary, teams' first attempts resulted in long grade-level lists of foundational reading skills that a single teacher couldn't manage. Striving to review data for each skill set student by student and skill by skill immediately overwhelmed teachers. So the teams at Bragg Elementary created skill sets that grouped skills together. After just three weeks of implementation, they saw proficiency rates soar in their data from 35 percent to 95 percent mastery! The victory came in grouping the skill sets in a sequential continuum so that teachers could more easily monitor students for intervention and acceleration.

At Wonderview Elementary, another critical turning point was the realization that teachers needed clarity on how they should assess each learning target and on what knowledge students had to demonstrate for teachers to declare them proficient. This clarity made it feasible for students to accelerate more quickly and for teachers to collect their common assessment data on the exact targets for students' individual needs. Figure 5.2 (page 118) illustrates an example of a data tracker the teachers at Wonderview Elementary used. (See page 127 for a reproducible version of this figure.) The purpose of this tracker is to determine whether students have mastered each skill set and to quickly accelerate those who have into the next skill set. Again, this needs to happen quickly. Having students wait until an entire group is ready to move up is too slow; the data tracker allows for faster movement.

In figure 5.2, you will notice the term *accelerationist*, a term the teachers at Wonderview Elementary coined. It best describes the person (or persons) most directly focused on getting students to grade level in reading. Teachers are often accustomed to using terms

Reading Acceleration									
Skill Set Group Number:	Skill set 36								
Skill Set Description:	Show proficiency by decoding or reading three syllable types, long-vowel digraphs.								
Name of Accelerationist:	Carol Jones								
Student Name	**Homeroom Teacher Name**	**Target 1:** Open syllables	**Target 2:** Closed syllables	**Target 3:** VCe words	**Target 4:** Long A digraphs	**Target 5:** Long E digraphs	**Target 6:** Long I digraphs	**Target 7:** Long O digraphs	**Target 8:** Long U digraphs
Gina Irwin	Mrs. Mckinney	M	M	M	M	M			
Rob Vaziri	Mrs. Mckinney	M	M	M	M	M	M	M	M
Brandon Magary	Mr. Balko	M	M	M	M				
Brianna Adams	Mr. Balko	M	M	M	M	M	M	M	
Sulome Patel	Ms. Zacny	M	M						

M = Mastery

Source: © 2019 Wonderview Elementary, Hattieville, Arkansas.

Figure 5.2: Student data tracker.

like *remediation* and *intervention*, when, in fact, the outcomes of these endeavors are frequently unsuccessful for getting students to grade level in basic reading skills. The unintentional outcome of reading remediation and intervention has become an acceptance of the status quo. When that happens, teams lose the intent that grade-level equivalency *must* be achieved. Therefore, teams must accelerate students to get them to grade level. The skill-set group number in figure 5.2 refers to a specific foundational reading skill set teachers identified and ranked in order of the sequence of the learning continuum. Within this skill set, there are specific learning targets students must achieve for mastery. For example, to master the skill set, students must be able to read words using *each* long vowel digraph, and their reading must not be haphazard. The learning targets must be specified for each long vowel to be taught and learned, and instruction must demonstrate each learning target, develop understanding of each target, and produce evidence that students have mastered the target. The letter *M* in this chart represents that the student has mastered the learning target. If the learning target has not been mastered, then the next step is to enter the continuous learning cycle for re-teaching to mastery as a requirement for the guaranteed and viable curriculum.

Perhaps the most critical lesson of this work is the fact that standardized test scores fuel the instructional focus for priority schools due to the sanctions states or provinces apply when students do not perform at high levels. In spite of the fact that it is a state or provincial sanction bringing the reading crisis to light, the urgency is apparent, and educators must get to work on this root cause of the achievement deficit. Expectations for content and comprehension increases by grade level on standardized tests, and without students having the ability to access and comprehend grade-level text, it is simply not possible to improve student achievement. Students who lack foundational reading skills cannot read to learn and cannot access texts necessary for them to work on the grade-level content and comprehension that states and districts heavily assess. Accelerating reading instruction for students who lack these foundational decoding and comprehesion skills provides them with opportunities to acquire the missing skills while continuing to access grade-level content. Thus, reading acceleration in both foundational decoding skills as well as comprehension is the key to improving every student's potential and performance. Schools and teams must analyze and restructure every program, resource, assessment, schedule, and use of human resources to improve student achievement and get students to grade level in reading. As the teachers at Bragg Elementary, James Matthews Elementary, and Wonderview Elementary have demonstrated, the right structural changes and a laser focus on reading acceleration that move students to higher levels of reading achievement is possible.

The Work of Collaborative Teams

Critical to the successful implementation of the reading-acceleration strategy within collaborative teams is teacher ownership. The reality is that if a leadership team or collaborative team leader just creates a continuum and passes it out to teachers, it will not change results. The power of this work lies within the crucial conversations that teachers must have to determine what students must learn in order to be proficient readers.

In the schools highlighted in this chapter, team members began the work with a clear understanding that students were struggling with foundational reading skills. They felt discouraged by the lack of reading achievement and low test scores and were eager to find a solution that would stop the failure cycle. If meeting the challenge meant using a continuum to help accelerate reading skills, then they were happy to own that solution. As a result of this mindset, many crucial conversations occurred among the teachers, in which they reached consensus on the critical foundational reading skills and the sequence of those skills in the continuum.

Some might say that a foundational reading skill continuum could be a viable product for schools to purchase and use as is, but it does not often work. Teachers must be involved in discerning what the skills are, how to sequence the skills, what the individual learning targets of each skill are, and how to determine proficiency. This requires collective inquiry and iterative work among team members. After implementing a continuum, the collaborative teams at Wonderview Elementary realized that their first attempt at identifying the foundational reading skills needed revision, as the continuum did not put the skills in the correct order. At James Matthews Elementary, chart paper lined the walls of the collaborative team meeting room for several months as teams worked to decide how to best place the skills into sets by grade level and then pace the skill sets for the school year. Once the teams had developed the continuum, each team created its own guaranteed and viable foundational reading skill curriculum that was vertically articulated with other grade-level teams' curricula. The continuum then becomes a road map providing teachers with clarity and focus for the foundational reading skills students must master by a specific date on the school calendar.

Once teams determine the continuum, the next crucial conversations center on identifying the learning targets students need to master within each skill set. For example, the kindergarten teams at Wonderview Elementary spent a great deal of time discussing how they wanted students to show mastery of their letters. These conversations become animated. Teachers might suddenly make a team decision about whether they should teach groups of letters for identification, sound, and letter formation or if they should expect mastery on only identification. Then, the conversation might shift to whether there should be simultaneous identification of lowercase and uppercase letters. Most often, teachers don't agree on learning targets, and each teacher has a different expectation for mastery. However, they work to build consensus, just as a PLC culture envisions (DuFour et al., 2016).

Upon reaching consensus on the essential foundational skills and the correlating learning targets, teams identify how to assess students and what the expectations for mastery are. Figure 5.3 shows an example template for checking skill set learning targets and mastery. (See page 128 for a reproducible version of this figure.)

Phases of Acceleration

The acceleration strategy involves multiple phases, and it is critical that teacher teams be involved in the necessary collaborative discussions during each phase of this work, shown in figure 5.4 (page 122). These discussions are very often the most important part of the process, as they provide shared learning opportunities for teachers. If school leadership simply develops a continuum and provides it to collaborative teams, then it robs those teams of vital learning experiences. Having teacher involvement in every phase of the process is critical in order for all team members to improve their practice and own the process to improve student reading achievement. As mentioned earlier in this chapter, the focus of foundational reading skills occurs during grades K–2 instruction; however, when students in grades beyond this range have not learned these skills, it is absolutely imperative that they learn to apply them. Accelerating these students in the foundational reading and comprehension skills must happen as fast as possible with all possible personnel and time allocated toward mastery.

Skill Set Learning Targets and Mastery Check

Student Name: _____

Homeroom Teacher Name: _____

Date When All Learning Targets Mastered: _____

Skill Set: Letter focus A–E; identify sound and write.			
Related Standard: • **RF.K.1.D**—Recognize and name all upper- and lowercase letters of the alphabet. • **RF.K.3.A**—Demonstrate basic knowledge of one-to-one letter-sound correspondences by producing the primary sound or many of the most frequent sounds for each consonant.			
Learning Target	**What Proficiency Looks Like**	**How We Will Assess**	**Mastery Date**
Identify uppercase letters A–E.	Automatic response	Flash cards Letter-identification recording sheet; correct four of five times in three sessions	August 25
Identify lowercase letters A–E.	Automatic response	Flash cards Letter-identification recording sheet; correct four of five times in three sessions	September 9
Pronounce the standard sound for A–E.	Automatic response	Flash cards Letter-identification recording sheet; correct four of five times in three sessions	September 16
Write uppercase letters A–E.	Writing with the correct formation on a handwriting line	Letter formation correct on the handwriting line; correct four of five times in three sessions	December 13
Write lowercase letters A–E.	Writing with the correct formation on a handwriting line	Letter formation correct on the handwriting line; correct four of five times in three sessions	December 13

Source for standard: National Governors Association (NGA) & Council of Chief State School Officers (CCSSO), 2010.

Figure 5.3: Skill set learning targets and mastery check.

Phase	Tasks
Phase 1: Create a continuum of K–2 foundational skills.	1. Grade-level teams work together to identify the foundational reading skills and the sequencing of skills for their respective grade levels. Teachers utilize the continua designed by vertically oriented teams as well as purchased materials, assessments, and any other research they can do for true inquiry into better understanding the skills. The teachers' professional judgment is most critical; they must make these decisions for their students.
	2. The skills should be grouped together per meaningful likeness. This allows for identification and mastery of learning targets within each skill set. Team members will have interesting conversations about these skills as teachers are not clear on what students need in order to demonstrate mastery.
	3. The building of the continuum will be an ongoing process. Teams may declare it complete, but then the teachers will begin to realize changes are needed as they implement the continuum and learn from their work.
	4. Teams need to determine a cutoff between kindergarten and first grade as well as between first and second grades. This is to provide pacing against what students should learn at each grade level. The continuum is built so that students can accelerate to the next skill set as soon as they prove mastery. The reason for this competency-based approach is to provide students with the opportunity to fill missing skills and accelerate quickly. Students who are advancing can continue and not be delayed waiting on peers.
	5. Once students have reached a point of completion with a skill set, teachers must implement and learn from their work to make revisions.
	6. Depending on the abilities and grade levels involved, teams may add a continuum for reading comprehension. Comprehension must be addressed simultaneously as it is foundational for students to perform related standards, such as literal questioning.
Phase 2: Identify learning targets within each skill set.	1. Teachers work on the part of the continuum that corresponds to their grade level. As a team, members analyze and research each skill set to determine the learning targets students must master for the skill set. This becomes challenging as the temptation is to leave out some blends or vowel teams because there are so many. The focus is on the concept of teaching for mastery instead of for coverage.
	2. Teams use the "Skill Set Learning Targets and Mastery Check" template (page 128) to enable teachers and students to document when students have mastered a learning target. The template has a section for teachers to determine what proficiency looks like. For example, teachers need to decide whether it is demonstrated in isolation or by decoding it in a text. In some cases, teachers want to see it demonstrated more than once, and teams can also document this progress on the template.

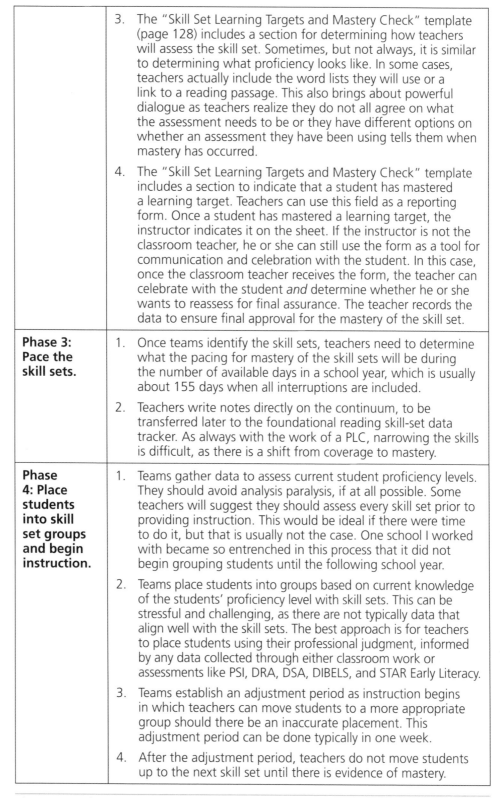

	3. The "Skill Set Learning Targets and Mastery Check" template (page 128) includes a section for determining how teachers will assess the skill set. Sometimes, but not always, it is similar to determining what proficiency looks like. In some cases, teachers actually include the word lists they will use or a link to a reading passage. This also brings about powerful dialogue as teachers realize they do not all agree on what the assessment needs to be or they have different options on whether an assessment they have been using tells them when mastery has occurred.
	4. The "Skill Set Learning Targets and Mastery Check" template includes a section to indicate that a student has mastered a learning target. Teachers can use this field as a reporting form. Once a student has mastered a learning target, the instructor indicates it on the sheet. If the instructor is not the classroom teacher, he or she can still use the form as a tool for communication and celebration with the student. In this case, once the classroom teacher receives the form, the teacher can celebrate with the student *and* determine whether he or she wants to reassess for final assurance. The teacher records the data to ensure final approval for the mastery of the skill set.
Phase 3: Pace the skill sets.	1. Once teams identify the skill sets, teachers need to determine what the pacing for mastery of the skill sets will be during the number of available days in a school year, which is usually about 155 days when all interruptions are included.
	2. Teachers write notes directly on the continuum, to be transferred later to the foundational reading skill-set data tracker. As always with the work of a PLC, narrowing the skills is difficult, as there is a shift from coverage to mastery.
Phase 4: Place students into skill set groups and begin instruction.	1. Teams gather data to assess current student proficiency levels. They should avoid analysis paralysis, if at all possible. Some teachers will suggest they should assess every skill set prior to providing instruction. This would be ideal if there were time to do it, but that is usually not the case. One school I worked with became so entrenched in this process that it did not begin grouping students until the following school year.
	2. Teams place students into groups based on current knowledge of the students' proficiency level with skill sets. This can be stressful and challenging, as there are not typically data that align well with the skill sets. The best approach is for teachers to place students using their professional judgment, informed by any data collected through either classroom work or assessments like PSI, DRA, DSA, DIBELS, and STAR Early Literacy.
	3. Teams establish an adjustment period as instruction begins in which teachers can move students to a more appropriate group should there be an inaccurate placement. This adjustment period can be done typically in one week.
	4. After the adjustment period, teachers do not move students up to the next skill set until there is evidence of mastery.

Figure 5.4: Phases of acceleration.

Conclusion

Any school can replicate this chapter's approach of creating a hierarchical continuum of foundational reading skill sets. Once a school is exposed to this approach and philosophy, staff find answers to questions that both students and teachers have long suffered to answer. Getting the continuum and assessments prepared requires commitment and diligence, but once the purpose is clear, most teachers are ready to dive in as the acceleration model restores the professional judgment to teachers to make the decisions needed for each student. The data collection for each skill set provides a roadmap and immediate feedback for each student to get exactly what they need in reading instruction. When teachers and students see immediate results, there is a tremendous surge of motivation; as a result, more students get to grade level faster in reading. Using this approach makes a daily difference for students in acquiring the foundational reading skills and the basic comprehension strategies that unlock the skills for grade-level content standards in all areas.

As a final note, know that many of the resources included in this chapter's References and Resources section are not cited in the chapter text but are valuable resources nonetheless because they recognize and support the critical nature of systematic phonics instruction and fundamental reading-comprehension strategies.

References and Resources

Castles, A., Rastle, K., & Nation, K. (2018). Ending the reading wars: Reading acquisition from novice to expert. *Psychological Science in the Public Interest, 19*(1), 5–51.

Collins, J. (2001). *Good to great: Why some companies make the leap . . . and others don't.* New York: HarperCollins.

Connor, C. M., Alberto, P. A., Compton, D. L., & O'Connor, R. E. (2014, February). Improving reading outcomes for students with or at risk for reading disabilities: A synthesis of the contributions from the Institute of Education Sciences Research Centers (NCSER 2014-3000). Washington, DC: National Center for Special Education Research, Institute of Education Sciences, U.S. Department of Education. Accessed at https://files.eric.ed.gov /fulltext/ED544759.pdf on September 16, 2020.

Connor, C. M., & Morrison, F. J. (2016). Individualizing student instruction in reading: Implications for policy and practice. *Policy Insights From the Behavioral and Brain Sciences, 3*(1), 54–61.

Dickinson, C. K. (2014). Accelerating first grade reading growth through systematic yet responsive phonics instruction. *School of Education Student Capstone Theses and Dissertations, 4062.* Accessed at https://digitalcommons.hamline.edu/hse_all/4062 on October 20, 2020.

DuFour, R., DuFour, R., Eaker, R., Many, T. W., & Mattos, M. (2016). *Learning by doing: A handbook for Professional Learning Communities at Work* (3rd ed.). Bloomington, IN: Solution Tree Press.

Eaker, R., & Marzano, R. J. (Eds.). (2020). *Professional Learning Communities at Work and High Reliability Schools: Cultures of continuous learning.* Bloomington, IN: Solution Tree Press.

Ehri, L. C. (2004). Teaching phonemic awareness and phonics: An explanation of the National Reading Panel meta-analyses. In P. McCardle & V. Chhabra (Eds.), *The voice of evidence in reading research* (pp. 153–186). Baltimore, MD: Brookes.

Hattie, J. (2012). *Visible learning for teachers: Maximizing impact on learning.* New York: Routledge.

Heck, R. H. (2009). Teacher effectiveness and student achievement: Investigating a multilevel cross-classified model. *Journal of Educational Administration, 47*(2), 227–249.

International Reading Association. (2019). *Children's rights to excellent literacy instruction.* Accessed at https://literacyworldwide.org/docs/default-source/where-we-stand/ila-childrens-rights-to-excellent-literacy-instruction.pdf on January 27, 2021.

Kramer, S. V. (2015). *How to leverage PLCs for school improvement.* Bloomington, IN: Solution Tree Press.

Kramer, S. V., & Schuhl, S. (2017). *School improvement for all: A how-to guide for doing the right work.* Bloomington, IN: Solution Tree Press.

Marzano, R. J. (2017). *The new art and science of teaching.* Bloomington, IN: Solution Tree Press.

McNamara, D. S. (Ed.). (2007). *Reading comprehension strategies: Theories, interventions, and technologies.* Mahwah, NJ: Erlbaum.

National Center for Education Statistics. (n.d.). *National assessment of educational progress.* Accessed at https://nces.ed.gov/nationsreportcard on September 17, 2020.

National Center for Education Statistics. (2019). *The nation's report card: Results from the 2019 mathematics and reading assessments.* Accessed at www.nationsreportcard.gov/mathematics/supportive_files/2019_infographic.pdf on October 1, 2020.

National Governors Association Center for Best Practices & Council of Chief State School Officers. (2010). *Common Core State Standards for English language arts and literacy in history/social studies, science, and technical subjects.* Washington, DC: Authors. Accessed at www.corestandards.org/assets/CCSSI_ELA%20Standards.pdf on October 1, 2020.

O'Reilly, T., Wang, Z., & Sabatini, J. (2019). How much knowledge is too little? When a lack of knowledge becomes a barrier to comprehension. *Psychological Science, 30*(9), 1344–1351.

Scanlon, D. M., Anderson, K. L., & Sweeney, J. M. (2017). *Early intervention for reading difficulties: The interactive strategies approach* (2nd ed.). New York: Guilford Press.

Seymour, P. H. K., Aro, M., & Erskine, J. M. (2003). Foundation literacy acquisition in European orthographies. *British Journal of Psychology, 94*(2), 143–174.

Shanahan, T. (2012). Developing fluency in the context of effective literacy instruction. In T. Rasinski, C. Blachowicz, & K. Lems (Eds.), *Fluency instruction: Research-based best practices* (pp. 17–34). New York: Guilford Press.

Sweller, J. (2010). Cognitive load theory: Recent theoretical advances. In J. L. Plass, R. Moreno, & R. Brünken (Eds.), *Cognitive load theory* (pp. 29–47). New York: Cambridge University Press.

Taylor, D. B., Mraz, M., Nichols, W. D., Rickelman, R. J., & Wood, K. D. (2009). Using explicit instruction to promote vocabulary learning for struggling readers. *Reading and Writing Quarterly, 25*(2–3), 205–220.

United Nations Educational, Scientific and Cultural Organization. (2017, September). *More than one-half of children and adolescents are not learning worldwide.* Accessed at http://uis.unesco.org/sites/default/files/documents/fs46-more-than-half-children-not-learning-en-2017.pdf on January 2, 2021.

Student Data Tacker for Reading Acceleration

			Target 1:	Target 2:	Target 3:	Target 4:	Target 5:	Target 6:	Target 7:	Target 8:
Skill Set Group Number:										
Skill Set Description:										
Name of Accelerationist:										
Student Name	**Homeroom Teacher Name**									

Skill Set Learning Targets and Mastery Check

Student Name: _____

Homeroom Teacher Name: _____

Date When All Learning Targets Mastered: _____

Skill Set:			
Related Standards:			
Learning Target	**What Proficiency Looks Like**	**How We Will Assess**	**Mastery Date**

Source: © 2019 Wonderview Elementary, Hattieville, Arkansas.

Sarah Schuhl, MS, is an educational coach and consultant specializing in mathematics, professional learning communities (PLCs), common formative and summative assessments, school improvement, and response to intervention (RTI). She has worked in schools as a secondary mathematics teacher, high school instructional coach, and K–12 mathematics specialist.

Schuhl was instrumental in the creation of a PLC in the Centennial School District in Oregon, helping teachers make large gains in student achievement. She earned the Centennial School District Triple C Award in 2012.

Schuhl designs meaningful professional development in districts throughout the United States. Her work focuses on strengthening the teaching and learning of mathematics, having teachers learn from one another when working effectively as collaborative teams in a PLC at Work, and striving to ensure the learning of each and every student through assessment practices and intervention. Her practical approach includes working with teachers and administrators to implement assessments for learning, analyze data, collectively respond to student learning, and map standards.

Since 2015, Schuhl has coauthored the books *Engage in the Mathematical Practices: Strategies to Build Numeracy and Literacy With K–5 Learners* and *School Improvement for All: A How-To Guide for Doing the Right Work.* She is a coauthor (with Timothy D. Kanold) of the *Every Student Can Learn Mathematics* series and the *Mathematics at Work*™ *Plan Book*, as well as an author and coeditor of the *Mathematics Unit Planning in a PLC at Work* series.

Schuhl previously served as a member and chair of the National Council of Teachers of Mathematics (NCTM) editorial panel for the journal *Mathematics Teacher* and is currently serving as secretary of the National Council of Supervisors of Mathematics (NCSM). Her work with the Oregon Department of Education includes designing mathematics assessment items, test specifications and blueprints, and rubrics for achievement-level descriptors. She has also contributed as a writer to a middle school mathematics series and an elementary mathematics intervention program.

Schuhl earned a bachelor of science in mathematics from Eastern Oregon University and a master of science in mathematics education from Portland State University.

To learn more about Sarah's work, follow @SSchuhl on Twitter.

To book Sarah Schuhl for professional development, contact pd@SolutionTree.com.

Working Together to Ensure All Students Learn Mathematics

Sarah Schuhl

Planning for meaningful and effective instruction
focuses primarily on the work teachers do
during core instruction and includes necessary
differentiation in lessons. However, teachers on a
collaborative team will have to address the learning
of students throughout the year and design
effective instruction for intervention, remediation,
and enrichment and extension as necessary during
additional time in the school day.

—*Sharon V. Kramer and Sarah Schuhl*

As a high school teacher, I often started each year with students entering algebra 1 unprepared. Students lacked conceptual understanding and procedural fluency with such skills as quick recall of basic facts, whole number operations, fractions, and basic graphing, as well as how to simplify expressions and solve equations. Yet, algebra 1 was the lowest level of mathematics offered at the school for high school and was, in fact, the proper placement for a student in ninth grade.. What was a teacher to do?

Later, as a K–12 mathematics instructional coach, I learned that even as early as kindergarten, some students entered school without any number experience, whether through playing games or through a preK program. Consequently, too many students initially struggled with the foundations of counting to tell how many or with subitizing (recognizing the number of dots in a configuration without counting), required skills for students to learn addition and subtraction. In the later elementary grades, students often grappled with place value and whole number operations as well as fractions. In middle school, students showed confusion with negative rational numbers, variables, and proportions.

How could we, as a school district and in our collaborative teams at each site, guarantee equity by addressing gaps in student learning while still having students learn foundational standards in their grade level or course? In other words, how could we accelerate mathematics learning? There is no one tactic to employ. Rather, through a variety of strategies used in core instruction and with intentional, targeted intervention on a unit-by-unit basis, I have seen students begin to believe in their ability to do mathematics and close gaps. I've even seen students choose an unrequired fourth-year mathematics or science course as a result.

My districtwide work and subsequent work with priority schools has reinforced the need to address gaps in students' mathematics learning as early as possible. Doing so guarantees equity of mathematics learning across a grade level or course and provides students with the knowledge and skills needed for graduation and beyond. Closing the gaps requires a focus on building number sense and utilizing strategies that show students there are multiple ways to reason through problems. Learning mathematics is more than getting the right answer; it means students can show the logical reasoning skills necessary to articulate and validate each solution.

This chapter focuses on how collaborative teams ensure students in priority schools learn grade- or course-level mathematics. It begins with how teams first clarify the essential mathematics their students need to learn, along with a plan to connect and integrate any prerequisite knowledge and skills needed. Later, the chapter explores how teams plan their approach to accelerate student learning through grade- or course-level instruction and establish a framework to provide team-delivered, mathematics-focused interventions for students who struggle with grade- or course-level concepts. The ideas shared promote equity and can be used for teams planning on-site or remote learning experiences in mathematics.

Clarify as a Team the Mathematics Students Must Learn

Many teachers wish students came to their grade level or course having learned the prior mathematics content necessary for the students to be successful. They envision building on that prior knowledge and growing each student's ability to quantify the world, logically reason, and justify conclusions. When they find out students are not prepared, teachers too often separate students into ability groups and set different learning expectations for each group or slow down learning for all students. Unfortunately, both of these responses contribute to gaps in student learning, often putting students further behind from one year to the next (National Council of Supervisors of Mathematics [NCSM], 2020; National Council of Teachers of Mathematics [NCTM], 2018).

In fact, the only way to close gaps in student learning is to *accelerate* student learning (Mattos, 2020). (See chapter 5, page 109, for insights into acceleration related to reading achievement.) Helping every student learn mathematics at grade or course level requires that teachers collaboratively address students' mathematics learning needs in a manner that scaffolds learning up to grade or course level and fills any learning holes, unit by unit. Thus, teacher teams accelerate learning to grade or course level for the essential learning standards.

Together, the teachers on your team answer the four critical questions of a PLC (DuFour, DuFour, Eaker, Many, & Mattos, 2016; see page 3). Answering these questions clarifies the mathematics students need to learn and gathers the data needed to make the most effective instructional decisions. When answering the first critical question to determine what students have to know and be able to do, your team first looks at the mathematics content standards and discusses what exactly a student must demonstrate to show he or she is proficient with the standards. Your team discusses how to teach for conceptual understanding, rather than first focusing on steps or procedures. Together, you and your colleagues determine strategies to employ that ensure students develop number sense, connect and transfer learning, and read and solve real-life problems.

At each grade level, there are state or provincial standards for mathematics describing the content standards and process standards students must learn. *Content standards* share the knowledge and skills students must learn related to grade- or course-level mathematics. The *process standards* share how students reason as mathematicians. Common examples of process standards are given in The Standards for Mathematical Practice (National Governors Association [NGA] & Council of Chief State School Officers [CCSSO], 2010) and NCTM's (2000) *Principles and Standards for School Mathematics*. Educator and mathematics specialist Marilyn Burns (2015) also shares the following characteristics she believes students must develop:

- Interest to figure out solutions to problems
- Willingness to persevere when solutions are not immediate
- Ability to check solutions by solving problems in a different way
- Understanding that incorrect answers are valuable for learning and, therefore, be willing to risk making errors at times
- Ability to accept frustrations that come from not knowing
- Understanding that there's a difference between not knowing an answer and not having figured it out *yet*

Students must intentionally and explicitly learn each of these characteristics while they are also learning grade- or course-level content. In other words, in addition to teaching content, teams must address *how* students engage in learning mathematics so they develop the habits of mind (Costa, n.d.) they need to be successful.

Addressing mathematics learning of process standards with content standards goes hand in hand with the need for students to have a growth mindset about their learning (Dweck, 2016). Consider: How well do students believe their intentional effort will produce mathematical learning? Students develop self-efficacy when they believe they are capable of learning mathematics. Jo Boaler (2016) writes about students' need for a growth mindset as they learn mathematics: "When students fail and struggle, it does not mean anything about their mathematical potential; it means that their brains are growing, synapses are firing, and new pathways are being developed that will make them stronger in the future" (p. 178). Creating a growth mindset means teachers notice for students what is productive in their work based on their reasoning and effort. NCTM (2018) adds, "Mathematics teaching involves not only helping students learn concepts and develop skills and understanding but also empowering students to see themselves as capable of participating in and being doers of mathematics" (p. 28).

There are many ways your team might think about and clarify its approach to growing student mindsets. Share with students the answers to tasks so they learn to persevere and see whether their solution pathway is working. Ask students to share solutions with each other so they see how to use multiple strategies to solve tasks. Celebrate mistakes and model making mistakes as a way to learn. Question and wonder how students can use mathematics to make sense of the world. Recognize when student effort leads to strong mathematical reasoning so students see they *can* think and reason mathematically.

When students are significantly below grade or course level, they may not learn all grade- or course-level standards because teachers will need to spend time on connected prerequisite concepts and skills necessary to reach those standards. Your collaborative team, with guidance, determines the essential standards students must learn to be successful in the next grade level or course. For guidance with essential mathematics standards, your team can consult several sources as to which standards are most critical for students to learn and which ones the team might minimize or let go of from one year to the next as it works to close gaps. You may reference district, state, or provincial documents; websites such as Achieve the Core (https://achievethecore.org); or the essential concepts identified in NCTM's (2018, 2020a, 2020b) *Catalyzing Change* series for elementary, middle, and high school. And, while teaching essential mathematics standards, your team works with students to help them believe they can learn mathematics through feedback in a culture that embraces errors as a critical component to learning.

Determine Student Learning of Grade- or Course-Level Mathematics

As your team considers the essential mathematics content standards and practices students learn in your grade level or course, team members begin to determine how to utilize core instruction (Tier 1) and any additional time and support they might have for intervention and extension (Tier 2; Buffum, Mattos, & Malone, 2018). Tier 1 includes the block of time or class period devoted to students learning grade- or course-level standards (and, at times, connected prerequisite standards). Every student is included in Tier 1 instruction and heterogeneously grouped, not tracked into lower- or higher-level mathematics courses (NCSM, 2020a, 2020b). Tier 2 includes additional time during the school day for students to have targeted and specific intervention (or extension) for grade- or course-level standards or the prerequisite standards needed to access grade- or course-level standards. (See chapter 8, page 171, for more information about tiered instruction.) Table 6.1 shares a few ideas of team actions to avoid and consider as you plan student mathematics learning in Tiers 1 and 2.

At the beginning of the year and at strategic intervals, your team will most likely use data from a progress-monitoring tool (for example, a district- or school-purchased bank of assessments) to determine which students need support and what strengths and challenges

Table 6.1: Team Actions to Avoid and Consider for Tier 1 and Tier 2

Actions to Avoid	Actions to Consider
Tier 1 • Teach page by page in the book through each unit, and get as far as you can. • Reteach everything students should have learned before starting grade- or course-level content. • Move students to a lower grade or course, or retain students. • Create ability groups, and teach each group separately with different learning expectations. • Talk louder and slower. • Only give steps and have students practice. • Use low-level tasks and skill-based problems only. • Slow instruction down for all students. • Teach everything from each lesson in the book. • Have students learn through memorization rather than understanding.	**Tier 1** • Clarify the guaranteed and viable curriculum all students will learn (DuFour et al., 2016). • Teach prerequisite skills students need to learn within appropriate units, always concluding with grade- or course-level standards (Schuhl, Kanold, Deinhart, Larson, & Toncheff, 2020). • Create and give common assessments for formative learning (DuFour et al., 2016). • Have students learn in mixed-ability groups of four with intentional tasks during each lesson (Kanold, Kanold-McIntyre, Larson, Barnes, Schuhl, & Toncheff, 2018). • Engage students in discourse so they learn from one another (Hattie, Fisher, & Frey, 2017). • Focus on students learning through conceptual understanding (NCTM, 2018, 2020a, 2020b). • Use a balance of high- and low-level cognitive-demand tasks that includes word problem (Smith & Stein, 2011). • Start each lesson with a connection to prior-knowledge and consider relevance (Kanold, Kanold-McIntyre, Larson, Barnes, Schuhl, & Toncheff, 2018). • Emphasize NCTM's (2014) productive beliefs.
Tier 2 • Send students out to other adults on campus to be "fixed." • Solely use a computer program that determines which standards a student has learned and creates a learning plan independent of the learning happening in class. • Group students for intervention based on an overall test percentage (for example, 65 percent), when the score does not detail by target what a student has learned, or has not learned *yet*. • Teach standards the same way they were taught during Tier 1 core instruction. • Focus solely on basic facts and algorithms. • Only use interim assessment data or progress-monitoring data to determine placement, and leave students in the same intervention for extended periods of time.	**Tier 2** • Use data from common assessments to target interventions using student misconceptions (Buffum et al., 2018). • Address prior knowledge needed for the current or next unit (Schuhl et al., 2020). • Use word problems to develop context for learning mathematics standards (NCTM, 2014). • Use the concrete-representational-abstract (CRA) model for learning: What *concrete* models or manipulatives can students use to make sense of mathematics (C)? What *representations* (drawings) can students use to see mathematics (R)? How can students use numbers and symbols to *abstractly* document the mathematics (A)? (Flores, Hinton & Burton, 2016). • Focus on number sense and an understanding of mathematics over memorized facts (NCTM, 2014). • Review the eight recommendations from the Institute of Education Sciences (Gersten, et al., 2009).

they have toward learning mathematics. However, your team's use of routine common mid-unit and end-of-unit assessments, written to specific learning targets, informs team members' daily differentiated instruction and their flexible and targeted interventions. Such assessments help your team answer all four critical questions of a PLC.

The evidence of student learning your team collects from its common assessments informs how team members will scaffold student learning up to grade- or course-level standards while addressing the targeted prior-knowledge content. Rather than purchasing a program or computer application solely to implement interventions, collaborative teams can best address students' learning needs on a unit-by-unit basis. During each unit, your team addresses keys to learning in core instruction (Tier 1) and provides needed timely interventions (Tier 2) with your students.

Plan Core Mathematics Instruction

For the purposes of equity and learning, all students should have access to core instruction and not be pulled out or sorted into ability groups during that time of the learning day (Boaler, 2016; Kanold & Larson, 2012; NCSM, 2015; NCTM, 2014, 2018; U.S. Department of Education, 2008). Throughout each unit, your team discusses how to engage all students in learning, determines the prior knowledge students need, and uses common assessment data to design re-engagement opportunities, at times using a portion of instructional time in intentional small group mini-lessons and extensions, as needed. Your team also uses the data to define targeted intervention groups (and extension groups) for Tier 2. Together, your team works to accelerate learning during core instruction to close gaps so team members can minimize the number of students needing Tier 2 or Tier 3 supports.

This unit-by-unit work includes multiple components, including planning a unit, planning how the team will help students achieve conceptual understanding, and planning the daily lessons.

Planning a Unit

When planning core instruction for each unit, your team does the following.

1. Determine the start and end dates for the unit.

2. Identify the essential standards students will learn.

3. Create student-friendly learning targets, written as *I can* statements, for each standard. Share these with students so they know what they are learning throughout the unit, place them on common assessments during and at the end of the unit, and use them when analyzing data derived from common assessments and interventions.

4. Determine dates for common mid-unit assessments to essential standards and the common end-of-unit assessment.

5. Create all common assessments needed for the unit, determine how student work will be equitably scored across the team, and determine proficiency levels.

6. Determine the prerequisite standards and skills to address during the unit.

7. Discuss instructional strategies and tools to use during the unit.

8. Teach and differentiate instruction, as needed.

9. Analyze data after each mid-unit and end-of-unit common assessment to (a) determine which students learned each learning target and which have not learned the targets *yet*, (b) determine effective instructional practices, and (c) plan for interventions, extensions, and student self-reflection and goal setting. See the *Every Student Can Learn Mathematics* series by Timothy D. Kanold and colleagues (2018) and the *Mathematics Unit Planning in a PLC at Work* series by Sarah Schuhl and colleagues (2020, 2021).

As your team plans each unit, it may want to consider planning for intervention using one or more flex days; that is, days team members can use to re-engage students in learning essential standards, if the data from a common mid-unit or end-of-unit assessment shows more learning is needed. Your team may also choose to allocate a set number of days (perhaps one to three days) to teach prior grade- or course-level standards students need to learn to access new learning in the unit. This means during each unit, your team probably won't be able to teach everything in the corresponding chapter from your textbook but instead will choose a balance of low- and high-level cognitive-demand tasks from the lessons that address grade- or course-level learning of the essential standards in each unit.

Planning for Conceptual Understanding

As your team considers teaching each unit, also consider how students will learn through a lens of conceptual understanding and application that will eventually lead to procedural fluency. For example, most U.S. state standards do not expect students to fluently use the standard addition and subtraction algorithm until fourth grade, the standard multiplication algorithm until fifth grade, and the standard division algorithm until sixth grade. The years leading to those grades are for building an understanding of place value and the meaning of the operations, ending with the shortcut of an algorithm. An algorithm alone, especially for a struggling student, can be very confusing. Students do not understand or remember the set of steps needed and confuse one set of steps for addition with another for multiplication if the concept of each operation has not been learned in a way that applies to different numbers and variables. Instead, consider having students start with base-ten blocks, ten frames, and linking cubes to see and understand each operation and eventually draw models to make sense of the operations with whole numbers. Teams should apply similar thinking to mathematics concepts and skills students learn later in middle school and in high school.

In their seminal book *Adding It Up: Helping Children Learn Mathematics*, Jeremy Kilpatrick, Jane Swafford, and Bradford Findell (2001) of the National Research Council describe *conceptual understanding* this way:

> Conceptual understanding refers to an integrated and functional grasp of mathematical ideas. Students with conceptual understanding know more than isolated facts and methods. They understand why a mathematical idea is important and the kinds of contexts in which it is useful. They have organized

their knowledge into a coherent whole, which enables them to learn new ideas by connecting those ideas to what they already know. Conceptual understanding also supports retention. Because facts and methods learned with understanding are connected, they are easier to remember and use, and they can be reconstructed when forgotten. (pp. 118–119)

Too often, teachers start with steps for fluency (algorithms) before developing conceptual understanding through the context of word problems and real-life modeling situations, if those are included at all. Unfortunately, that means students are not able to reason through a context to plan a solution pathway that helps develop an understanding of the numbers and symbols in equations they are solving. Students instead focus solely on an answer and skip thinking about the meaning behind the numbers and symbols in equations and expressions. Without making sense of the mathematics and developing an understanding of the reasoning required, along *with* practicing fluency, retention and future application of mathematics suffers. With algebra 1 as the entry course for high school freshmen and algebra 2 or its equivalent needed for high school graduation, the National Mathematics Advisory Panel recommends, "To prepare students for algebra, the curriculum must simultaneously develop conceptual understanding, computational fluency, and problem-solving skills" (U.S. Department of Education, 2008, p. xix).

Determine as a team the mathematical tools and strategies to use that will develop students' conceptual understanding leading to procedural fluency. How might your team use ten-frames, base-ten blocks, fraction tiles, algebra tiles, or technology (including calculators) to explore and justify concepts? What are the different strategies to use for teaching operations, fractions, equations with variables, proportions, functions, geometry, and statistics? Discuss as a team the tools and strategies students have used in previous grades or courses that you can utilize in your current unit.

Connections between mathematical standards and strategies are also critical. Your team identifies how each essential standard is connected to prior knowledge students should have learned earlier in the current school year or in a previous year, as well as determines how the standard connects to future learning. For example, in third grade, an understanding of division and equal parts of a whole leads to an understanding of fractions; in middle school, an understanding of fractions leads to an understanding of ratios and proportions; and in high school, proportional reasoning leads to an understanding of slope and linear functions. Understanding connections strengthens how students learn concepts and minimizes teaching gimmicks and tricks to get answers, which impedes later learning.

Figure 6.1 shows an example of connections using the distributive property and area models, starting with an understanding of a rectangle in kindergarten and moving to an understanding of the area of a rectangle in third grade. In fourth grade, students find the product of multidigit numbers using area models based on place value; in fifth grade, students find the product of improper fractions using area models based on place value; and finally, in algebra 1, students find the product of binomials using the same model. Each of these connections shows an application of the distributive property, and students connect their learning from one year to the next to develop a conceptual understanding of this property.

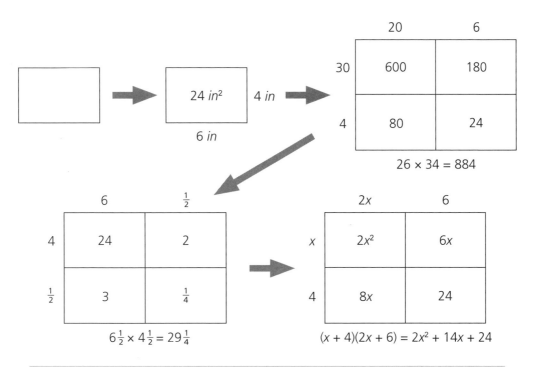

Figure 6.1: Vertical mathematics connections using area and the distributive property.

As your team determines connections between concepts and strategies for each essential standard in a unit, consider questions such as the following.

- What have students learned earlier in the school year or in prior years that connects to this unit?

- What is the concept of each standard in the unit? How do the standards relate to one another? How might students show they have learned the standards (without a focus on algorithms)?

- What tools and strategies can students use to make sense of the unit mathematics?

- What word problems and high-level tasks should the team include in the unit to give meaning to the learning in the unit?

- What algorithm (set of steps) is most common to this skill? Is this something students need to know how to do by the end of the unit or sometime later in the future? In either case, how will the team build to that understanding instead of starting with the algorithm?

Fluency in mathematics does not simply mean students can complete a timed test without errors. NCTM (2014) generally defines *fluency* as having accurate, efficient, and flexible strategies for solving problems. Consider how to use number talks (Parrish, 2010), number lines, and various representations (drawings, tables, equations, and graphs) to have students develop fluent methods of solving problems. Discuss as a team how students will learn from one another through sharing strategies and discussing solution pathways. Sharing student work and thinking during instruction grows each student's toolkit of strategies to try in future learning experiences and develops perseverance and an understanding that there is more than one way to tackle a task.

Literacy and language can also be stumbling blocks for mathematics students. Consider as a team how to have students predict reasonable answers (much like inferences), read word problems (unlike literary text, in mathematics, the main idea in the informational text of word problems is often the last sentence; key details come first), utilize K-W-L charts (graphic organizers), and communicate using mathematics vocabulary (which includes the reading of symbols, notations, and numbers), among other literacy connections. For more examples of strategies for improving mathematics students' literacy and language abilities, see *Engage in the Mathematical Practices: Strategies to Build Numeracy and Literacy With K–5 Learners* (Norris & Schuhl, 2016).

As mentioned in table 6.1 (page 135) for Tier 2 interventions, also consider how to incorporate the concrete-representational-abstract (CRA) model during initial core instruction (The Access Center, 2004; Flores et al., 2016). For example, when teaching addition, a *concrete* model might include linking cubes or a ten-frame; when teaching fraction operations, use fraction tiles; and when teaching graphing, you might use human graphs or graph paper and pipe cleaners to physically make each graph. The *representations* then become corresponding pictures, which might include dots, number lines, bar models, or graphs. The *abstract* parts of the CRA model are the equations with numbers and symbols that correspond to the concrete objects and pictures. In middle school, consider how to use manipulatives to make sense of ratios and percentages such as base-ten hundredths and tenths blocks or colored disks; in high school, consider using algebra tiles to simplify expressions and solve equations and tactile grids with pipe cleaners for functions in order to support student understanding of key features in graphs and the information they reveal.

In *Principles to Actions*, NCTM (2014) states, "An excellent mathematics program integrates the use of mathematical tools and technology as essential resources to help students learn and make sense of mathematical ideas, reason mathematically, and communicate their mathematical thinking" (p. 78). Using the CRA model helps teams achieve this outcome.

Planning Lessons

Incorporating a focus on conceptual understanding, connections to prior and future learning, use of language and vocabulary, sharing of solution pathways, and learning through the CRA model into daily core instruction lessons can be a lot to manage. To make it more doable, Timothy D. Kanold, Jessica Kanold-McIntyre, Matthew R. Larson, Bill Barnes, Sarah Schuhl, and Mona Toncheff (2018) ask teachers to plan for six elements in order to design high-quality lessons:

1. Essential learning standards—the *why* of the lesson
2. Prior-knowledge warm-up activities
3. Academic language vocabulary as part of instruction

4. Lower- and higher-level-cognitive-demand mathematical task balance

5. Whole-group discourse and small-group discourse balance

6. Lesson closure for evidence of learning (p. 10)

Mathematics Instruction and Tasks in a PLC at Work (Kanold, Kanold-McIntyre, et al., 2018) provides many examples and protocols for each of these six lesson elements.

When planning each lesson, first be clear about the *why* of the lesson: What will students learn that day about an essential mathematics standard? Next, start the lesson with a task that requires students to use prior learning they will need later in the lesson. Identify the vocabulary and notations students will use and learn in the lesson and determine the most effective tasks (always at least one at grade level every day) to use during instruction. Finally, consider how you can account for whole-group and small-group discourse (for example, during whole group, every student answers using pair-share; during small group, define individual roles) as well as how students will reflect at the end of the lesson on whether they learned the target for the day.

How teams design core instruction and plan units is critical, especially when many students are in need of intervention. This means core instruction will most likely include some intervention (some prerequisite skills needed to tackle the essential standards on a unit-by-unit basis) because doing it all during Tier 2 (or Tier 3) is not feasible in priority schools. Every day, students should experience grade- or course-level mathematics. At times, during a lesson, teachers must accelerate student learning to grade level for an essential standard utilizing small-group instruction to address prior knowledge needed for the essential standard. At other times, they may use a whole-group experience to address prior knowledge. It takes a team to determine how to support every student in learning at grade level for the essential standards.

Provide Mathematics Interventions

In a priority school, when the majority of students may be below grade level in their mathematics understanding, teachers incorporate real-time interventions during core instruction throughout Tier 1. They observe and listen to student thinking, give feedback, and make adjustments during the lesson or form targeted small groups for mini-lessons during part of the instructional time. Yet, additional time and support is also needed through dedicated Tier 2 interventions to accelerate the learning of prior standards leading to the essential grade- or course-level standards students must learn. Or, this additional Tier 2 time may be necessary for students to learn a current essential standard when it is time to move on to the next unit and new essential standards.

Collaborative teams design any Tier 2 intervention (and possibly extension) to ensure equity in student learning. In addition to daily formative assessment experiences, teams use the data from common mid-unit and end-of-unit assessments, organized by standard or target. See chapter 7 (An Intentional Data-Analysis Protocol, page 153) and figure 6.7 of *School Improvement for All* (Kramer & Schuhl, 2017; visit www.SolutionTree.com

/free-resources/PLCbooks/sia). This process (1) gives your team information about how many students have learned targets or not learned them *yet*, (2) allows your team to discuss the effectiveness of instructional practices used so far, and (3) helps your team identify and use the misconceptions that appear in student work to drive interventions (and extensions) at Tier 2. Teams can then share students and each teach a group needing learning of a specific target or skill. Just as discussed with core instruction, a focus on conceptual understanding and application leading to procedural fluency is critical in Tier 2 interventions.

As stated, in a response to intervention (RTI) model, collaborative teams design Tier 1 and Tier 2 instruction related to mathematics teaching and learning (Buffum et al., 2018). In *Visible Learning for Mathematics*, John Hattie and colleagues (2017) state, "RTI focuses on providing high-quality instruction and interventions matched to student need, monitoring progress frequently to make decisions about changes in instruction or goals, and applying child response data to important educational decisions" (p. 214). Hattie and colleagues (2017) list RTI as the third most powerful action teachers can take to improve student learning of mathematics. In an RTI model, Tier 3 is for students far below grade level and often in several content areas. Priority schools often have too many students in need of Tier 3 interventions, and teams may need to address some of these mathematics learning gaps during their Tier 2 time of the day or via mini-lessons in Tier 1.

In *It's TIME: Themes and Imperatives for Mathematics Education*, NCSM (2014) similarly shares, "More than a decade of research and experience suggests that leaders can increase achievement by ensuring that, in addition to high-quality classroom experiences, students also have access to intensified learning opportunities (Kilpatrick et al., 2001)" (p. 37). These experiences should include a focus on conceptual understanding and not just rote memorization of facts or steps. If teams share students across grade levels to work on basic facts, for example, consider how Tier 2 lessons may grow an understanding of operations, first using the CRA model or number talks, so students understand there are several mental strategies to use for each fact.

Since intentional Tier 1 and Tier 2 learning experiences accelerate student learning of mathematics to an understanding of grade- or course-level essential standards, what are considerations for a strong Tier 2 mathematics intervention? From the Institute of Education Sciences, Russell Gersten and colleagues (2009) have eight recommendations for K–8 mathematics interventions:

1. Screen all students to identify those at risk for potential mathematics difficulties and provide interventions to students identified as at risk.

2. Instructional materials for students receiving interventions should focus intensely on in-depth treatment of whole numbers in kindergarten through grade 5 and on rational numbers in grades 4 through 8. These materials should be selected by committee.

3. Instruction during the intervention should be explicit and systematic. This includes providing models of proficient problem solving, verbalization of

thought processes, guided practice, corrective feedback, and frequent cumulative review.

4. Interventions should include instruction on solving word problems that is based on common underlying structures.

5. Intervention materials should include opportunities for students to work with visual representations of mathematical ideas and interventionists should be proficient in the use of visual representations of mathematical ideas.

6. Interventionists at all grade levels should devote about 10 minutes in each session to building fluent retrieval of basic arithmetic facts.

7. Monitor the progress of students receiving supplemental instruction and other students who are at risk.

8. Include motivational strategies in Tier 2 and Tier 3 interventions. (p. 6)

Just as is true of Tier 1 instruction, Tier 2 interventions happen during the school day and are focused on a conceptual understanding of mathematics, leading to application and procedural fluency. Students use concrete models and make predictions and then draw pictures and write equations. If a team is using a computer program, the teachers select and use the modules that cover the prior-knowledge standards students need in order to learn the grade- or course-level essential standards. They blend any online learning with mini-lessons and time spent with a teacher for immediate feedback and learning. These practices are true for grades K–8 as well as high school–mathematics interventions.

Conclusion

Closing gaps in mathematics sometimes takes a back seat to closing gaps in literacy. However, both literacy and numeracy are important to students' success in school, and both help students make sense of their world. The ability to read, write, reason, and provide logical justifications allows students more choices in elective classes in middle school and high school and opens up college and career opportunities beyond high school. Addressing gaps in mathematics learning does not come at the expense of literacy but rather works in partnership with growing student learning related to reading, writing, speaking, listening, and language.

In priority schools, students are often not at grade level in their mathematics understanding and application. When the majority of students are below grade level, your team first addresses the issue through thoughtful essential standards and core instruction. Team members will allocate days in each unit to teaching prior-knowledge standards students need to learn to be successful (not use the first few months of school to focus solely on prior grade- or course-level learning). They will do so to ensure every student learns each essential standard for the grade level or course.

Additional time and support will also be necessary, so your team will consider how to provide that time and how to best use that time through your use of common formative assessments. It is easy to slow everything down and not teach every essential standard or leave out critical units. Instead, strategically use small-group and whole-group experiences in Tier 1 while always exposing students to grade-level experiences. Also, use Tier 2 additional time to grow student learning to grade level for each essential standard.

Clarify as a team the essential standards students must learn in the unit and the prior knowledge that needs to be addressed in Tier 1 and Tier 2. Consider how teams will use tools to grow conceptual understanding. When students are still struggling with mathematics facts related to addition, subtraction, multiplication, and division, work as a team to determine how to teach the grade- or course-level concept while still working toward computational fluency. There are times where students can use manipulatives or a calculator to grow an understanding of a concept during core instruction. Such approaches help ensure students do not fall farther behind but rather begin accelerating to grade- or course-level understanding while also learning the strategies for basic facts during targeted interventions.

Answering the four critical questions of a PLC with your team members will help you ensure every student learns mathematics and provide equitable learning experiences across your team. Through careful unit planning and a focus on essential standards and intentional interventions, team members will accelerate student learning to grade or course level, and your students will develop numeracy and make sense of their world. Your students will make connections from one concept to the next and grow in their belief they can do mathematics—opening up a world of possibilities for their future.

References and Resources

The Access Center. (2004). *Concrete-representational-abstract instructional approach.* Accessed at http://165.139.150.129/intervention/ConcreteRepresentationalAbstractInstructionalApproach .pdf on December 30, 2020.

Boaler, J. (2016). *Mathematical mindsets: Unleashing students' potential through creative math, inspiring messages and innovative teaching.* San Francisco: Jossey-Bass.

Buffum, A., Mattos, M., & Malone, J. (2018). *Taking action: A handbook for RTI at Work.* Bloomington, IN: Solution Tree Press.

Burns, M. (2015, June 4). *Starting point 4: Helping students become effective math learners* [Blog post]. Accessed at https://mathsolutions.com/blog/helping-students-become -effective-math-learners on September 25, 2020.

Costa, A. L. (n.d.). *What are habits of mind?* Accessed at www.habitsofmindinstitute.org/what -are-habits-of-mind on December 7, 2020.

DuFour, R. (2015). *In praise of American educators: And how they can become even better.* Bloomington, IN: Solution Tree Press.

DuFour, R., DuFour, R., Eaker, R., Many, T. W., & Mattos, M. (2016). *Learning by doing: A handbook for Professional Learning Communities at Work* (3rd ed.). Bloomington, IN: Solution Tree Press.

Dweck, C. (2016). *Mindset: The new psychology of success* (Updated ed.). New York: Random House.

Flores, M. M., Hinton, V. M., & Burton, M. E. (2016). Teaching problem solving to students receiving tiered interventions using the concrete-representational-abstract sequence and schema-based instruction. *Preventing School Failure, 60*(4), 345–355.

Gersten, R., Beckmann, S., Clarke, B., Foegen, A., Marsh, L., Star, J. R., & Witzel, B. (2009, April). *Assisting students struggling with mathematics: Response to intervention (RtI) for elementary and middle schools* (NCEE 2009-4060). Washington, DC: National Center for Education Evaluation and Regional Assistance, Institute of Education Sciences, U.S. Department of Education. Accessed athttps://ies.ed.gov/ncee/wwc/Docs/PracticeGuide /rti_math_pg_042109.pdf on March 27, 2021.

Hattie, J., Fisher, D., & Frey, N. (2017). *Visible learning for mathematics: What works best to optimize student learning, grades K–12.* Thousand Oaks, CA: Corwin Press.

Kanold, T. D., Barnes, B., Larson, M. R., Kanold-McIntyre, J., Schuhl, S., & Toncheff, M. (2018). *Mathematics homework and grading in a PLC at Work.* Bloomington, IN: Solution Tree Press.

Kanold, T. D., Kanold-McIntyre, J., Larson, M. R., Barnes, B., Schuhl, S., & Toncheff, M. (2018). *Mathematics instruction and tasks in a PLC at Work.* Bloomington, IN: Solution Tree Press.

Kanold, T. D., & Larson, M. R. (2012). *Common Core mathematics in a PLC at Work: Leader's guide.* Bloomington, IN: Solution Tree Press.

Kanold, T. D., Schuhl, S., Larson, M. R., Barnes, B., Kanold-McIntyre, J., & Toncheff, M. (2018). *Mathematics assessment and intervention in a PLC at Work.* Bloomington, IN: Solution Tree Press.

Kanold, T. D., Toncheff, M., Larson, M. R., Barnes, B., Kanold-McIntyre, J., & Schuhl, S. (2018). *Mathematics coaching and collaboration in a PLC at Work.* Bloomington, IN: Solution Tree Press.

Kilpatrick, J., Swafford, J., & Findell, B. (Eds.). (2001). *Adding it up: Helping children learn mathematics.* Washington, DC: National Academies Press.

Kramer, S. V., & Schuhl, S. (2017). *School improvement for all: A how-to guide for doing the right work.* Bloomington, IN: Solution Tree Press.

Marzano, R. J. (2017). *The new art and science of teaching.* Bloomington, IN: Solution Tree Press.

Mattos, M. (2020). *Mind the gaps, session 1: Designing a master schedule to target learning gaps next fall* [Webinar]. Accessed at www.solutiontree.com/mind-the-gaps-session-1.html on May 13, 2020.

Mattos, M., DuFour, R., DuFour, R., Eaker, R., & Many, T. W. (2016). *Concise answers to frequently asked questions about Professional Learning Communities at Work.* Bloomington, IN: Solution Tree Press.

Mid-Continent Research for Education and Learning. (2010). *What we know about mathematics teaching and learning* (3rd ed.). Bloomington, IN: Solution Tree Press.

National Council of Supervisors of Mathematics. (2014). *It's TIME: Themes and imperatives for mathematics education.* Bloomington, IN: Solution Tree Press.

National Council of Supervisors of Mathematics. (2015, Spring). *Improving student achievement by infusing highly effective instructional strategies into multi-tiered support systems (MTSS)— Response to intervention (RtI) Tier 2 instruction.* Accessed at http://rapps.pbworks.com/f /NCSM_TierII.pdf on October 5, 2020.

National Council of Supervisors of Mathematics. (2020a, Spring). *Closing the opportunity gap: A call for detracking mathematics.* Accessed at www.mathedleadership.org/docs/resources /positionpapers/NCSMPositionPaper19.pdf on December 31, 2020.

National Council of Supervisors of Mathematics. (2020b). *NCSM essential actions: Framework for leadership in mathematics education.* Reston, VA: Author.

National Council of Teachers of Mathematics. (2000). *Principles and standards for school mathematics: An overview.* Reston, VA: Author.

National Council of Teachers of Mathematics. (2014). *Principles to actions: Ensuring mathematical success for all.* Reston, VA: Author.

National Council of Teachers of Mathematics. (2018). *Catalyzing change in high school mathematics: Initiating critical conversations.* Reston, VA: Author.

National Council of Teachers of Mathematics. (2020a). *Catalyzing change in early childhood and elementary mathematics: Initiating critical conversations.* Reston, VA: Author.

National Council of Teachers of Mathematics. (2020b). *Catalyzing change in middle school mathematics: Initiating critical conversations.* Reston, VA: Author.

National Governors Association Center for Best Practices & Council of Chief State School Officers. (2010). *Common Core State Standards for mathematics.* Washington, DC: Authors. Accessed at www.corestandards.org/assets/CCSSI_Math%20Standards.pdf on August 6, 2020.

Norris, K., & Schuhl, S. (2016). *Engage in the Mathematical Practices: Strategies to build numeracy and literacy with K–5 learners.* Bloomington, IN: Solution Tree Press.

Parrish, S. (2010). *Number talks: Helping children build mental math and computation strategies.* Sausalito, CA: Math Solutions.

Schuhl, S., Kanold, T. D., Barnes, B., Jain, D. M., Larson, M. R., & Monzingo, B. (2021). *Mathematics unit planning in a PLC at Work, High School.* Bloomington, IN: Solution Tree Press.

Schuhl, S., Kanold, T. D., Deinhart, J., Lang-Raad, N. D., Larson, M. R., & Smith, N. N. (2021). *Mathematics unit planning in a PLC at Work, Grades PreK–2.* Bloomington, IN: Solution Tree Press.

Schuhl, S., Kanold, T. D., Deinhart, J., Larson, M. R., & Toncheff, M. (2020). *Mathematics unit planning in a PLC at Work, Grades 3–5.* Bloomington, IN: Solution Tree Press.

Schuhl, S., Kanold, T. D., Kaynold-McIntyre, J., Chuang, S., Larson, M. R., & Smith, M. (2021). *Mathematics unit planning in a PLC at Work, Grades 6–8.* Bloomington, IN: Solution Tree Press.

Smith, M. S., & Stein, M. K. (2011). *Five practices for orchestrating productive mathematics discussions.* Reson, VA: National Council of Teachers of Mathematics.

U.S. Department of Education. (2008, March). *Foundations for success: The final report of the National Mathematics Advisory Panel*. Washington, DC: Author. Accessed at www2.ed.gov /about/bdscomm/list/mathpanel/report/final-report.pdf on October 5, 2020.

Van de Walle, J. A., Karp, K. S., & Bay-Williams, J. M. (2019). *Elementary and middle school mathematics: Teaching developmentally* (10th ed.). New York: Pearson.

 **Dana Renner** is assistant superintendent of Stillwater Public Schools in Stillwater, Oklahoma. She has more than twenty-five years of experience in education as a teacher, instructional facilitator, assistant principal, head principal, and director of human resources. Dana has extensive experience in large urban and suburban districts and has worked at all levels of education.

As principal, Dana led Central Middle School, in Edmond Public Schools, Edmond, Oklahoma to model PLC status. As principal of the Freshman Academy at U.S. Grant High School, she was part of an administrative team that led the school to become the first model PLC in the state of Oklahoma. Dana has extensive experience in continuous school improvement and school turnaround, the PLC at Work process, common formative assessments, data-analysis protocols, diverse student populations and student achievement.

Dana was recognized as the Oklahoma State Middle School Principal of the Year for 2015–2016 and was a representative at the National Association of Secondary School Principals Leadership Institute in Washington, DC. She was selected by the Oklahoma state superintendent of public instruction to serve on the Principal's Advisory Committee and Teacher Leader Effectiveness Advisory Committee.

Dana has a bachelor's degree in secondary education from Oklahoma State University and a master's degree in school administration from the University of Central Oklahoma. Dana is pursuing her doctorate in curriculum and leadership at Oklahoma State University.

To book Dana Renner for professional development, contact pd@SolutionTree.com.

Understanding the Story Data Tell

Dana Renner

These teachers do not see the data related to
student learning as an evaluation or judgment;
rather, they see it as an opportunity to learn from
one another, to become better educators, and to
better meet the needs of each student.

—*Sharon V. Kramer and Sarah Schuhl*

Throughout my years in education, I've seen and even utilized a variety of strategies designed to help collaborative teams analyze student learning and see the outcomes of every hit or every miss in each student's academic career. It's easy to see the allure of data. Analyzing test scores and achievement data represents accountability at its finest, right? When students fail, we know how to hold them accountable: *You failed this. You missed that. You need to come to school more. You need to read more. You need to write more. You need to study before a test. You need to pay attention. You need to focus.* And it doesn't stop. *You need to behave, come to class prepared, prioritize school, care about your future, sleep more at night, eat better, come to class on time, memorize this, know that, take notes, read the chapter*, and on and on.

Sadly, throughout my experiences with these data-analysis strategies, I often saw a negative outcome—labeling students into groups. This was especially common where failure was involved. You've surely seen or even unconsciously applied many of the labels: *underachieving, at risk, underprivileged, low performing, below grade level, below basic, unsatisfactory*, and so on.

In 2011, I joined U.S. Grant High School in Oklahoma City, Oklahoma, as an assistant principal. I was responsible for the Freshman Academy, which was like a school within a school, and managed the course offerings, staff professional development and evaluations, scheduling, and so on. I also managed student transitions from middle school into high school and from ninth grade into tenth grade. As the lead assistant principal, I filled in during the head principal's absence at any point in time.

By every definition, the school was a failing school and had been for several years. Every student had a label with negative connotations, and no one had projections for success. Given most students never had any success, making such projections didn't feel worthwhile. As a result, I could see where these well-intended strategies of connecting student faces to data had continuously failed.

Many define *accountability* as acceptance of responsibility. For those of us who work in the world of education, it's a word that takes on a negative connotation. How do teachers prioritize and hold themselves accountable when the data tell them that *everything* is a need? I see it a little differently. In 2011, Sharon Kramer, a leader in the field of education and a PLC-focused school-improvement coach, stood before me and said, "Do you believe that all means all? Do you believe in 100 percent of students performing at or above grade level 100 percent of the time?" When I answered *yes* to both of those questions, I knew she would hold me accountable for that response. I knew that not only was I accepting responsibility for the academic achievement and individual growth of *every* student at U.S. Grant High School, but I was committing the school's many collaborative teams to that goal too.

If you read chapter 3 (page 51), you know that, at this time and for six years in a row, the state of Oklahoma had labeled U.S. Grant High School as a failing school. The district labeled it as a Turnaround School in 2010, making it possible for the school to receive additional funding for school-improvement efforts. We chose the PLC process and culture as the pathway for school improvement. Along this journey of improved achievement, the school's collaborative teams became Sharon's willing students. She gave us a crash course in essential PLC concepts, like the three big ideas, the four pillars, and the four critical questions (DuFour, DuFour, Eaker, Many, & Mattos, 2016; see page 3). Then, she charged us with the work. And work we did!

When we began, we knew we needed data to inform our efforts. But we needed to collect and analyze those data differently than we had in the past. We needed data that did not merely label students but instead told our school's story and enabled us to act to improve learning for all students. We started with the senior students to see who was on track for graduation and who wasn't. We discovered 204 seniors had not met the state testing requirements for graduation. We made it imperative that these students receive the opportunities and resources they needed to meet those graduation requirements. By looking closely at all students' data, a story began to unfold for each student. The running theme was failure.

This work was the gut check for myself and my leadership team. If I truly believed that all meant *all*—100 percent of students, 100 percent of the time—we needed to find a way to help our collaborative teams change the story's end. This was when data analysis became my impassioned labor of love for every student at U.S. Grant High School. Our school's collaborative teams began examining data multidimensionally, digging deeply into each student's data to reveal where learning got lost. Teams charted their course for every student, which meant making evidence-based decisions to improve learning.

Knowing this information allowed all teams to establish an intentional plan for *every* student. And it worked.

Our approach to data analysis and the way our collaborative teams used data to tell a story that would improve equitable instruction and learning outcomes can work for your school too. In this chapter, you will explore how your collaborative team can embark on or refine its data journey. The following sections establish what analyzing data *really* means, dispense with the illusion of will versus skill, provide a data-analysis framework and protocol, and explain how teams conduct research to reveal their students' data story.

The Real Purpose of Data

You've likely heard the expression *data rich but information poor*. In this age of accountability, collaborative teams are not short on data-derived information about student learning. What most often challenges teams is discovering the meaning within the data and how to interpret, question, and comprehend what the data say. There is a story that data tell educators about each student's learning. The data either uncover problems, reveal strengths, or show that a student is right on target. Instructionally, you can't manage what you can't measure, and when data uncover problems, they reveal the problems' nature and point the way to next steps and solutions (Bloomberg, 2020). Good data do not replace good judgment, but they are essential to informing it (Bloomberg, 2020). If your team is information poor, then team members are likely making decisions about what *they* think learners need, based on opinion or experience. These factors matter, but it's more important that team members collectively use evidence for decision making.

In a feature article for the American Association of School Administrators, Ronald Thomas (2011), associate director of the Center for Leadership in Education at Towson University, shares eight ingredients that ensure productive data analysis for improving student learning.

1. **Have the right teams in place:** Teams should be content specific and grade-level compatible, including vertical teams with those teachers that teach content above and below the grade level teacher. Similarly, teams can be virtual and interdisciplinary; however, interdisciplinary teams can focus on an overarching schoolwide goal or a content-specific goal related to a larger schoolwide goal. If the purpose of collaboration is to help more students achieve at higher levels (DuFour et al., 2016), then this can only be accomplished when the right teams focus on the right work (the four critical questions that drive the work of a PLC).

2. **Build a culture of trust:** Teacher teams establish a culture of trust as they focus on the right work. This can take time.

3. **Use a protocol to increase collaboration:** It is helpful for teams to identify norms and other protocols to guide them through their work together. Refer to the "Critical Issues for Team Consideration" reproducible (page 168) at the end of this chapter.

4. **Articulate a compelling reason to analyze data collaboratively:** Focus on the learning, and take ownership of what the data are telling your team about student learning.

5. **Have clarity about your team's autonomy:** Teams should know the loose (negotiable) and tight (non-negotiable) aspects of their PLC and school culture (DuFour et al., 2016). School leadership should expect teacher teams to be content experts in their own field and respond accordingly.

6. **Ensure access to ongoing time, support, and coaching:** Teams require their leadership build in protected collaboration time within the school day. This time must be free of interruptions.

7. **Build in self-accountability mechanisms:** Team members should encourage each other to use templates or artifacts to document their work, as the leadership team will need teachers to show evidence of the team's work.

8. **Connect small victories to specific actions, and celebrate them:** Celebrate successes by sharing them at a faculty meeting, via staff email, or by providing another form of public recognition. Do this as often as possible.

The essential understanding of these eight ingredients is that simply coming together with your team will not yield the desired outcome of increased student achievement. When teams come together, they must know the work to focus on that will most impact student learning. When teams work together on common goals, they generate a common purpose, yielding collective efficacy, which can positively impact student achievement.

The Illusion of Will Versus Skill

When teachers talk to me about why their students are or are not successful in a classroom, their comments frequently include a common thread. They often say that a student can't do the work or is choosing not to do the work. Such statements and discussions shift the focus away from student learning and strategic teaching. As a PLC instructional coach working with teacher teams, I can say that, in these moments, teachers must become the students and must be ready to learn their way through their struggles. For teachers, data analysis becomes a will-versus-skill scenario (Muhammad & Hollie, 2012). As individuals, do teachers have the *will* to analyze data based on their attitude, other incentives, confidence, or personal feelings related to what the data might say? Do teachers have the *skill*—the capability and proficiency—to analyze data? Much like students, individual teachers are prone to avoid what they don't know how to do or don't see the value in.

Understanding the will-versus-skill matrix within collaborative teams' work is significant to the desired outcomes of student achievement. There is a continuum or a progression: low skills and low motivation, low skills and high motivation, high skills and low motivation, and high skills and high motivation. Optimal results for students depend on optimal work from teachers. When analyzing data, teachers need to be highly skilled and highly motivated as they collaborate as a team.

About this, Thomas (2011) says:

> Whether schools have productive data-analysis sessions leading to instructional improvements and increased student learning or meetings that are a waste of time and resources could well hinge on the structures that are put in place by the expectations of school and district leadership. As I have worked with more than 200 school teams as a data coach for the past 20 years, I have seen team after team struggle to become a truly collaborative professional learning community that effectively analyzes and acts on data. Why is this so, and what can school system leaders do to equip teams with the tools they need to be successful?

In my personal experience, school leaders who establish PLC processes effectively in their schools are doing things right toward establishing a collaborative culture. *Effectively* is the key word in the preceding passage. Many schools I visit build collaboration time into the school day for teachers to meet; however, I repeatedly see teams that don't know how to effectively use this time. Ineffective collaboration time is wasted time. In these situations, teacher teams always think they are part of a high-functioning, sustaining PLC. No matter how many years they have been operating in this way, I typically find the opposite; these teams are in the initiating stages of collaboration and have yet to take needed steps forward in their work. I often find the largest disconnect appears through a team's use of a data-analysis protocol.

An Intentional Data-Analysis Protocol

Teams must engage in an intentional exploration of data to determine the direction and actions they need to take so every student will successfully learn. Whether teams analyze state or provincial testing data, district benchmark data, or teacher team–level data like common formative and summative assessments, using a data-analysis protocol reveals the following.

- Patterns of strengths and weaknesses

- Individual student successes or failures

- A correlation between teaching strategies and student learning

- A connection between the lesson planning and the learning targets and intentionality through instruction

- Rigor as it relates to depth of knowledge (DOK; Francis, 2017; Webb, 1997)

- Whether there is a correlation between school or district data results and state or provincial testing results

- Improvements in student growth and content mastery from year to year

- Individual student growth from day to day, week to week, lesson to lesson, and unit to unit

When teams consistently use a data-analysis protocol throughout an instructional year, it enables them to look at snapshots (individual moments in time) of the learning that has happened or to look at an entire year in review for all students.

A misconception about data-analysis protocols is that teachers use them to work toward some desired accountability measure on the end-of-year state or provincial test. But when analyzing student data, teams are really working toward understanding individual student learning and improving instructional practices. Where there is learning, there will likely be an improvement on the end-of-year state or provincial test, which could also positively impact the school's accountability measure. However, to build trust essential to the collaborative process, team members must all understand that using a data-analysis protocol is not a compliance measure for end-of-year outcomes, either in the classroom or schoolwide. As Thomas (2011) states:

> The message to teachers must be this: These are our kids and their learning. Our work is not about abstract concepts of state accountability or school improvement. We did not get into this business to increase state test scores. We are here to help children learn. In the midst of our hard work, we all need to recall and remind our staff of why we do what we do.

I have worked with many schools and teacher teams in priority schools where team members would say they have a solid data-analysis process. It takes only one or two probing questions from me to reveal that they *think* they have a protocol in place, but in plain and simple terms, they do not. Many one-liners and oft-repeated idioms and proverbs come to mind when I am amid these discussions: "How's that working out for you?" "The proof is in the pudding," and "Put your money where your mouth is." You get the idea. The most common breakdowns occur at the point where teachers want to defend their work *against* the evidence that drives their decisions. My response is for collaborative teams to each work through the following nine-step data-analysis process.

1. As a team, generate a comparative colored chart of stoplight data (overall), arranged by standard, by learning target, by teacher (figure 7.1). In this case, *stoplight data* refers to a color-coding system aligned to student proficiency levels. A green (light gray) level indicates proficiency with one more standards students have met or mastered. Yellow (medium gray) indicates approaching proficiency. Red (dark gray) indicates below proficiency. Although this example shows just one common formative assessment (CFA) and one common summative assessment (CSA), there can, of course, be more than one common formative assessment for an instructional unit. Teams simply add columns to the chart based on the data they've collected. As a team, examine and study the data. Although we show just one example of a data chart in this section, you will find several additional examples of data-analysis configurations in Extend the Team's Use of Data (page 160).

2. For a braoder view of overall learning, generate a comparative graph of team-by-team stoplight data with the data arranged by teacher, by assessment question, and by class.

3. Generate a comparative graph that shows stoplight data just by teacher and student. As a team, examine and study the data.

Learning Standard	Proficiency Target	Teacher A		Teacher B		Teacher C	
		CFA	CSA	CFA	CSA	CFA	CSA
RI.8.1	65	59	71	53	62	61	74
RI.8.2	72	43	68	41	59	59	70
RI.8.5	70	51	70	47	61	60	72
RI.8.6	78	78	80	60	62	50	65

Figure 7.1: Data chart—Comparison by standard, by target, by teacher.

4. Use the data-analysis protocol in figure 7.2 (page 156) to summarize the team's data and then answer questions about the data to drive the team's conversation about next steps.

5. Determine intervention and extension strategies to differentiate instruction so you better support students who have yet to show proficiency and extend students who demonstrate mastery. For example, will the team utilize whole-group instruction, small-group instruction, or individual student instruction? What scaffolds do the data indicate students might need? See chapter 3, Respond to Data (page 75), to learn more about this work.

6. Plan *when* you will respond to data. Is there intervention time built into the instructional day through the master schedule, or does the team need to incorporate tiered lesson design into its classroom planning and lesson delivery? Perhaps team members could arrange a before- or after-school meeting time?

7. Engage in instruction for reteaching and extension (either by student, in student groups, or through whole-class instruction) using the strategies established in step 5.

8. Reassess students' learning after reteaching and extension, and determine next steps. That is, if necessary interventions did result in learning for students who have not shown proficiency with essential standards, determine and execute your team's next steps to advance learning for those students.

9. Generate a student-intervention data-tracking sheet. (See Extend the Team's Use of Data, page 160, for an example.)

This data-analysis process starts with a wide lens by looking at broad-level data. With each step, teams tighten their focus on the data to see the individual student needs come into focus. How did the team perform on a specific essential standard? How did each individual teacher's classes perform by individual period or by all periods? As teachers grow increasingly comfortable sharing data, they also grow more comfortable asking questions about the data to one another and among the group. You will hear comments like, "Wow, your students did really well! What did you do differently to teach this standard that might help my students." Or, "How did you get your class to grow so much?" Or, "What strategies can we try in the intervention to better support this specific student's learning gap?"

1. Determine the percentage of students proficient on the assessment for each standard or target by teacher and then for all students within the team. Write the information in the following chart.

	Target 1	Target 2	Target 3	Target 4
Teacher A				
Teacher B				
Teacher C				
Teacher D				
Total Team				

2. For each standard or target, determine the number of students who are proficient, close to proficient, and far from proficient by teacher and by team. (Write the number or the names of the students.)

Target 1

	Proficient	Close to Proficient	Far From Proficient	Total
Teacher A				
Teacher B				
Teacher C				
Teacher D				
Total Team				

Target 2

	Proficient	Close to Proficient	Far From Proficient	Total
Teacher A				
Teacher B				
Teacher C				
Teacher D				
Total Team				

Target 3

	Proficient	Close to Proficient	Far From Proficient	Total
Teacher A				
Teacher B				

Teacher C				
Teacher D				
Total Team				

Target 4				
	Proficient	Close to Proficient	Far From Proficient	Total
Teacher A				
Teacher B				
Teacher C				
Teacher D				
Total Team				

3. What skills did the proficient students demonstrate in their work that set their work apart? Which instructional strategies did teachers use that effectively produced those results?

4. In which area or areas did my students struggle? In which areas did our team's students struggle? What is the cause? How will we respond? Which strategies will we try next?

5. Which students need additional time and support to learn the standards or targets? What is our plan?

6. Which students need extension and enrichment? What is our plan?

7. Do these data show we are on track to meet our SMART goal? Why or why not?

Source: Kramer & Schuhl, 2017, pp. 103–104.

Figure 7.2: Data-analysis protocol.

*Visit **go.SolutionTree.com/PLCbooks** for a free reproducible version of this figure.*

Research That Reveals Students' Data Story

The data-anlaysis process I describe in the previous section covers a lot of ground. However, at its core is a focus on researching and understanding the data students generate from a variety of lessons and assessments. If a collaborative team wants students to learn, the team and individual team members must be clear about the work that's layered under the four critical questions of a PLC and the products the team needs to generate to improve student learning (Eaker & Keating, 2012). Consider how the following products and actions associate with each critical question (DuFour et al., 2016). (See chapter 3, page 51, for more information about many of these items.)

1. What do we want all students to learn and be able to do in each course and unit?

    ‣ A list of learning standards

    ‣ A list of essential (power) standards

    ‣ A list of learning targets (content and skills), clarifying the meaning of each standard and the DOK it requires

    ‣ A learning progression for each standard, clarifying the teaching progression of learning targets to meet the overall standard

    ‣ Instructional strategies to teach students the learning progression content

2. How will we know what students have learned and can do?

    ‣ State or provincial assessments

    ‣ Benchmark assessments

    ‣ Common formative assessments

    ‣ Common summative assessments

3. How will we respond when students experience difficulty in their learning?

    ‣ Classroom-based differentiated grade- and course-level instruction

    ‣ Interventions to support students who continue to struggle with grade- or course-level instruction

    ‣ Interventions for students who lack prerequisite skills for the grade or course level

4. How will we celebrate and extend and enrich the learning of students who demonstrate proficiency?

    ‣ Classroom-based differentiated instruction, given individually or in student teams

    ‣ Deeper instruction on content within essential standards

    ‣ Instruction on supporting or nonessential (nice-to-know) standards

By obtaining or developing these products and combining them with team actions in the classroom, collaborative teams acquire the data they need and determine instructional plans based on the story their data tell. This includes the following.

- Understand any concerns, obstacles, or restraints within the data.
- Monitor data progression.
- Revise instructional approaches.
- Extend the team's use of data.

Understand Concerns, Obstacles, and Restraints

Collecting data is not where most teachers or teacher teams struggle. They struggle in determining what the data communicate about student learning. In addition to needing guidance on how to interpret data to make them meaningful, teams need tools to help them analyze data and, in so doing, take ownership of the data. Specialized and detailed reporting tools are much more beneficial to both teachers and the cause of learning than receiving a generic report from some software program that the school or district purchased to record and disaggregate data on teams' behalf. Such reports might be more convenient to generate, but without collaborative data analysis of student proficiency on team-generated and team-assessed essential standards and learning targets, the value of that initial collaborative work is lost. Intentionally digging into the data has value, but leveraged against restraints in time, teachers may voluntarily opt out of doing so, which devalues the whole process. Teams must protect their collective data analysis by allotting time for it and using appropriate supporting documents to guide their work.

Monitor Data Progression

Over time, teacher teams will collaboratively analyze data and use the information they glean from the data to seek and share best practices, take collective responsibility for learning outcomes, and seek improvement (Eaker & Keating, 2015). By frequently analyzing data, teachers can graphically demonstrate learning growth by comparing changes as time goes on.

Revise Instructional Approaches

In my experience, once teams develop a data-analysis protocol that enables them to interpret data at a deep level, they begin to realize they need built-in time to respond to what the data are telling them. Those responses might include adjustments to core grade- or course-level instruction or adjustments to the master schedule to build in more remediation and extension time, for example. Whatever the response, teams must take an intentional next step that responds to the exact need the data communicate. After issuing that response, teams need to reassess and determine whether it was appropriate and resulted in learning.

Extend the Team's Use of Data

Throughout North America, multiple schools have incorporated the data-analysis protocol and process I have outlined in this chapter. When schools use this process to connect deeply with data and read their stories, it results in learning growth. This framework is the trigger for teacher teams; it is the light-bulb moment where teachers connect with the information and make the data meaningful and impactful. Think of the process like a laundry cycle: wash, rinse, and repeat; analyze, interpret, and respond.

Teams can utilize the data-analysis protocol with any assessment data, including data from preassessments, formative and summative assessments, benchmark assessments, and state or provincial assessments. Schools' or teams' formats for organizing collected data can also vary significantly but still provide quality and actionable information for teams to improve learning outcomes. The following figures provide a series of graphical representations showing various outputs teams might analyze while confronting student learning data. Note that these are not full data sets but representative aggregates and excerpts used for illustrative purposes. Each figure presents a different data focus relative to an eighth-grade English language arts (ELA) common formative assessment.

- **Figure 7.3:** This figure organizes data by assessment question and lists data according to each teacher's overall class scores (merging separate class periods). Using this graphical representation, team members need to note each assessment question's source. For example, is it a team- or teacher-generated question? Is it from a previous state or provincial template? Further, each question must align to a team-determined essential standard or learning target. In this example, shaded standards are the essential standards. Scores with light-gray shading have met or exceeded the target score. Scores with medium-gray shading are below the target, and teams with dark-gray shading are well below the target. Subsequent figures use similar formatting.

- **Figure 7.4 (page 162):** This figure replicates the format of figure 7.2 (page 156) but focuses on student performance in the first-period class only. The team members would replicate these data for each class period.

- **Figure 7.5 (page 163):** This figure organizes data based on the individual students in a single class period. It presents each student's overall score.

- **Figure 7.6 (page 164):** This figure takes a more granular look at students' scores by comparing data on each student's answer within a single classroom. It lists overall data at the top and individual student answers underneath. Checkmarks for a question indicate the student gave the correct answer. Letters indicate an incorrect answer the student gave.

- **Figure 7.7 (page 165):** This example helps teams target student interventions based on the student and several metrics related to their learning, such as performance on state- or province-issued benchmark assessments, team-issued common formative assessments, and so on. Teams can organize such collections according to their needs. Utilizing data in this way, teams can target interventions and begin closing the learning gap.

Question Number	Source	Skill Assessed	Learning Standard	DOK Level	Target Score	Teacher A Class Score	Teacher B Class Score	Teacher C Class Score	Teacher D Class Score
1	Team-generated	Making inferences	RI.8.1	2	79	66	68	53	66
2	State template	Making inferences	RI.8.1	2	57	69	74	58	63
3	Curriculum resource	Making inferences	RI.8.1	2	65	64	61	31	56
4	Team-generated	Identify text structure and organizational patterns	RI.8.5	2	70	43	69	37	51
5	State template	Determining the author's purpose	RI.8.6	3	78	60	75	38	58
6	Curriculum resource	Paraphrasing or summarizing	RI.8.2	2	72	59	70	42	51
7	Curriculum resource	Identify text structure and organizational patterns	RI.8.5	4	62	56	51	48	52
8	State template	Determining the author's purpose	RI.8.6	3	60	48	58	38	52

Source for standards: NGA & CCSSO, 2010.

Figure 7.3: Eighth-grade ELA CFA—Comparison by teacher, by class.

Question Number	Source	Skill Assessed	Learning Standard	DOK Level	Target Score	Teacher A Period 1 Score	Teacher B Period 1 Score	Teacher C Period 1 Score	Teacher D Period 1 Score
1	Team-generated	Making inferences	RI.8.1	2	79	60	64	50	62
2	State template	Making inferences	RI.8.1	2	57	68	72	52	60
3	Curriculum resource	Making inferences	RI.8.1	2	65	38	66	32	48
4	Team-generated	Identify text structure and organizational patterns	RI.8.5	2	70	58	72	34	52
5	State template	Determining the author's purpose	RI.8.6	3	78	56	72	40	48
6	Curriculum resource	Paraphrasing or summarizing	RI.8.2	2	72	54	68	50	50
7	Curriculum resource	Identify text structure and organizational patterns	RI.8.5	4	62	52	48	46	50
8	State template	Determining the author's purpose	RI.8.6	3	60	42	58	34	48

Source for standards: NGA & CCSSO, 2010.

Figure 7.4: Eighth-grade ELA CFA—Comparison by teacher, by period.

Teacher	Period	Student	Raw Score	Proficiency Level (Target Score)	Percentage of Correct Responses
Teacher A	1	Student 1	40	55	73%
Teacher A	1	Student 2	38	55	69%
Teacher A	1	Student 3	37	55	67%
Teacher A	1	Student 4	36	55	65%
Teacher A	1	Student 5	36	55	65%
Teacher A	1	Student 6	26	55	47%
Teacher A	1	Student 7	26	55	47%
Teacher A	1	Student 8	19	55	35%
Teacher A	1	Student 9	19	55	35%
Teacher A	1	Student 10	19	55	35%

Figure 7.5: Eighth-grade ELA CFA—Comparison by single class, by student (overall score).

Teacher: Teacher A

Period: 1

	Raw Score	Percent Correct	Question 1	Question 2	Question 3	Question 4	Question 5	Question 6	Question 7	Question 8
Assessment Question Number			1	2	3	4	5	6	7	8
DOK Level			2	2	2	2	3	2	4	3
Class Percentage of Correct Responses			55%	43%	53%	40%	47%	39%	40%	16%
Total Points Possible			1	1	1	1	1	1	1	1
Correct Response			A	C	C	D	B	B	A	D
Student										
Student 1	20	36%	D	A	✓	B	C	✓	B	✓
Student 2	19	35%	B	A	D	B	A	✓	D	A
Student 3	16	29%	B	B	A	C	C	A	✓	B
Student 4	18	33%	✓	✓	D	B	✓	C	✓	A
Student 5	15	27%	✓	A	A	B	✓	D	D	B
Student 6	15	27%	D	✓	✓	C	D	✓	✓	✓
Student 7	15	27%	D	✓	✓	B	D	✓	B	B
Student 8	24	44%	✓	A	✓	B	C	✓	✓	C
Student 9	31	56%	✓	✓	D	✓	✓	✓	D	A
Student 10	17	31%	✓	B	D	✓	✓	D	✓	A

Figure 7.6: Eighth-grade ELA CFA—Comparison by student, by question.

Teacher	Student	Absences	English Learner	Currently Receiving Intervention	Intervention Teacher	Current Grade	State Test Grades		CFA 1: Vocabulary	CFA 2: Inference	Benchmark 1	CFA 3: Summary
A	1	2		Yes	Alcindor	57	15	4.8	60	60	49	60
A	2	1		No		75	25	3.8	100 (retake)	80	59	60
B	1	4	✓	Yes	Duncan	80	17	4.3	100 (retake)	100 (retake)	59	80
C	1	0	✓	No		76	33	5.9	80 (retake)	80	63	80
C	2	9		Yes	Petchesky	66		5.1	60	80	45	80
A	3	0	✓	No		76		4.8	100	60	82	60
A	4	4	✓	Yes	Alcindor	74	18	3.8	100	60	74	60
B	2	3		No		76	35	6.4	80	80	63	80
C	3	7	✓	No		83	39	5.8	100	80	72	80
C	4	1		Yes	Duncan	82		6.3	100	80	68	80
A	5	2		No		88	39	6.1	100	100	70	80
B	3	0		No		81	35	4.8	80	100	72	70
B	4	0	✓	No		88	19	4.5	100	80	72	100
B	5	1		No		85	36	10	90	80	84	85
C	5	1		No		90	39	6.7	M	90	80	100

Figure 7.7: Eighth-grade ELA CFA—Student intervention-tracking sheet.

Note that several students in this example are color-coded as far below proficiency but have benefitted from assessment retake opportunities that have raised their overall grade. In subsequent reports, these students' color-coding would change to reflect their current status, but that does not necessarily mean such students won't require future interventions.

Conclusion

In *Time for Change*, educational consultants and coauthors Anthony Muhammad and Luis F. Cruz (2019) state, "Data should be used to develop collaborative ownership of a problem and a collective desire to solve that problem" (p. 28). After staff at U.S. Grant High School had reviewed comprehensive data and established a plan to triage students' needs, student learning growth started happening. As this work continued, the school focused simultaneously on student learning and student and staff culture, the results of which you read about in chapter 3 (page 51). The team collaboration and data analysis allowed teachers to peel data down to the individual student level and provide individual remediation and extensions, thus focusing on the third and fourth critical questions of a PLC. The resulting academic growth highlighted in chapter 3 raised the bar for all students, and it only took three years to achieve tremendous growth. U.S. Grant High School was no longer a priority school in need of improvement, yet the work of collaborative teams merely provided a foundation for continued growth. The work doesn't stop. The same will happen in your school should it accept the challenge of gathering, confronting, and reacting to its data. A PLC's work is an ongoing journey that you can learn more about from *School Improvement for All: A How-To Guide for Doing the Right Work* (Kramer & Schuhl, 2017), which effectively blends priority schools' school-improvement needs within the PLC process.

References and Resources

AllThingsPLC. (n.d.). *Tools & resources*. Accessed at www.allthingsplc.info/tools-resources on September 14, 2020.

Bloomberg, M. (2020, January 10). *You can't manage what you can't measure*. Accessed at www .linkedin.com/pulse/you-cant-manage-what-measure-mike-bloomberg on February 8, 2020.

DuFour, R., DuFour, R., Eaker, R., Many, T. W., & Mattos, M. (2016). *Learning by doing: A handbook for Professional Learning Communities at Work* (3rd ed.). Bloomington, IN: Solution Tree Press.

Eaker, R., & Keating, J. (2015). *Kid by kid, skill by skill: Teaching in a Professional Learning Community at Work*. Bloomington, IN: Solution Tree Press.

Francis, E. M. (2017, May 9). *What is depth of knowledge?* [Blog post]. Accessed at https:// inservice.ascd.org/what-exactly-is-depth-of-knowledge-hint-its-not-a-wheel on May 4, 2020.

Kramer, S. V., & Schuhl, S. (2017). *School improvement for all: A how-to guide for doing the right work.* Bloomington, IN: Solution Tree Press.

Muhammad, A., & Cruz, L. (2019). *Time for change: Four essential skills for transformational school and district leaders.* Bloomington, IN: Solution Tree Press.

Muhammad, A., & Hollie, S. (2012). *The will to lead, the skill to teach: Transforming schools at every level.* Bloomington, IN: Solution Tree Press.

National Governors Association Center for Best Practices & Council of Chief State School Officers. (2010). *Common Core State Standards for English language arts and literacy in history/social studies, science, and technical subjects.* Washington, DC: Authors. Accessed at www.corestandards.org/assets/CCSSI_ELA%20Standards.pdf on October 1, 2020.

Thomas, R. (2011). Why school teams don't analyze data. *School Administrator, 68*(9). Accessed at www.aasa.org/SchoolAdministratorArticle.aspx?id=20448 on September 28, 2020.

Webb, N. L. (1997, April). *Criteria for alignment of expectations and assessments in mathematics and science education* (Research Monograph No. 8). Washington, DC: Council of Chief State School Officers.

Critical Issues for Team Consideration

Team Name:

Team Members:

Use the following rating scale to indicate the extent to which each statement is true of your team.

1	2	3	4	5	6	7	8	9	10

Not True of Our Team   **Our Team Is Addressing This**   **True of Our Team**

1. _____ We have identified team norms and protocols to guide us in working together.

2. _____ We have analyzed student achievement data and established SMART goals to improve on this level of achievement we are working interdependently to attain (SMART goals are specific and strategic, measurable, attainable, results oriented, and time bound.

3. _____ Each team member is clear on the knowledge, skills, and dispositions (that is, the essential learning) that students will acquire as a result of our course or grade level and each unit within the course or grade level.

4. _____ We have aligned the essential learning with state and district standards and the high-stakes assessments required of our students.

5. _____ We have identified course content and topics we can eliminate to devote more time to the essential curriculum.

6. _____ We have agreed on how to best sequence the content of the course and have established pacing guides to help students achieve the intended essential learning.

7. _____ We have identified the prerequisite knowledge and skills students need in order to master the essential learning of each unit of instruction.

8. _____ We have identified strategies and created instruments to assess whether students have the prerequisite knowledge and skills.

9. _____ We have developed strategies and systems to assist students in acquiring prerequisite knowledge and skills when they are lacking in those areas.

page 1 of 2

10. _____ We have developed frequent common formative assessments that help us determine each student's mastery of essential learning.

11. _____ We have established the proficiency standard we want each student to achieve on each skill and concept examined with our common assessments.

12. _____ We use the results of our common assessments to assist each other in building on strengths and addressing weaknesses as part of an ongoing process of continuous improvement designed to help students achieve at higher levels.

13. _____ We use the results of our common assessments to identify students who need additional time and support to master essential learning, and we work within the systems and processes of the school to ensure they receive that support.

14. _____ We have agreed on the criteria we will use in judging the quality of student work related to the essential learning of our course, and we continually practice applying those criteria to ensure we are consistent.

15. _____ We have taught students the criteria we will use in judging the quality of their work and provided them with examples.

16. _____ We have developed or utilized common summative assessments that help us assess the strengths and weaknesses of our program.

17. _____ We have established the proficiency standard we want each student to achieve on each skill and concept examined with our summative assessments.

18. _____ We formally evaluate our adherence to team norms and the effectiveness of our team at least twice each year.

Source: DuFour, R., DuFour, R., Eaker, R., Many, T. W., & Mattos, M. (2016). Learning by doing: A handbook for Professional Learning Communities at Work (3rd ed.). Bloomington, IN: Solution Tree Press, p. 69.

 **Gerry Petersen-Incorvaia, PhD,** is assistant superintendent for educational services at Glendale Elementary School District in Arizona. He has served as a teacher, principal, university professor, and director for curriculum and instruction. He has worked at both school sites and district offices while implementing professional learning communities (PLCs). In the time that Gerry has worked as director for curriculum and instruction and assistant superintendent at Glendale Elementary School District, the district has become a model PLC, implementing best practices of the PLC process.

In addition to working with Solution Tree and PLCs, Gerry has trained and presented with Rick Stiggins and Jan Chappuis regarding assessment, presented with the State Collaborative on Assessment and Student Standards, and written curriculum and presented with Jay and Daisy McTighe regarding Understanding by Design. The diverse experiences he has had in schools and school districts have invigorated his philosophy that all students should have equity of access to a rigorous education.

Gerry earned his bachelor's degree from Luther College in elementary education and music and his master's and doctoral degrees from the University of Arizona in music education, with post-doctoral work in educational leadership.

To learn more about Gerry's work, follow @DrGerryPI on Twitter.

To book Gerry Petersen-Incorvaia for professional development, contact pd@SolutionTree.com.

Moving From a Flooded to a Balanced Intervention Pyramid

Gerry Petersen-Incorvaia

Response to learning or interventions and remediation are more powerful than the negative effects of poverty.

—*Sharon V. Kramer and Sarah Schuhl*

In 2015, I worked as the director for curriculum and instruction at Glendale Elementary School District in Arizona. At the time, our schools were bottom heavy; that is, the majority of our students were performing in our state's lowest proficiency label creating an impossible imbalance in our response to intervention (RTI) efforts.

RTI, which is a specific approach to a multitiered system of supports (MTSS), is a method of intervention for ensuring all students who are behind grade- or course-level learning proficiency catch up and then stay on grade or course level (Buffum, Mattos, & Malone, 2018). RTI at Work clarifies this goal by envisioning tiered intervention as an inverted pyramid, with all students receiving Tier 1 instruction at the broad top level, with progressively fewer students in need of Tier 2 and Tier 3 interventions (see figure 8.1, page 172). Unfortunately, the bottom of our district's pyramid was flooded with students.

Since 2015, our staff have worked collaboratively and intently to move students from this flooded pyramid floor to ensure all students benefit from Tier 1 instruction, and they have succeeded. But how did our collaborative teams establish the high-functioning culture of learning to accomplish this?

With state requirements, district expectations regarding new curriculum, and student academic and social-emotional needs, some of our district's schools found it hard to know where to start. One collaborative team at a school in the district figured out a system that worked to move all students, including the lowest quartile of students, to higher proficiency levels. This case illustrates any collaborative teacher team's power to influence learning not just at the team level but at the district level, ensuring equitable

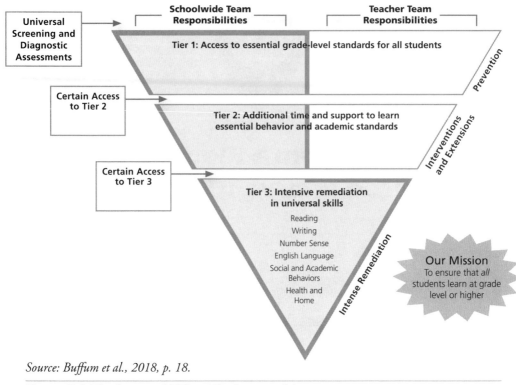

Source: Buffum et al., 2018, p. 18.

Figure 8.1: The inverted RTI at Work pyramid.

access to instruction for all students. The team's research, problem solving, and implementation of its problem of practice helped the team become stronger and resulted in higher student proficiency.

To comprehend this team's work, it's necessary to have a clear understanding of tiered instruction. RTI at Work defines three tiers of instruction and intervention.

1. Tier 1 instruction and intervention involves teaching in the moment while modifying and differentiating instruction for students who did not learn the content that was just taught.

2. Tier 2 intervention occurs for students who have struggled to gain proficiency with grade- or course-level content, standards, and learning targets so that teachers can keep these students in the curriculum.

3. Tier 3 intervention involves remediation that helps support students to learn prerequisite skills that may be creating a gap between learning from past years and grade- or course-level learning.

With an effect size of 1.07, RTI is a powerful system of targeted support for students to close academic gaps and sustain growth on par with their classmates (Hattie, 2012). Given that an effect size of 0.40 is equal to experiencing a year's growth in a year's time, an effect size of 1.07 represents double the impact of no intervention measures at all. The key understanding teams must have about RTI is that it is a system of support to ensure all students learn at high levels.

Oftentimes, priority or underperforming schools have a flooded intervention pyramid. When the majority or close to the majority of students need Tier 3 intervention or remediation, there are unique needs these schools must consider regarding time and the organization of people, resources, and support. In this chapter, you will learn how your collaborative team's efforts can help your school move from a flooded pyramid to a balanced one. You'll next explore the role of intervention and Tier 1 instruction, how to provide dedicated time for team intervention in a school's master schedule, and how to find additional time in the crowded schedule to offer Tier 2 and Tier 3 instruction. Note that all of this work can be accomplished regardless of whether students are receiving in-person or distanced instruction.

Response to Intervention and the Role of Tier 1

Although I address the three RTI tiers in the chapter introduction, to understand and effectively deliver Tier 1 instruction, it's important to understand its place among the tiers and, specifically, the timing most appropriate for each intervention tier.

- Tier 1 is less about intervention than it is about core grade- or course-level instruction (Buffum et al., 2018). Included in Tier 1 are individual teacher checks for student understanding of daily lessons. Teachers adjust and differentiate subsequent instruction based on these formative check-ins.

- Tier 2 interventions occur at the end of a unit of study, after collaborative teams administer a common assessment. Teams may consider these assessments formative or summative in nature, but they should always use the resulting data for formative purposes.

- Tier 3 interventions typically occur after a benchmark assessment, such as a universal-screener at the start of a school year or semester, a state or provincial assessment, or an end-of-semester assessment. Tier 3 interventions can occur at any time throughout the year.

Teams discuss and act on all three tiers as part of the learning cycle when addressing the third and fourth critical questions of a PLC (DuFour, DuFour, Eaker, Many, & Mattos, 2016): What do we do when students don't learn? What do we do when the students already know it? This chapter focuses on the third critical question, but you can learn more about answering the fourth in chapter 9 (page 189). Table 8.1 (page 174) sums up the *who, when, how, where,* and resources of each intervention level.

A balanced pyramid of intervention has about 5 to 8 percent of students in a Tier 3 intervention (Buffum et al., 2018). However, priority schools often find themselves locked into a perpetual cycle where between 40 and 80 percent of students are in a Tier 3 intervention (Buffum et al., 2018). This can be overwhelming for collaborative teams throughout a school and district, especially when they have a lack of resources.

Table 8.1: Summary of Tiered Intervention

Tier	Who	When	How	Where	Resources
Tier 1	Teacher	Within first-best instruction	Check for understanding	Small-group instruction	Standard adopted resources
Tier 2	Team	Within flex time	Common formative assessment	Flexible groups, shared throughout the team	Differentiated resources
Tier 3	School	Within intervention time	Benchmark universal screener	Flexible groups with supplemental services	Evidence-based intervention program

Robert Eaker (2018), author and coarchitect of the PLC at Work process, shares, "As a profession, shouldn't we expect the same standard of care for *all kids* that we expect for *our own kids?*" (p. 5). This is the moral and ethical oath educators take. Collaborative team members want all students to be at least on grade and course level, demonstrating mastery of essential standards and ensuring there is room for all students at the top of the inverted RTI pyramid. Figure 8.2 illustrates an ideal balance for student access to tiered intervention. When a majority of students require intensive remediation, the pyramid becomes unbalanced and floods (figure 8.3).

Tier 1
(access to essential grade-level standards):
100 percent of students

Tier 2
(additional support to master
grade-level standards):
5–15 percent of students

Tier 3
(intensive remediation
in universal skills):
5–8 percent of students

Source: Adapted from Buffum et al., 2018.

Figure 8.2: A balanced intervention pyramid.

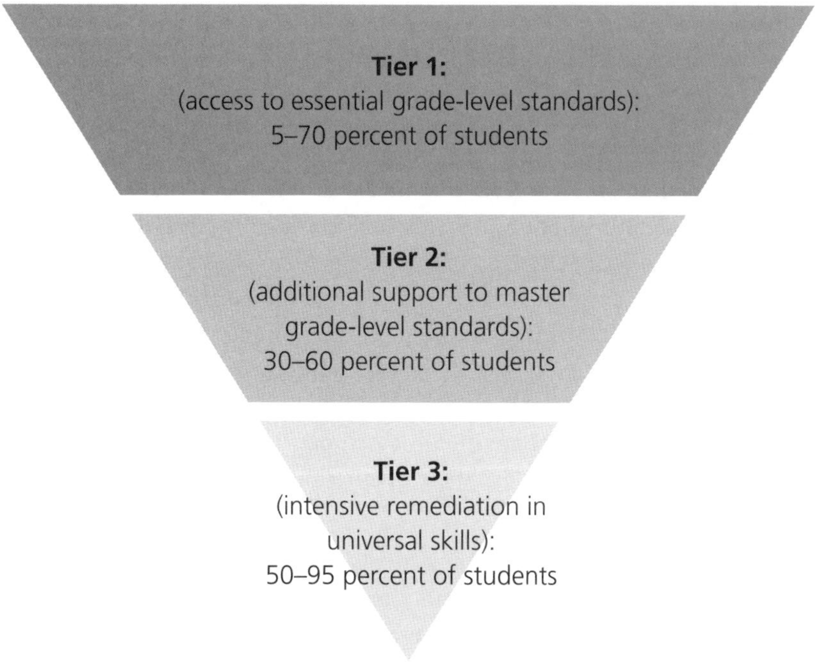

Tier 1:
(access to essential grade-level standards):
5–70 percent of students

Tier 2:
(additional support to master
grade-level standards):
30–60 percent of students

Tier 3:
(intensive remediation in
universal skills):
50–95 percent of students

Source: Adapted from Buffum et al., 2018.

Figure 8.3: A flooded intervention pyramid.

Maintaining students' access to grade- and course-level content is paramount to helping students accelerate so they get on and stay on level (Tier 1). The philosophy of how to help this work in a priority school is that any student who needs Tier 3 instruction may lack the skills or knowledge necessary to access Tier 1 curricula. When this happens—that is, when the student needs remediation on foundational skills from prior years' content—the student is in need of all three tiers of intervention. The student receives Tier 1 and Tier 2 instruction to stay current in grade- or course-level curricula and Tier 3 instruction to fill any foundational academic gaps. Another way to put this is that a student needs core instruction, plus intervention on the core learning, plus more intervention on remediation that amounts to core instruction, plus more, plus more. This begs the questions, When does all this intervention happen? and How does it happen?

As part of a PLC's first big idea (a focus on learning to ensure all students can learn at high levels; DuFour et al., 2016), Paul Goldberg (2017) stresses that "staffs work cohesively and collaboratively to close the achievement gap and measure that progress by high achievement for all students" (p. 23). But how do teams get all students to high levels of achievement with a lack of time, people, and resources and a flooded pyramid? Closing this achievement gap requires ensuring a strong Tier 1 is in place. Gayle Gregory, Martha Kaufeldt, and Mike Mattos (2016a, 2016b) suggest a powerful Tier 1 curriculum has the following five components.

1. Essential standards

2. Success criteria for mastery

3. 21st century skills

4. Meaningful, relevant, and student-centered instruction

5. Evidence-based best practices

Along with these components, teams need to utilize scaffolds and differentiated instruction to ensure mastery of essential standards for all students. When Tier 1, or *first-best*, instruction is strong, there is less need for Tier 2 and Tier 3 interventions. Although easier said than done, it is important that teams continually engage in embedded professional learning and that school structures help Tier 1 be as successful as possible. To clarify this point, when collaborative teams focus on a learning cycle (unit-by-unit instruction), which includes deconstructing or unwrapping standards, building proficiency maps or detailed pacing guides with calendared common formative assessments, and clarifying high-leverage teaching practices, their professional learning is embedded in this process. School structures are then focused on providing teachers with increased time to focus on evidence-based, first-best instruction. Together, these conditions lead to student success.

When students do not master the Tier 1 learning, it takes collaboration and an entire team effort to ensure all students are grade- or course-level ready. Austin Buffum and Mike Mattos (2015) state that with Tier 1 instruction and planning in collaborative team time, teachers must be flexible, enabling them to address "the overall standard and targets at three levels: (1) scaffolded learning, (2) core learning, and (3) extensions of learning. Teams, rather than individual teachers, work together to design specific activities that ensure all students will learn the standards" (p. 22). Educational consultant and author Casey Reason (2018) corroborates this while sharing a philosophy of collaborative teams: "They have abandoned the notion of 'my students' or 'your students' or 'my job' or 'your job.' It's 'our students,' 'our collective commitment,' and 'our results'" (p. 40). This philosophy permeates all three tiers.

Ensuring that strong Tier 1 instruction includes small-group instruction (guided reading, small-group skill work, extended activities, re-engagement of content, and so on) and occurs each day for every student is important. Without this, a team, school, or district will never successfully intervene its way out of a flooded pyramid. But it's also necessary to ensure a targeted, strategic, evidence-based practice of Tier 3 is in place at the other end of the pyramid. Combined with a focused Tier 2 that activates as teams complete common formative assessments, teams can keep all students steeped in rich, grade-level curricula.

Oftentimes, intervention resources demand that small student groups access instruction via a scripted program that teams must follow with strict fidelity for the resources to have optimum results. This may not always allow for the 80 to 95 percent of students who need Tier 3 instruction in priority school to be a part of such intensive interventions. So, what to do? How do *all* students get what they need? What if 80 percent of students in a grade level need Tier 3 intervention, but only 20 percent of the students fit into the Tier 3 program, and they also still need access to Tier 1 and Tier 2 to stay in the curriculum? What is the plan for the other 60 percent of students? Team members' throwing up their hands and giving up is not an option. All hands and minds need to be on deck to ensure a strategic plan is in place.

Scheduled Time for Intervention

When it comes to supporting intervention, finding time to provide those supports is at the top of every team's list. As Sharon V. Kramer (2015) states, "Because academic diversity in many classrooms is so great, school-improvement efforts must focus on both intervention and remediation" (p. 31). (And don't forget extensions!) Education experts Jeff Craig and Joe Mack (2019) give examples of different names for intervention time: *WIN* (what I need) and *TEAM* (together everyone achieves more) time. Some schools may implement an RTI period into their schedule. However, when schools set a designated time for intervention, it often has a subsequent and perhaps an unintended impact on the time that teams have to collaborate. During collaborative team time, the team members focus on lesson planning for interventions, particularly Tier 3 support, instead of focusing on the teaching and learning cycle unit by unit for Tier 1 and Tier 2. How do collaborative teacher teams and leadership teams school- and districtwide find the right balance for each tier?

Finding balance isn't the only question teams face. When the majority of students need Tier 3 interventions, and therefore also need Tier 2 interventions and access to Tier 1 instruction, teams require additional personnel to do the instruction. However, priority schools do not always have access to funding to add interventionists or educational assistants who can work with teacher teams and take on these responsibilities. So how do teacher teams honor the learning of all students in a grade level, not just all students who need Tier 3 intervention? How do teams split classrooms of students and not split the teachers?

The school leadership team can work with teacher teams to reconfigure the school's master schedule to help organize time and people for Tier 3 intervention during the school day. The following sections examine options for creating blocked time for intervention, building interventions (unblocked time) into regular instruction, and utilizing intervention time effectively.

Blocked Intervention Time

Sometimes, master schedules have a block of time for intervention in place; that is, a set amount of time is given to intervention for a grade or course. If this is the case in a priority school, I recommend using this intervention time specifically for Tier 3 intervention and extension. However, and as we've established, the challenge is to ensure students who need access to Tier 2 instruction retain access to Tier 1 as well.

A best practice is to ensure Tier 2 intervention occurs within three weeks of Tier 1 instruction; therefore, collaborative teams should be on at least a three-week cycle (DuFour et al., 2016). However, in priority schools, a five- to ten-day cycle for common formative assessments that factor into Tier 2 intervention is needed in order to respond to the number of students who may not learn the content in a timely manner. (See chapter 3, page 51.) Teams may *also* use the block of Tier 3 intervention time for Tier 2 as well (not *instead* of). The use of flex days in the Tier 3 intervention schedule helps collaborative teams respond not only to students' Tier 3 needs but also to their Tier 2 needs.

Supposing collaborative teams have a five-day cycle for Tier 1 instruction and common formative assessment implementation, table 8.2 shows the structure for the work over eight days, which also includes intervention.

Table 8.2: Adding Intervention Time in Eight-Day Cycles

Days	The Work
1–4	Tier 1 instruction of the unit of study
5	Implementation of common formative assessment
6	Analysis of the common formative assessment, and grouping of students for Tier 2 intervention
7	Flex time during Tier 3 intervention to intervene for Tier 2
8	Flex time during Tier 3 intervention to intervene for Tier 2

Figure 8.4 offers a look at a two-week collaborative team schedule for English language arts (ELA).

	Monday	Tuesday	Wednesday	Thursday	Friday
Week 1	Tier 1 instruction during ELA block Tier 3 remediation during intervention block	Tier 1 instruction during ELA block Tier 3 remediation during intervention block	Tier 1 instruction during ELA block Tier 3 remediation during intervention block	Tier 1 instruction during ELA block Tier 3 remediation during intervention block	Tier 1 instruction during ELA block Implementation of common formative assessment Tier 3 remediation during intervention block
Week 2	Tier 1 instruction during ELA block Team analysis of common formative assessment Tier 3 remediation during intervention block	Tier 1 instruction during ELA block Tier 2 intervention flex time during intervention block	Tier 1 instruction during ELA block Tier 2 intervention flex time during intervention block	Tier 1 instruction during ELA block Tier 3 remediation during intervention block	Tier 1 instruction during ELA block Tier 3 remediation during intervention block

Figure 8.4: Adding intervention time over two weeks.

Table 8.3 shows how schools can organize intervention time by combining continuous Tier 3 intervention time with two-day pauses for Tier 2 interventions.

Table 8.3: Continuous Tier 3 Interventions With Two-Day Pauses for Tier 2

Continuous Tier 3 Interventions	Two-Day Pause for Tier 2	Continuous Tier 3 Interventions	Two-Day Pause for Tier 2
Conduct Tier 3 program.	Pause for Tier 2 instruction. Review common formative assessment data.	Conduct Tier 3 program.	Pause for Tier 2 instruction. Review common formative assessment data.

Unblocked Intervention Time

Sometimes, it's not possible to add an intervention period to the master schedule. Depending on the length of a school day, the number of content areas to cover, or the content rotations, this may be impossible. When that is the case, thinking creatively can reveal flexible ways to utilize time. For example, there may be some flexibility during small-group reading or mathematics instruction. Best practices for an ELA or mathematics block allow time for small-group instruction, such as guided reading.

Because students who are below grade level need direct instruction, their time *after* meeting with the teacher for their guided-reading rotation or small-group instruction rotation is a perfect opportunity for their Tier 3 intervention, instead of perhaps center time. If a school has a staff member available to help provide Tier 3 support during only part of the day and only for certain grade levels, the school schedule could be set up like the one in figure 8.5 (page 180), which allows for Tier 3 support for grades K–4. In upper elementary and secondary schools, teams can request that a staff member be scheduled-in during learning time for nonessential standards in other content areas. To understand how intervention factors into the table, follow the Tier 1 instruction and first small group (called *group 1*) in each grade level. This schedule allows every student to have time with the classroom teacher for first-best instruction and small-group instruction before students are pulled out for intervention.

Figure 8.6 (page 181) shows an excerpted example of what a full-day schedule could look like for a single grade level. For our purposes, this could represent a schedule for any grade, K–4.

Utilization of Intervention Time

For each tier of intervention, different resources and personnel represent best practice in providing support for the tier. Table 8.4 (page 182) illustrates which resources and personnel teams can apply to make effective use of intervention time.

Monday	8:00–8:20 a.m.	8:20–8:40 a.m.	8:40–9:00 a.m.	9:00–9:20 a.m.	9:20–9:40 a.m.	9:40–10:00 a.m.
Kindergarten	Tier 1 instruction	Group 1 with teacher	Group 2 with teacher Group 1 with interventionist	Group 3 with teacher Group 1 with interventionist	Group 4 with teacher	Tier 1 instruction
First Grade	Tier 1 instruction	Tier 1 instruction	Group 1 with teacher	Group 2 with teacher	Group 3 with teacher Group 1 with interventionist	Group 4 with teacher Group 1 with interventionist
Second Grade	Tier 1 instruction	Tier 1 instruction	Tier 1 instruction	Tier 1 instruction	Group 1 with teacher	Group 2 with teacher
Third Grade	Tier 1 instruction	Tier 1 instruction	Tier 1 instruction	Tier 1 instruction	Tier 1 instruction	Tier 1 instruction
Fourth Grade	Tier 1 instruction	Tier 1 instruction	Tier 1 instruction	Tier 1 instruction	Tier 1 instruction	Tier 1 instruction

Monday	10:00–10:20 a.m.	10:20–10:40 a.m.	10:40–11:00 a.m.	11:00–11:20 a.m.	11:20–11:40 a.m.	11:40 a.m.–12:00 p.m.
Kindergarten	Tier 1 instruction	Tier 1 instruction	Tier 1 instruction	Tier 1 instruction	Tier 1 instruction	Tier 1 instruction
First Grade	Tier 1 instruction	Tier 1 instruction	Tier 1 instruction	Tier 1 instruction	Tier 1 instruction	Tier 1 instruction
Second Grade	Group 3 with teacher Group 1 with interventionist	Group 4 with teacher Group 1 with interventionist	Tier 1 instruction	Tier 1 instruction	Tier 1 instruction	Tier 1 instruction
Third Grade	Group 1 with teacher	Group 2 with teacher	Group 3 with teacher Group 1 with interventionist	Group 4 with teacher Group 1 with interventionist	Tier 1 instruction	Tier 1 instruction
Fourth Grade	Tier 1 instruction	Tier 1 instruction	Group 1 with teacher	Group 2 with teacher	Group 3 with teacher Group 1 with interventionist	Group 4 with teacher Group 1 with interventionist

Figure 8.5: One-day schedule excerpt for grades K–4 (partial day).

Monday	7:45–10:35 a.m.	10:35–10:55 a.m.	10:55–11:35 a.m.	11:35 a.m.–12:05 p.m.	12:05–12:45 p.m.	12:45–2:00 p.m.	2:00–2:45 p.m.
Content Area	English language arts	Mathematics	Lunch and recess	Science and social studies	Specials areas (music, visual arts, physical education)	Mathematics	Intervention
Daily Lessons	Word study (fifteen to twenty minutes) Launch lesson (twenty minutes) Guided reading (sixty to ninety minutes) Writing (forty minutes)	Mathematics fluency (twenty minutes)		Focus on most-essential standards	Performance tasks instruction	Launch lesson (twenty-five minutes) Small-group instruction (forty minutes) Cognitive closure (ten minutes)	Tier 3 program Pause to implement an intervention for the data-driven response to a common formative assessment

Figure 8.6: One-day schedule for a single grade.

Table 8.4: Resources and Personnel of Tiered Interventions

Tier	Time	Assessments Utilized	Students	Organization of Educators	Curricular Resources
Tier 1 (Core)	During the content-area block of time	Checks for understanding and exit tickets	All students (Each day, they receive Tier 1 instruction that includes small groups.)	Teacher of record	Core curriculum, standardized for all students
Tier 2 (Core plus more)	During a flexible time or day	Common formative assessments	Students who have not mastered the common formative assessment learning targets or standards	Grade-level or content-area collaborative teacher team	Reteaching with scaffolding, differentiation, and reconceptualization of Tier 1 resources
Tier 3 (Core plus more plus more)	Scheduled and consistent time based on the resource used	Summative assessments, such as benchmark and state or provincial assessments	Students who are not on grade or course level and need remediation	All hands on deck, which includes: • Grade-level or content-area collaborative teacher team • Interventionists • Educational assistants • Site administration	Resources specifically for remediation

Not only do collaborative teams need to work with leadership to support organizing the master schedule to support Tier 3 intervention, but collaborative teams also need to decide what to do during intervention time; this is key to moving students out of remediation. Table 8.5 shows an example of how a school or collaborative team can go about this.

Table 8.5: Deciding How to Spend Tier 3 Intervention Time

Step	Considerations
Triangulate data for the bottom two quartiles of students.	**Data needed:** Determine all the data points teams can use to make triangulated decisions. Some examples are state or provincial assessments, benchmark assessments, reading assessments, common formative assessments, and Lexile levels. **Questions to ask:** Are there discrepancies in the data? Are students proficient in some areas and not others? What do the data tell us? Which students need additional screeners to diagnose areas of need? How might we organize the data in one spreadsheet?
Give additional diagnostic screeners.	**Questions to ask:** Which students take the screeners? What are the cutoff scores for our work? **Actions:** Add the data to the spreadsheet for collaborative decision making.
Have a team dialogue to get to know students' needs student by student, skill by skill.	**Actions:** Discuss the needs of like groups, and for each group, identify the two to three skills that the students within the grouping need.
As a collaborative team, select resources to support the intervention.	**Considerations:** Fidelity to the identified skills and needs is imperative. The resources identified must fit the needs and the skills. Consider that each student group needs support with multiple skills, and then find the resources that can help with those skills.
As a collaborative team, make a flexible grouping and assessment plan.	**Actions:** Biweekly, discuss needed grouping changes. Teachers may use formative observational data to recommend changes in grouping; formative data should be presented to the collaborative team for discussion. Reassess needs regularly. Select the assessment your team will use to monitor progress based on skill needs. Teams should select a two- to four-week cycle and determine dates when they will commit to reassessing student proficiency.

continued →

Step	Considerations
Consider administrative topics.	**Questions to ask:** Can the learning or leadership team provide additional staff for intervention time to make smaller groups? Does the schedule need to be modified across grade levels to stagger this time so that the extra staff can effectively support the grade levels that have the most students in need of intervention? Given that collaborative team meetings should engage and empower all individuals on the team, do the school and team norms allow each teacher to have a voice in this work?
Consider Tier 3 program placements.	**Actions:** Once the placement test is executed, administer mastery tests until students fail. • If the students show mastery, continue with mastery tests until you find the students' specific struggle point or misconception. Begin lessons there. • If a student intervention group is continuing from the previous year, give the mastery test from the last lesson taught. If the students show mastery, continue with mastery tests until you find the students' specific point of need. Begin lessons there. • If a student intervention group is continuing from the previous year, even though it may not be advised by the evidence-based Tier 3 program being implemented, administer the placement test again to see if the students can advance to the next level.
Ponder how the group's practices can help improve student learning.	**Questions to ask:** Ask the following questions as a team. • How frequently is the group meeting? Groups should be meeting four days a week at a minimum. Cancellation should not be an option. • How long is your group time? Tier 3 intervention is program dependent, but group time should be forty to sixty minutes in order to teach the lessons fully and to build on the skills practices to implement them in one sitting for best results. • Are you monitoring progress and tracking student data? Keep staff accountable for assessing students and tracking the student data. • Are you following the program with fidelity? Are you cutting out portions of the lessons to speed the lessons along? This does not mean you cannot move past lessons the students quickly show mastery in. It is not advised to hold students back in order to go lesson by lesson. • Who is the point person to ensure accountability for other teachers? How do your team and leadership check in with this person on lesson progress, lesson pacing and timing, mastery tests, data sheets, and so on? Having consistency in your conversation supports program implementation.

Where to Find More Tier 2 and Tier 3 Time

Finding more time in the schedule is hard to do, as all content is scheduled bell to bell. Although many who create master schedules start with the specials areas or related arts to create the collaborative team times, another effective practice is to schedule all Tier 1 instruction first. Once the master schedule accounts for all Tier 1 instruction, leadership teams work with teacher teams to input specials areas or related arts or electives as well as lunch and recess. Teams can utilize any remaining available time for intervention. However, with state or provincial and local requirements for time allotments per content area, many schools find no extra time available.

The following are some other examples of where to create time.

- Time before and after school, as long as this is not the only intervention, because not all students may be able to stay at school beyond school hours

- Flex time during nontested areas as needed; however, ensure instruction in those nontested contents still occurs on the most-essential standards

- Center time or time during small-group instruction rotations as long as all students still get Tier 1 instruction with time in a small group with the teacher

- Electives or reading and mathematics labs for secondary students

Finding time for a complete intervention system that allows for all three tiers of intervention is important to support student learning. With possible academic gaps occurring not only during in-person learning but also from distance learning, it is even more imperative a strategic and systematic approach to time is needed. When student learning is required, collaborative teams of staff can find the time to ensure all three tiers of intervention occur for every student who is in need.

Conclusion

Moving students not only out of the bottom quartile but also to proficiency is important in priority schools. This, many times, means interventions must accelerate the learning of remediation content and necessary prerequisite skills to grade- or course-level standards. Moving from a flooded pyramid to a more balanced intervention pyramid is no easy task. It takes all hands on deck for a long period of time. This process does not escape the continuous improvement cycle, which consists of looking at how the process is working and, if it's not working at the level desired, making changes to get better results.

Reorganizing their master schedules and time allocations can help schools ensure that the majority of instructional time is part of Tier 1 and that there is a solid system of intervention for those students needing both Tier 1 and Tier 2 and those needing all three tiers. Any school can replicate the approaches to intervention time present in this chapter, as these strategies take resources teacher teams already have access to and make them work within a system of support for student learning. As Buffum and Mattos (2015) state:

> There are three foundational elements supporting the pyramid to help combat these lower standards and ensure all students learn at high levels—(1) collective capacity and efficacy building, (2) vertical anchors, and (3) baseline supporters—as well as the glue holding all three tiers together. (p. 138)

Building students' and teachers' capacity and efficacy will help ensure the entire system of support stays fundamentally in place and allow the vertical anchors and baseline supporters to, in essence, do the job the system needs. Schools should also schedule celebrations of small academic wins as well as lessons learned and progress toward goals for all students. Celebrating progress, whether through the implementation of new processes or through academic gains, will help a strong, reliable system of intervention support all students.

References and Resources

Buffum, A., & Mattos, M. (Eds.). (2015). *It's about time: Planning interventions and extensions in elementary school.* Bloomington, IN: Solution Tree Press.

Buffum, A., Mattos, M., & Malone, J. (2018). *Taking action: A handbook for RTI at Work.* Bloomington, IN: Solution Tree Press.

Craig, J., & Mack, J. (2019, Summer). High schools can win, too! *AllThingsPLC Magazine,* 29–32.

DuFour, R., DuFour, R., Eaker, R., Many, T. W., & Mattos, M. (2016). *Learning by doing: A handbook for Professional Learning Communities at Work* (3rd ed.). Bloomington, IN: Solution Tree Press.

Eaker, R. (2018, Fall). First thing: The divine right to muddle through. *AllThingsPLC Magazine,* 4–5.

Goldberg, P. (2017, Spring). Giving students what they need when they need it. *AllThingsPLC Magazine,* 22–28.

Gregory, G., Kaufeldt, M., & Mattos, M. (2016a). *Best practices at Tier 1: Daily differentiation for effective instruction, elementary.* Bloomington, IN: Solution Tree Press.

Gregory, G., Kaufeldt, M., & Mattos, M. (2016b). *Best practices at Tier 1: Daily differentiation for effective instruction, secondary.* Bloomington, IN: Solution Tree Press.

Hattie, J. (2009). *Visible learning: A synthesis of over 800 meta-analyses relating to achievement.* New York: Routledge.

Hattie, J. (2012). *Visible learning for teachers: Maximizing impact on learning.* New York: Routledge.

Kramer, S. V. (2015). *How to leverage PLCs for school improvement.* Bloomington, IN: Solution Tree Press.

Kramer, S. V., & Schuhl, S. (2017). *School improvement for all: A how-to guide for doing the right work.* Bloomington, IN: Solution Tree Press.

Mattos, M. (2016, November 2). *Connecting PLCs and RTI* [Blog post]. Accessed at www
.allthingsplc.info/blog/view/335/connecting-plcs-and-rti on September 28, 2020.

Reason, C. (2018, Fall). When you say everyone, do you mean everyone? How a culture of
"every" makes every bit of difference. *AllThingsPLC Magazine*, 37–41.

Sonju, B., Kramer, S. V., Mattos, M., & Buffum, A. (2019). *Best practices at Tier 2:
Supplemental interventions for additional student support, secondary.* Bloomington, IN:
Solution Tree Press.

 **Michael Roberts** is an author and consultant with over two decades of experience in education. He has been an administrator at the district level and has served as an on-site administrator at the high school, middle school, and elementary school levels.

Prior to becoming the director of elementary curriculum and instruction at the Scottsdale Unified School District in Scottsdale, Arizona, Michael was the principal of Desert View Elementary School (DVES) in Hermiston, Oregon. Under his leadership, DVES produced evidence of increased learning for all students each year from 2013 to 2017, and it met the challenges of 40 percent growth over four years, a rising population of English learners, and a dramatic increase in the number of trauma-affected students.

Michael served as an assistant principal in Prosser, Washington, where he was named the Washington Association of School Administrators' 2010–2011 Assistant Principal of the Year for the Three Rivers region. In 2011–2012, he was a finalist for Washington State's Assistant Principal of the Year. He is the author of *Enriching the Learning: Meaningful Extensions for Proficient Students in a PLC at Work* and *Shifting From Me to We: How to Jump-Start Collaboration in a PLC at Work*.

Michael earned his bachelor's degree in elementary education from Washington State University and his master's degree in educational leadership from Azusa Pacific University.

To learn more about Michael's work, visit https://everykidnow.com or follow @everykidnow on Twitter or Instagram.

To book Michael Roberts for professional development, contact pd@SolutionTree.com.

Making Proficient Students a Priority

Michael Roberts

> Teams must also serve students who are ready
> to learn and in need of extensions. This is a
> large task and the stakes are high. By working
> together in a culture of accountability, however,
> teacher teams can meet these demands.
>
> —*Sharon V. Kramer and Sarah Schuhl*

Look closely at any classroom in any priority school, and you are likely to see a scenario like the following. The issue in the classroom is clear. There are twenty-five students. Twenty of those students perform below the proficient level on assessments. Eleven of those twenty have serious prerequisite skill gaps. These students are reading at least two grade levels below where they should be, and they have serious gaps in their fundamental mathematics skills. For the teacher, it seems as though all twenty-five students have serious behavioral issues that prevent her executing any lesson the way she plans. It is a very frustrating situation. The principal has added to the teacher's stress by informing the staff the state has, once again, identified the school as being in the bottom 5 percent of all the schools in the state. If things do not change immediately, the state might step in. In the mind of a teacher, the state might as well be saying the school will be quarantined and its teachers required to wear signs in public that say, "I failed my students."

But the teachers in this school work hard. They care about the students in their charge. The teacher in this particular classroom arrives every day thirty to forty-five minutes before she is contractually required to do so. She stays an extra hour or two every day after the students leave. She comes in on Saturdays, Sundays, and holidays. She wants very much for all her students to be successful. It is obvious that she is working very hard to ensure that all her students learn at high levels. She loses sleep trying to come up with new ways to help her students. She reads articles and listens to podcasts about social-emotional learning. She has used all the tricks she has learned over her extended career to help these students. But, in spite of all her work, nothing seems to be working.

The students who are behind take up almost all the space in her mind. But in truth, a big key to turning things around largely rests where she is not looking: the five proficient students; the green students. Systematically planning extensions for these students will change the paradigm for the class and the teacher.

In *Learning by Doing*, Rick DuFour, Rebecca DuFour, Robert Eaker, Thomas Many, and Mike Mattos (2016) lay out four critical questions for collaborative teams to answer effectively. (See page 3.) Over the years, I have supported the work of many schools, including priority schools. When I ask the teachers I work with which question they have the hardest time answering, the vast majority point to critical question 4 (DuFour et al., 2016): How will we extend learning for students who are already proficient? It's incumbent on collaborative teams to confront why this is the question that befuddles teachers the most. Further, if team members are unable to answer this question, what is happening to these students who will benefit from extension?

Often, a lack of resources blocks the road to teams' establishing effective extensions and clearly understanding the benefits of extending students' learning in a systematic, meaningful way. Also, if they are totally honest, teachers in priority schools feel pressure to focus their thoughts, planning, and time on the students who are not on grade level. Students who regularly attain proficiency are simply not a priority in a priority school.

Schools identified as being unsuccessful cannot afford to lose any students, especially those students who are some of the most successful on campus. By not intentionally planning for students whom critical question 4 is designed to serve, collaborative teams and the teachers who compose those teams unintentionally shortchange their school and their students. By planning to extend student learning, teachers communicate to students that high levels of learning will be rewarded, teachers raise their own expectations for students, and the students get excited to learn more, which often results in decreased negative behavior (Gregory, Kaufeldt, & Mattos, 2016). Just as important, it is often true that when you raise the bar for some students, you raise the bar for *all* students (Gregory et al., 2016).

In this chapter, I explore how collaborative teams in priority schools can develop effective extensions for proficient students. This chapter focuses on what it means to make these green (proficient) students visible, why doing so is important, and how to make it happen. The process I detail is the kind of approach that is often expected at affluent schools, where more students show up prepared, well fed, and with most of their needs fulfilled outside of school. This work is a different challenge in priority schools, where the second and third intervention tiers covered in chapter 8 (page 171) are flooded with 60, 70, or 80 percent of students in need of additional time and targeted support. As a result, green (proficient) students are often left waiting for their peers to catch up rather than continuing to learn. The process in this chapter will help teams break this cycle. To conclude the chapter, I follow up with a look at how teams can establish extension standards to further support proficient students' learning. It is important to note that the processes in this chapter don't change based on the mode of instruction. Whether students receive their extensions in person or remotely, the process is the same.

Making Green Students Visible

In an effort to make student data easier to consume and understand, schools often color-code students. As teams place proficient students in a team-created shared document (such as a shared Google Doc or Microsoft Word document), teams often highlight them in green (see the examples in chapter 7, page 154). Some schools prefer physical cards, with a student's picture and the scores from district benchmarks and state assessment printed boldly on them. These cards are then placed in pocket charts. If a student achieves a proficient or above score here, he or she then is defined by the tell-tale green border or highlighter used to show at a glance this child is now a "given" when it comes to a team determining which students are or aren't gaining proficiency with essential standards. Both of these processes are fine, but teachers tend to focus on students in the yellow and red categories, which represent students who are operating at slightly below grade level or are in need of serious remediation in prerequisite skills. These students need support and supportive instruction, but teams must not forget about students they place in the green category. Instead, they must systematically plan to extend the learning of these students.

Schools and districts ignore proficient students at great risk to those students' future learning. By not extending students who are demonstrating proficiency, teams can unwittingly contribute to a student developing a fixed mindset when it comes to his or her own cognitive abilities. In *Mindset*, Carol Dweck (2016) explains that a *fixed mindset* makes one see everything as finite. In students' case, having a fixed mindset makes them see their ability to be successful as having a limit, which they will one day reach and then cease to grow any further. Teachers can easily identify students with a fixed mindset by listening to how students talk about themselves. Fixed-mindset students say things like, "I used to be smart," or "I am not good at mathematics anymore." When students make statements like these, they are really saying, "I once was regularly proficient, but not any longer."

Some students reach these conclusions on their own, but they can also draw these ideas from the unintentional actions of the adults around them. For example, if a student shows up to kindergarten well prepared by his or her parents, having run through basic mathematics flash cards every morning and been read to for thirty minutes every night, the student may receive extra free time while peers receive more foundational mathematics and reading support. In some cases, the prepared student becomes an ad hoc student aide, attempting to support peers who are not yet proficient. But, when instruction becomes more rigorous, the well-prepared student may not be ready to productively struggle with a standard. It doesn't matter if the student reaches that point in second grade or their junior year of high school. When the extra free time becomes intervention time at a kidney table with a small group in primary grades, or the *A* at the top of the paper becomes a *D* in a student's first advanced-placement class, a student who has not been effectively challenged by extensions may feel the end of his or her intellectual abilities has arrived.

According to Kathryn S. Davis and David R. Dupper (2004), students who are regularly proficient yet not extended sometimes begin to have resentment toward teachers because they feel as though they are being ignored or even disrespected. Carol Ann Tomilson and Susan D. Allan (2000) point out that when differentiation in the classroom does not take place, students become uncommitted to developing their learning at a deeper level. This research is echoed in John Hattie's (2017) findings that teacher credibility and student-teacher relationships can greatly change the way a student learns and behaves in class. For example, when a student is no longer committed to learning, there is often an emergence of negative student behaviors. These negative behaviors can range from quiet off-task behavior to outright defiance. When regularly proficient students begin exhibiting negative behaviors, it can especially disconcert a teacher and signal to the rest of the class that "even the smart kids do not care."

However, by intentionally planning to address the needs of students who will benefit from extension, collaborative teams can mitigate or even prevent these behaviors. In the article "Differentiation Does, in Fact, Work," Carol Ann Tomlinson (2015) lays out evidence that, when teams plan extensions for proficient students *before* planning interventions, not only are the interventions more effective but staff's expectations of student learning increase. Tomlinson's (2015) work provides a compelling reason for collaborative teams to build meaningful extensions for these students in spite of a team feeling that only a handful of students will be proficient. When teams build extensions, students have their learning supported, teachers head off any negative behaviors that may arise, and all students benefit from these higher adult expectations and more thoughtful interventions.

In the following sections, I look more closely at the data supporting these conclusions, relate a real-world example of how extensions benefit all students, and conclude by showing how valuing data keeps green students visible.

Extensions and Effect Size

John Hattie's (2009, 2017) research supports Tomlinson's (2015) assertion that planning extensions before interventions better supports both efforts. In *Visible Learning Plus*, Hattie (2017) lists more than 250 influences that affect student learning; many of the highest-impact influences align directly with teachers' planning meaningful extensions for students and raising their vision of what their students can accomplish. *Effect size*, in this case, refers to the measurable differences in learning when teams adopt a new learning initiative or practice, as compared to teams' not making any changes at all. According to Hattie's (2009) research, the average student should grow 0.40 of a standard deviation each year. In other words, teachers can expect students to learn a full year of content during a single school year. A student's socioeconomic status carries a 0.52 effect size (Hattie, 2017), meaning that students who come from wealthier and more privileged backgrounds are often more prepared for school or, as they age, travel more, and have a wider range of experiences that can build their interests in learning. This sets students of poverty at a distinct disadvantage to their more affluent peers. However, poverty does not define students.

A student's living conditions determine how well he or she lives outside the school building, not how much that student can learn *in* school. Students can overcome poverty's detrimental effects on learning through a variety of factors that are firmly within the collaborative team's and individual teacher's control (Jensen, 2019). For example, collective teacher efficacy, which is when all teachers believe they can positively affect all students, carries a 1.57 effect size (Hattie, 2017). When teachers simply believe and act with the knowledge that they are the most powerful variable in students' learning experience, they can redefine the levels at which students learn and help students become academically successful. According to Tomlinson (2015), a key factor in this redefining process is the planning of extensions. When collaborative teams regularly plan extensions, team members increase their estimates of what the students can achieve, and teacher estimates of student achievement carry a 1.29 effect size (Hattie, 2017).

Ultimately, collective teacher efficacy is roughly three times more powerful than the detrimental effects of poverty (Hattie, 2017). Teachers' estimates of achievement can affect a student two and a half times more than poverty, and student effort is approximately one and a half times more powerful than poverty (Hattie, 2017). By building efficacy, raising staff expectations for students, and providing engaging lessons for all students that lead to more student effort, students will learn at a quicker pace, and more students will be successful.

The Effect of Team-Driven Extensions

Once teams start taking advantage of collective efficacy by working collaboratively, and they have a higher estimate of what the students can accomplish, the whole paradigm of a school begins to change. In 2019, I began working with Gibbs PreK Center in Huntsville, Texas, a school consisting entirely of three- and four-year-old students. Staff were struggling to mitigate negative student behaviors to the point that those behaviors, rather than learning, had become the school's focus. This misplaced focus dropped the staff's collective efficacy and their expectations of what students could learn.

In September of that year, I supported the teachers and administration as they began working on changing the focus of the school and determining what all students needed to learn and how teams would assess those essential standards. In effect, they focused on answers to the first two critical questions of a PLC (DuFour et al., 2016). The school leadership team, with input from its teacher teams, selected the essential learning and skills all students would acquire. Team members used the tool depicted in figure 9.1 (page 194) to facilitate these conversations.

The leadership team, again with support from the teacher teams, further agreed that teachers would place assessments for this essential learning and skill development in notebooks for the students. The leadership team members then trained the rest of the staff, including long-term substitute teachers and alternatively certified staff, on how to effectively implement the notebooks. This included providing team members with a tracking sheet, similar to the one pictured in figure 9.2 (page 195), that teachers would use to track each student, skill by skill. (See page 204 for a reproducible version of this figure.) Dark gray shading indicates red color-coding, medium gray indicates yellow, and light gray indicates green.

Subject: _____   Grade level: _____

1. What essential knowledge and skills should students in this subject and grade learn?

2. What essential knowledge and skills should students in this subject in the previous grade learn to be successful in this grade?

Source: Kramer & Schuhl, 2017, p. 59.

Figure 9.1: Tool to determine essential knowledge and skills.

*Visit **go.SolutionTree.com/PLCbooks** for a free reproducible version of this figure.*

		Essential Standards								
Student Name	Teacher Name	Standard or Outcome: Letter Recognition	Target 1	Target 2	Target 3	Running Record	Standard or Outcome: Letter Construction	Target 1	Target 2	Target 3	Running Record
Burrell	Jones										
Halladay	Thomas										
Howard	Thomas										
Lee	Cruz										
Lidge	Jones										
Madson	Cruz										
Meyers	Jones										
Rollins	Thomas										
Utley	Cruz										
Victorino	Thomas										
Werth	Jones										

Figure 9.2: Skill tracker with color-coding.

Students each received a notebook with essential standards and assessments with the understanding that, as they received instruction from teachers, they were in charge of monitoring their own learning. Even in early childhood, schools can develop students' self-efficacy and monitoring skills, and teachers and students can have discussions together about academic and social-emotional successes and challenges (Kerr, Hulen, Heller, & Butler, 2021).

Teacher teams regularly assessed students as they reached proficiency with standards, and students marked the standards in which they had become proficient in their notebooks. Students who struggled with assessments received additional time and support because, in a PLC culture, all students learning means *all*. What the school as a whole was not prepared for was how the students would take to the notebooks and how much the notebooks would motivate students. When students gained proficiency on a standard, they asked for "the next thing." Teachers could not forget about the green students because the students were always reminding their teachers they were ready to learn more. As a result, the teacher teams found they needed to create extensions for these students in the same manner they were creating interventions for the students who were not yet proficient.

According to Jessie Anderson, principal of the Gibbs PreK Center, almost all negative behaviors disappeared, which helped maximize learning time (personal communication, March 3, 2020). As a result, a large percentage of students demonstrated mastery over the essential standards by January of that year, and staff had to quickly get back together to organize their important-to-know and nice-to-know standards to extend learning. The room to teach to these supporting standards exploded the number of successful students who felt enthusiastic about their learning.

Prior to the adoption of this approach, this Gibbs PreK Center typically produced three to six emerging readers a year out of a student body of around 350. By January of the same school year, the school had twelve emerging readers and was expecting another thirty by the end of the school year, a 700 percent increase (J. Anderson, personal communication, March 3, 2020).

The takeaway of this story is it does not matter if the students you serve are in preK, elementary, middle, or high school; this is a universal approach to learning. Collaborative teams must be very clear on what is essential for students to know and how they will assess that learning. Leadership teams need to provide these teams with the additional time and support they need to support students who are not yet proficient. There must also be a schoolwide willingness to come together and dig into nonessential standards to keep the proficient students' learning moving forward.

Imagine the valuable learning time lost if, instead of extending learning, proficient students at Gibbs PreK Center became teacher aides or had to wait until their peers caught up. This approach not only diminishes the enthusiasm of students for mastering essential standards but also eliminates the urgency for students to do so. If students are going just wait academically for the rest of the class, there is no incentive for students to master essential content quickly. Further, without this focal point and the successful use of student notebooks, the negative classroom behaviors would surely have returned because the proficient students would have had nothing meaningful to do.

The Value of Data

When collaborative teams plan extensions for proficient students, even though there may only be a few students who are demonstrating proficiency in the beginning, all students benefit. When those students in the green column remain featured in collaborative teams' data discussions and visible to the staff, all students benefit from higher expectations from the teachers and put forth more effort, raising the bar for all students (Tomlinson, 2015). Success in this endeavor, of course, relies on reliable data.

Unfortunately, the data proficient students produce often keep them in the shadows. That is because, in priority schools, *data* are often looked at as a four-letter word. Often, leaders try to spin the data, and collaborative teams ignore them. This happens for a very specific reason: the data are usually negative. Educators are working hard, and they care about the students they support. But in spite of the educators' best efforts, the students are not getting the results the teachers crave. I have been a long-term coach in many priority schools from California to Arkansas, and once these sites receive the *priority school* or *underachieving school* label, staff tend to shy away from discussing data in any meaningful way.

The important thing to know about even bad data is that there are always good results mixed in. In *Good to Great*, Jim Collins (2001) writes that a successful organization must face brutal facts. Priority schools see their data as one big lump of brutal. However, collaborative teams must understand the messages within the data so that they can focus on what is going well. They should ask, "Which practices are working best for the students we serve?"

According to Mark Weichel, Blane McCann, and Tami Williams (2018), authors of *When They Already Know It*, teachers sometimes develop a bias against the low-performing school they work in, a school where years of low scores have trained staff not to expect too much from the students attending the school. Once this occurs, staff will not expect a student who attends a failing school to need systematic extensions. This is why it is imperative that teams look at the data, because the data will tell a different story. Even in a school that resides on a given state's double-secret probation list, there are pockets of proficiency and, as chapter 2 (page 31) explains, pockets of *near* proficiency. Students who reside in these pockets deserve to have their teachers advance their learning, and collaborative teams need to understand what *is* working that helped support these students to or near proficiency. In turn, recognizing there are students who are becoming proficient will help bolster the staff morale and keep them from being overwhelmed by their current status.

Chip Heath and Dan Heath (2008) explore why some ideas in business stick around and become part of an organization's DNA while other ideas simply drift away. In *Made to Stick* (Heath & Heath, 2008), the brothers coin the acronym SUCCESs to sum up their finding that ideas must be *simple, unexpected, concrete, credible, emotional,* and attached to a *story* to become ingrained in any organization. In a school setting, an idea that needs to become sticky is teachers' using specific student data instead of broad definitions—such as, "Our students come from poverty"—to define student needs. Teachers in priority schools can always find simple and unexpected examples of students' beating the odds and becoming proficient readers or excellent mathematicians. The data these students produce are both concrete and credible, and teachers need to bring these examples to their team meetings. When teachers attach students' faces and stories to the data, these students' stories can become very emotional. Most teachers began their careers with the goal of changing students' lives for the better. In reflecting as a team on the work that helps proficient students succeed and extending those successful practices to help more students, the team can see they are literally living their dream. In short, proficient students are the personification of the SUCCESs acronym.

Through systematically building extensions and studying the data proficient students produce, collaborative teams raise their expectations for all students' success, increase the number of students in the green, and keep all the green students visible during their planning and discussions of what practices work best.

Establishing Extension Standards

In 2019, I worked with a first-grade team in Texas. The team members were discussing their students' data. When I asked about what their next steps would be for the students, I was met with silence. I pushed a little further and asked how the team was extending students who have achieved proficiency. Only one of the teachers responded. She said she uses her proficient students to teach the students who are not proficient in basic reading skills. She went on to explain this supported the goals of both extension and intervention.

This sort of plan is very common in priority schools. But this setup is not a meaningful extension, nor is it a strong intervention. This team, like many other teams I have worked with, had attempted to answer the first two critical questions of a PLC but had not answered the third and fourth critical questions in a systematic way.

I tell this story not to make light of the hard work of caring teachers but to highlight that an ad hoc approach to student aid is often the best idea many teachers come up with for proficient students. In spite of their best intentions, this is not an extension. Some educators will argue that if students can teach something, they truly understand it. It is true that evaluating, analyzing, and applying are all part of teaching, and they all represent higher-level-thinking levels in Bloom's taxonomy revised (Anderson & Krathwohl, 2001). However, very few students are trained to analyze other students' errors and evaluate the best way to correct those errors, especially when the students in question are still in early childhood grades (preK–2).

Often, these student-to-student sessions break down into the proficient student taking a book from the other student and saying, "I'll just read it." Or, if it is in mathematics, the proficient student who is meant to be helping the nonproficient student gets frustrated and says, "Write down seven; the answer is seven."

I have worked with well-meaning teachers in and out of priority schools who say, "Students like helping other students," and that is often true. But these proficient students are often not advancing their own learning during this time. At best, the proficient student is simply staying busy and perhaps cementing existing learning. At worst, not only is the proficient student not acquiring any new learning, but a wedge is also developing between students deemed to be smart enough to be aids and students deemed to be not smart and in need of help.

To create meaningful extensions in a systematic way, teams need to look in the same place their essential standards came from: their state or provincial standards. Teams can follow the recommendation of Gayle Gregory and colleagues (2016) in *Best Practices at Tier 1, Elementary* and sort their standards into the following groups:

- Essential to know and do
- Important to know and do
- Worth being familiar with
- Nice to know (p. 79)

Teams build their essential standards around the essential-to-know-and-do and important-to-know-and-do groups and guarantee that all students receive the time and support to ensure success with these essential standards. Students who attain proficiency on the essential standards can then receive extensions around the important-to-know, worth-being-familiar-with, and nice-to-know groups. Teams should refer to these standards as *extension standards*; these provide team members with a logical, standards-based progression to advance students' learning.

When teams create these extensions, they need to make sure that proficient students see their extensions as different and interesting work, not more work. If students see their extensions as more work, they will not fully engage in them. To avoid this, teams should use extension standards to accomplish the following.

- **Develop unique skills:** A *skill extension* involves supporting proficient students as they work on skills that are new or that they rarely use. For example, as part of a standards-based extension, charge students with writing a play, constructing blueprints for a model, or planning for and executing a debate.

- **Engage proficient students in an area of high interest:** In an *interest extension*, teachers focus on an area of high student interest as a vehicle for students to access an extension standard. For example, a teacher might ask extension students to understand fraction-decimal equivalents through baseball batting averages. Or a teacher might ask elementary students to extend their ability to compare and contrast two characters by comparing portrayals of Pegasus in classic Greek myths to the portrayals of Pegasus in My Little Pony. A middle or high school teacher might show students scenes from the two *Clash of the Titans* movies and ask the extension students to develop a similar comparison.

- **Build social connections:** The focus of a social extension is for proficient students to build stronger social skills as they explore extension standards. This type of extension is most effective when there is a small group of proficient students who, for whatever reason, do not connect with their peers. A *social extension* example could involve students' working together to construct a joint multimedia presentation on how to best find areas and perimeters of various polygons. Students could also work together to write a Lincoln–Douglas debate between the protagonist and the antagonist of a given story.

Developing unique skills, engaging students' interests, and building social extensions provide enough differentiation for students to be willing to engage in the extensions by providing the students with different work, not more work. If students perceive extensions as more of the same—for example, ten more mathematics problems or writing an extra two paragraphs—they will not be inclined to do the extension.

Figure 9.3 shows a template teams can use when planning extensions for their students. (See page 205 for a reproducible version of this template.) The tool begins, like everything the teams should be looking at, with the essential standard all students must master. Then teams identify starting and ending dates for the extension as well as the type of extension they will employ and which staff member will deliver the extension. Teams should then agree on which extension standards they will cover and identify by name students who will be participating in the extension and how the team will assess those students' near learning.

Conclusion

Students maintain their enthusiasm for learning when collaborative team members, be they on a high school team or a first-grade team, work together to establish both essential standards and a plan for where students will go in their learning progression once they master essential standards. If students are enthusiastic about learning, it is very easy for staff to expect a lot from them. In a priority school, having that adult expectation can be one of the most powerful things a teacher can do for his or her students. Students in a priority school are not predisposed to learn less; they may simply need more intentional supports. In a keynote presentation at the Solution Tree Summit on PLC at Work, Anthony Muhammad (2020) summed up that idea this way: "Free and reduced lunch tells you how [students] will pay for lunch, not how much they can learn."

The benefits that accrue, for both individual students and the school as a whole, are such that it is imperative that teachers on collaborative teams systematically and meaningfully extend proficient students in priority schools. When proficient students are extended in their learning, no matter how few they number at the beginning, the whole paradigm of adult expectations and student results shifts to the positive.

Essential standard: 3.OA.A.1—Interpret products of whole numbers, e.g., interpret 5 × 7 as the total number of objects in 5 groups of 7 objects each. For example, describe a context in which a total number of objects can be expressed as 5 × 7.

Date to begin extension: November 1, 2019

Date to conclude extension: November 15, 2019

Type of extension: Interest

Team member delivering extension: Smalls

Extension Standards	Extension Students	Formative Assessments During Extension
3.OA.A.3—Use multiplication and division within 100 to solve word problems in situations involving equal groups, arrays, and measurement quantities, e.g., by using drawings and equations with a symbol for the unknown number to represent the problem.	Charles, Rob, Arjun, Jon, Penny, Sofia, Camila, Timmy, Kavya, Carlos, Tristan, Stefani, Tatum, Mikhail, Jean-Paul, Glenn, Juan V., Scott, Amanda, Martha, Geoffrey, Isabella, Eddie, Pamela	Group-created story Individual solutions provided to peers' stories
3.OA.A.4—Determine the unknown whole number in a multiplication or division equation relating three whole numbers. *For example, determine the unknown number that makes the equation true in each of the equations* $8 \times ? = 48$, $5 = $ _____ $\div 3$, $6 \times 6 = ?$		Group-created story Individual solutions provided to peers' stories

Source for standard: NGA & CCSSO, 2010b.

Source: Roberts, 2019, pp. 66–67.

Figure 9.3: Example filled-in extension planning template.

References and Resources

Anderson, L. W., & Krathwohl, D. R. (Eds.). (2001). *A taxonomy for learning, teaching, and assessing: A revision of Bloom's taxonomy of educational objectives.* Boston: Allyn & Bacon.

Collins, J. (2001). *Good to great: Why some companies make the leap . . . and others don't.* New York: HarperCollins.

Davis, K. S., & Dupper, D. R. (2004). Student-teacher relationships: An overlooked factor in school dropout. *Journal of Human Behavior in the Social Environment, 9*(1–2), 179–193.

DuFour, R., DuFour, R., Eaker, R., Many, T. W., & Mattos, M. (2016). *Learning by doing: A handbook for Professional Learning Communities at Work* (3rd ed.). Bloomington, IN: Solution Tree Press.

Dweck, C. (2016). *Mindset: The new psychology of success* (Updated ed.). New York: Random House.

Gregory, G., Kaufeldt, M., & Mattos, M. (2016). *Best practices at Tier 1: Daily differentiation for effective instruction, elementary.* Bloomington, IN: Solution Tree Press.

Hattie, J. (2009). *Visible learning: A synthesis of over 800 meta-analyses relating to achievement.* New York: Routledge.

Hattie, J. (2017). *Visible learning plus: 250+ influences on student achievement.* Accessed at https://visible-learning.org/wp-content/uploads/2018/03/VLPLUS-252-Influences-Hattie -ranking-DEC-2017.pdf on January 29, 2020.

Heath, C., & Heath, D. (2008). *Made to stick: Why some ideas survive and others die.* New York: Random House.

Kaplinsky, R. (2015, February 4). *Depth of Knowledge matrix: Elementary and secondary math* [Blog post]. Accessed at https://robertkaplinsky.com/tool-to-distinguish-between-depth-of -knowledge-levels on October 8, 2020.

Jensen, E. (2019). *Poor students, rich teaching: Seven high-impact mindsets for students from poverty* (Rev. ed.). Bloomington, IN: Solution Tree Press.

Kerr, D., Hulen, T. A., Heller, J., & Butler, B. K. (2021). *What about us? The PLC at Work process for grades preK–2 teams.* Bloomington, IN: Solution Tree Press.

Kramer, S. V., & Schuhl, S. (2017). *School improvement for all: A how-to guide for doing the right work.* Bloomington, IN: Solution Tree Press.

Muhammad, A. (2020). *Moving beyond PLC lite: Nurturing full commitment to the PLC process.* Paper presented at the Solution Tree Summit on PLC at Work, Phoenix, AZ.

National Governors Association Center for Best Practices & Council of Chief State School Officers. (2010a). *Common Core State Standards for English language arts and literacy in history/social studies, science, and technical subjects.* Washington, DC: Authors. Accessed at www.corestandards.org/assets/CCSSI_ELA%20Standards.pdf on October 1, 2020.

National Governors Association Center for Best Practices & Council of Chief State School Officers. (2010b). *Common Core State Standards for mathematics*. Washington, DC: Authors. Accessed at www.corestandards.org/assets/CCSSI_Math%20Standards.pdf on August 6, 2020.

Roberts, M. (2019). *Enriching the learning: Meaningful extensions for proficient students in a PLC at Work*. Bloomington, IN: Solution Tree Press.

Tomlinson, C. A. (2015, January 27). Differentiation does, in fact, work. *Education Week*. Accessed at www.edweek.org/ew/articles/2015/01/28/differentiation-does-in-fact-work.html on September 28, 2020.

Tomlinson, C. A., & Allan, S. D. (2000). *Leadership for differentiating schools and classrooms*. Alexandria, VA: Association for Supervision and Curriculum Development.

Weichel, M., McCann, B., & Williams, T. (2018). *When they already know it: How to extend and personalize student learning in a PLC at Work*. Bloomington, IN: Solution Tree Press.

Student Data Tracker,
By Standard and Learning Targets

Student Name	Teacher Name	Essential Standards Standard or Outcome: ___ ___	Target 1: ___ ___	Target 2: ___ ___	Target 3: ___ ___	Target 4: ___ ___	Target 5: ___ ___	Running Record						

Extension Planning Template

Essential Standard: _____

_____

_____

_____

Date to Begin Extension: _____

Date to Conclude Extension: _____

Type of Extension: _____

Team Member Delivering Extension: _____

Extension Standards	Extension Students	Formative Assessments During Extension

Source: Roberts, M. (2019). Enriching the learning: Meaningful extensions for proficient students in a PLC at Work. Bloomington, IN: Solution Tree Press, pp. 66–67.

Index

Charting the Course for Leaders
Edited by Sharon V. Kramer
This all-encompassing anthology delivers clear steps that leaders can take throughout the PLC at Work® process to turn their priority school around. Over the course of thirteen chapters, readers will grow in their role as leaders and gain a clear vision of how to evolve their school into a thriving place of learning.
BKF979

School Improvement for All
Sharon V. Kramer and Sarah Schuhl
Ensure all students learn at high levels by targeting specific needs with an immediate course of action within a professional learning community. Each chapter includes space for teacher teams to determine next action steps and questions to bring greater focus to improvement efforts.
BKF770

The Big Book of Tools for Collaborative Teams in a PLC at Work®
William M. Ferriter
Build your team's capacity to become agents of change. Organized around the four critical questions of PLC at Work®, this comprehensive resource provides an explicit structure for collaborative teams. Access tools and templates for navigating common challenges, developing collective teacher efficacy, and more.
BKF898

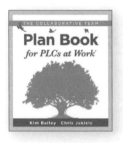

The Collaborative Team Plan Book for PLCs at Work®
Kim Bailey and Chris Jakicic
Designed exclusively for teacher teams, this plan book provides practical PLC information and resources. Access forty weekly planning pages, in-depth examples, succinct summaries of PLC concepts, and many more tools that will help you and your team thrive throughout the year.
BKF981

Solution Tree | Press
a division of
Solution Tree

Visit SolutionTree.com or call 800.733.6786 to order.

"Tremendous, tremendous, tremendous!

The speaker made me do some very deep internal reflection about the **PLC process** and the personal responsibility I have in making the school improvement process work **for ALL kids.**"

—Marc Rodriguez, teacher effectiveness coach, Denver Public Schools, Colorado

PD Services

Our experts draw from decades of research and their own experiences to bring you practical strategies for building and sustaining a high-performing PLC. You can choose from a range of customizable services, from a one-day overview to a multiyear process.

Book your PLC PD today!
888.763.9045

Solution Tree